THE *THÉÂTRE DES VARIÉTÉS* IN 1852
FM16

Copyright © David Hillery 1996

The right of David Hillery to be identified as the author of this work has been asserted by him in accordance with the Copyright, Designs and Patents Act 1988.

Published by Manchester University Press
Oxford Road, Manchester M13 9NR, UK
and Room 400, 175 Fifth Avenue, New York, NY 10010, USA
www.manchesteruniversitypress.co.uk

Distributed exclusively in the USA by
Palgrave, 175 Fifth Avenue, New York NY 10010, USA

Distributed exclusively in Canada by
UBC Press, University of British Columbia, 2029 West Mall, Vancouver, BC, Canada V6T 1Z2

British Library Cataloguing-in-Publication Data
A catalogue record for this book is available from the British Library

Library of Congress Cataloging-in-Publication Data
A catalog record for this book is available from the Library of Congress

ISBN 978 0 7190 8777 6 *paperback*

First published 1996 by Durham Modern Languages Series

This edition first published 2012 by Manchester University Press

Printed by Lightning Source

The *Théâtre des Variétés* in 1852

by
David Hillery

Durham Modern Languages Series 1996

University of Durham

The *Théâtre des Variétés* in 1852

by
David Hillery

Durham Modern Languages Series 1996

University of Durham

For Godfrey

Contents

Preface	i
Acknowledgements	ix
Glossary	x

I.	John Bowes and the *Théâtre des Variétés*	1
II.	The Troupe: actors and actresses — Impressions	6
III.	1852 — A Year at the Variétés	47
IV.	A Financial Overview	87
V.	Index of Plays and Playwrights in 1852	107
VI.	Monthly distribution of Performances in 1852	115
VII.	Monthly accounts April – December, 1852	121
VIII.	Nightly Box-office Takings 9 April – 31 December 1852	157
IX.	Tables	245
	i) Nightly Box-office Totals for 1852	246
	ii) Monthly totals and daily averages	252
X.	A List of authors used in 1852	253
XI.	Bibliography	259

Preface

It was the late Louis Allen who first suggested that I should have a look at the material in the Bowes Museum archives. Archives was perhaps too misleading a word. What I was introduced to was a dusty attic room containing dozens of cardboard boxes (mainly shirt boxes), a few trunks and random piles of ledgers. The boxes had been numbered and a brief indication of their contents penned on the lid; but they were in no particular order. What sorting of the contents had been done had produced only the vaguest arrangements of the material. It was not a promising start; particularly when a preliminary perusal of the correspondence for the years when John Bowes was the owner of the *Variétés* produced virtually nothing that was directly related to the theatre or to his involvement in it. And the published book on *John Bowes and the Bowes Museum* by Charles Hardy remained too general and too unfocused for my own purposes, though it did provide a useful starting point.

Then came an important find: the nightly box-office receipts for April 1852 right through to December of the same year. I can only assume that they survived by sheer chance. Normally such sheets would have been destroyed once their totals had been incorporated in the monthly accounts. The monthly accounts were there too (September was missing). Other bits of the jigsaw turned up in some of the ledgers; yet others in notebooks. What became clear was that it would be possible to construct a financial profile of the *Variétés'* activities in 1852 — and in some detail. This, at least, was a solid enough factual framework. Added to that it was possible to determine which *comédie-vaudevilles* had been performed and on precisely which nights.

Published material in the Bibliothèque de l'Arsenal (the collection Rondel) provided more information: actors' names, anecdotes, cuttings from newspapers and newspapers themselves. Eventually a picture – incomplete, impressionistic in parts — emerged. I offer it as it now stands, a paper-thin slice shaved from the huge bulk of nineteenth-century theatrical activity. The statistics I have reproduced in full in the hope that they may be of use to others working on nineteenth-century vaudeville. The rest of it might have been more interesting in the hands of an imaginative novelist, but I did think it necessary to attempt to add a little flesh to the bare bones of the accounts.

Acknowledgements

First of all I must express my thanks to the staff of the Bowes Museum and in particular to Mrs Conran, the Director, for her encouragement and to Sarah Medlam who cleared a space in her office and allowed me to work there off and on over a period of three years. The librarians at the Bibliothèque de l'Arsenal could not have been more helpful; it would be a shame if that delightful workplace were to succumb to modern technology or, worse still, be closed down in the current attempt at centralisation.

Finally, I must thank Janet Starkey, who alone, has made a readable book out of my pages of sometimes disorganized scribble. Without her invaluable help I would *never* have met the publishing deadline.

Glossary

charge : au théâtre, exagération dans la manière de jouer un rôle, de représenter un personnage.

feux : terme de théâtre. Ce qu'un acteur reçoit en sus de ses appointements fixes, chaque fois qu'il joue.
Origines: Les chanteurs et symphonistes de la musique du roi recevaient, en sus de leurs appointements, du pain, du vin et de la viande à six bonnes fêtes de l'année, ces aliments furent appréciés en argent en 1700, et chaque musicien reçut ainsi un supplément. A la fin du XVIIIe siècle ce supplément fut appliqué aux bougies, que les premiers sujets voulaient avoir au lieu de chandelles dans leurs cabinets, et dès lors la somme allouée prit le nom de feux.

jeton : jeton de présence, honoraire payé pour chaque séance.

I

John Bowes and the *Théâtre des Variétés*[1]

The received opinion regarding the period of John Bowes's ownership of the *Variétés* is briefly summed up in the most recent account of the theatre's history: 'At this date [1847] the theatre was purchased as a speculative venture by an English gentleman named John Bowes, but it was to prove a misguided investment. Directors continued to succeed one another with little success, and Bowes attempted to direct the theatre himself in 1854. The following year Hippolyte Cogniard took command, and was soon to restore to health the ailing fortunes of the *Variétés*'.[2] Cogniard achieved financial stability in the theatre by doing two things. To begin with he made the *Variétés*' revue an annual and increasingly spectacular event; then he persuaded Hortense Schneider to join the *Variétés* (at a salary of 2,000 francs per month) with Offenbach's *La Belle Hélène*. This operetta opened on 16 December 1864 and proved an overwhelming success. It was the first of a series of fruitful collaborations with Offenbach. The Bowes' years appear insignificant by comparison; and Joseph Long's summary only accentuates what, even as early as 1880, was fast becoming received opinion. In that year Bouffé, one of the early nineteenth-century comedians, published his *mémoires*. The Bowes era — which after all lasted nearly eleven years (sufficient indication in itself of Bowes's

---

[1] The basic information for this chapter is drawn largely from two main sources: James V. Wilkinson, 'John Bowes and Mrs Josephine Benoîte Bowes' (with special reference to their connection with France), an unpublished thesis in the Bowes Museum archive; and Charles E. Hardy, *John Bowes and the Bowes Museum* (Newcastle upon Tyne, Frank Graham, 1970). The printing referred to throughout will be the fourth, 1989, published by the Friends of the Bowes Museum.

[2] In Joseph Long, *Théâtre des Variétés* (Cambridge, Chadwyck-Healey; New Jersey, Teaneck, 1980). The book has no page numbers.

serious involvement with the theatre, even at some considerable cost)[3] — is dismissed in a few, not very accurate, lines: 'La série de mes nouveaux chagrins commença par le départ de Nestor [Roqueplan — in 1847] ... après avoir vendu les *Variétés* à un M. Bans [sic.], millionnaire anglais, n'entendant rien aux choses du théâtre et ne voulant être directeur que pour produire sur la scène Mlle Delorme, qu'il épousa plus tard'.[4]

It was true, no doubt, that Bowes knew next to nothing about running a theatre, but he was a keen theatre-goer and had been since the early 1830s. It was in 1846 that he first took an interest in the *Variétés* as a business venture, thinking it a worthwhile and profitable activity. He had begun to spend considerable periods of time in Paris and had an address there in 1846: 8, rue de Rougemont, only a short distance from the theatre. He was, in addition, a member of the French Jockey Club (the Cercle de la Société d'Encouragement pour l'Amélioration des races de chevaux en France) and of the Cercle de l'Union. It was also true that he took an active pleasure in close, friendly relationships with actresses, notably one Mlle Ernestine, an ongoing dalliance from 1842 to 1847. But in 1847 Mlle Delorme became the focus of his attention and no further reference was made to the discarded Mlle Ernestine.[5] The point, however, was that Bowes had had a business eye on the *Variétés before* he became enamoured of Joséphine Coffin-Chevallier. (Mlle Delorme was her stage name.) But the conjunction of business and pleasure must have had its attractions.

The financial side looked promising. Nestor Roqueplan had given the *Variétés* a secure financial base, his directing abilities producing weekly takings of between 15,000 and 25,000 francs. With expenditure running

---

[3] Bowes gained control of the *Variétés* in July 1847 and ultimately sold it to a M. Chabrier on 23 April 1858. Hippolyte Cogniard *leased* the theatre in 1855, he did not buy it. In an article in *L'Estampille / L'Objet d'Art*, octobre 1995, 'Le Bowes Museum, terre française au cœur de l'Angleterre', pp.71–81, Sarah Kane writes '[en 1847] John Bowes engagea de vastes sommes dans le Théâtre des Variétés, qui était alors une entreprise prospère'.

[4] Bouffé, *Mes Souvenirs 1880–1880* (Paris, Dentu, 1880), p.263.

[5] See C. Hardy, op. cit., pp.78–80 (and the entire chapter *Le Théâtre des Variétés*, pp.78–91).

at between 12–13,000 francs a week, the prospects were not unattractive. Profit margins, even the minimal ones (say 2,000 francs per week), were enticing and appeared to offer a profit of at least £1,000 per annum. One reason for this state of affairs was the presence of both Bouffé and Virginie Déjazet among the *Variétés* personnel. But this would soon change. Déjazet retired, Roqueplan was replaced by Morier and Bouffé felt undervalued.

In *Les Variétés 1850–1870*, Roger Boutet de Monvel writes:

> Tandis que M. Morin prenait comme directeur la place de Nestor Roqueplan, la propriété du théâtre passait des mains de M. Thayer dans celles de M. Bowes, un fastueux Anglais, renommé pour ses chevaux et les sommes considérables dont il fit usage pour restaurer le château de Luciennes [sic. — Louveciennes].[6] Non content de posséder l'ancienne demeure de la Dubarry, M. Bowes souhaita d'avoir un théâtre à lui et, pour satisfaire son envie, il acheta les *Variétés*. Mal lui en prit, car, à dater de ce jour, commença pour la scène du boulevard Montmartre toute une période obscure et désastreuse. Jusqu'en 1855, à l'arrivée d'Hippolyte Cogniard, auteurs et directeurs se succédèrent avec une égale mauvaise fortune, et ce fut un défilé ininterrompu de fours noirs, comédies fastidieuses et mornes vaudevilles dont aujourd'hui la nomenclature sans fin n'éveillerait chez personne l'ombre d'un souvenir.[7]

Morin lasted as director until 8 November 1849 and was succeeded by Jean-Baptiste-Joseph Thibaudeau in December of that year. He remained as director until March 1851, at which point Bowes himself took over for three months until Aimé Carpier was appointed on 6 June 1851. He lasted until the 16 January 1854 when Bowes again took control and remained as sole director until 5 June 1855. In fact the *Variétés* had closed its doors on the 26 May. A ministerial decree declared: 'À partir du 5 juin 1855, le directeur est nommé par arrêté ministériel, sans intervention des propriétaires de l'immeuble.' The situation was henceforth out of John Bowes's hands as far as the

---

[6] Bowes did not buy this château until 1852.
[7] R. Boutet de Monvel, op. cit., pp.8–9 (Paris, Plon, s.d. [1905?]).

director was concerned. But, as has been noted, it took him nearly three more years to find a buyer.

Twentieth-century commentators on the *Variétés* either ignore the Bowes period or regard it as a disaster: 'Il est certain que l'entrée de Bouffé aux *Variétés* [5 November 1843 in *Le Gamin de Paris*], avec des appointements fabuleux pour l'époque [1,000 francs a month plus 50 francs for each play he starred in], contribua beaucoup à la fortune de la salle du boulevard Montmartre, et à faire d'une scène de second ordre un théâtre à la mode; mais après le départ de Roqueplan, des jours néfastes se montrèrent de nouveau et ce ne fut que sous le Second Empire, alors que les frères Cogniard les dirigeaiant, que les *Variétés* connurent leur plus grande vogue, beaucoup grâce aux célèbres opérettes d'Offenbach'.[8]

Occasionally the Carpier *direction* gets a mention, but the terms are identical: 'En vain chercha-t-il à renouveler son personnel, à attirer chez lui des comédiens tels qu'Arnal, Lassagne ou Numa, le public des boulevards n'en trouva pas moins ses spectacles détestables'.[9]

Such overviews are not without their truth. Comparatively the 1850s did represent a downturn in the *Variétés'* fortunes. But they gloss over (necessarily) and obscure the weekly and, even more so, the daily ups and downs of a working theatre. Within the overall pattern there exists a considerable range of success and failure even during a period of general mediocrity. Not *all* the vaudevilles were failures; the period had

---

[8] D'Ariste, P., *La Vie et le monde du Boulevard, 1830-1870* (Paris, Jules Tallandier, 1930), p.85. The Bowes era is dismissed in *seven* words! Later, p.104, the author refers to 'son [Bowes's] incompétence en matière théâtrale' and on the previous page had repeated Bouffé's assessment.

[9] Boutet de Monvel, R., op. cit., p.10. For further information on the *Variétés* see Samuel, F., 'Le Théâtre des Variétés, 1777-1900', in *Le Théâtre*, No.27, février, 1900; Nozière, 'Le Théâtre des Variétés, 1779-1907', in *Le Théâtre*, no.201, mai, 1907 (a special number because of the centenary of the present building) and Pougin, A., 'Le Centenaire des Variétés'. See, in the Rondel collection, the côtes Rt.3439 (1) to (7) inclusive. The overall view remains the same; the mid-40s to the mid-50s represents one of the *Variétés* poor periods.

its high spots as well as its lows. And 1852 was no exception to that more detailed pattern.

For John Bowes 1852 was an eventful year: he became High Sheriff of County Durham; his horse Daniel O'Rourke won the Derby; the steam-ship *John Bowes* was launched; he bought the Dubarry Château at Louveciennes and, in August, he and Joséphine signed a marriage contract.[10]

At best he spent no more than a few months in Paris. And it is certain that for 1852, at least, he left the running of the theatre pretty much entirely in the (apparently) capable hands of Aimé Carpier.

---

[10] See Hardy, C., op. cit., p.93. (I have quoted one short paragraph virtually *verbatim*.)

II

The Troupe: actors and actresses — Impressions

The *Almanach les Spectales*[1] for 1853 contained, in fact, the annual theatrical statistics for 1852. It was not the only publication of its kind. Considerable numbers of similar or related publications came out annually or, if not annually, with reasonable frequency: *Les Acteurs et les actrices de Paris*;[2] *Galerie Illustrée des Célébrités contemporaines: Les Théâtres de Paris*;[3] or *Nouvelle Galerie des Artistes dramatiques vivants*,[4] and these are only the tip of the iceberg.[5] Some of these publications — the various *Almanachs* in particular — were cheaply produced and cheaply sold. Others, especially some of the *Galeries*, were much more 'soignées' and contained numerous contemporary engravings of the actors and actresses in roles that had made them their reputations. The sheer volume of these productions suggests an enormous public appetite for information about favourite theatres and their 'celebrities'. In addition to the statistics (which were properly the province of the *Almanachs*) there were biographical sketches (in the *Galeries*), brief and usually repetitive; the same few snippets of information and the almost identical anecdotes were served up time after time. This at least had the advantage of hammering home a few facts; but, equally, it forced the readers (the audiences in another guise), to stereotype and to pigeon-hole the actors and (indirectly) actresses. And the result of this was to oblige the directors to maintain and reinforce the stereotype by choosing roles for the better-known actors that barely differed from one *comédie-vaudeville* to the next. Not that such constrictions were new. [And actors still suffer, or profit, from them]. But it did mean that audiences' expectations could not be disappointed with impunity. The corollary was, of course, that actors were wary of venturing outside their normal type-casting; doing so meant running two main risks; disappointing the audience (which

[1] Sous la direction de L. Palianti, Paris, Librarie Nouvelle, 1853.
[2] By V. Dartheny, Paris, chez les Editeurs, rue Grange-Batelière, 13, 1853.
[3] Paris, Martinon Libraire, 1854, 2 vols.
[4] Paris, Libraire Théâtrale, 1855.
[5] See Bibliography.

showed in smaller box-office returns and smaller runs) and/or revealing their own limitations. Whenever such transgressions took place there was discontent both in the audiences and in the critical reviews (because the critics were as much responsible for the labelling of actors as were the normal theatre-goers).[6]

There were very few further sources of information. Sometimes actors and actresses were articulate enough to write or, in some cases, to have written for them, their autobiographies.[7] Very rarely, during their acting careers, would a critic (friendly) produce a brief, laudatory biography — and this accolade was reserved only for the very few acknowledged greats.

Information was therefore scarce and what there was was repetitive. It was also confined, with virtually no exceptions, to the main artistes within a troupe. In 1852 the *Variétés* possessed only one such actor: Etienne Arnal. It imported, for a four-month season, one of the great dramatic actors of his day, Frédérick Lemaître. Beyond that a number of the male actors were considered good in certain types of rôle and some of the female actors had their loyal fans both in the audiences and in the regular daily drama columns of those critics interested in the *comédie-vaudeville*. But the women were secondary. No actress at the *Variétés* in 1852 had achieved anything approaching the popularity of Mlle Déjazet of the previous decades. The result is a relative dearth of information regarding the vast majority of the actresses (and a good number of the actors). And, indeed, the main rôles — with few exceptions — were for men; and the gist of the critical reviews were equally devoted to the men — the women receiving perhaps a few lines (rarely more) of conventional, sometimes warm, mention.

The troupe at the *Variétés* was of a standard size: *twenty-two men* (if, for 1852 Frédérick Lemaître is included and Numa is not since he only joined late in the year) and *twenty-one women* (excluding Mlle Delorme who, although she figures on the salaries sheet until March 1852, does not figure as a regular acting member in the lists produced in the *Almanach*).

---

[6] See some of the critics' reactions to Arnal's role in *Une Queue rouge* or Frédérick Lemaître's in *Le Roi des drôles*.
[7] cf. Arnal and Céleste Mogador respectively.

The *Almanach* lists them in terms of their perceived importance within the troupe (see the section on salaries which, in the main, reflects the mens' position in the list fairly accurately). The men were:

Arnal, Leclère, Cachardy, Perey, Kopp, Mutée, Danterny, Numa, Lassagne, Moreau-Sainti, Frédérick Lemaître, Nestor, Henri Alix, Duvernoy, Nanteuil, Villot, Charier, Dellère, Jeault, Rhéal, Gautier, Burgny.

Once you get to Lemaître (whose position here has nothing at all to do with his perceived stature which, even in 1852, was enormous) the main names have been mentioned. The remainer usually, if not often in some cases, play bit parts and walk-on rôles.

The women were:

Page, Ozy, Virginie, Clarisse Miroy, Boisgontier, Potel, Ceneau, Duclay, Génot, Morel, Esther, Fitz-James, Blonval, Duparc, Bertin, Constance, Céleste, Chevalier, Gabrielle, Victorine, Joly.

Of these twenty-one, only the first five receive anything like frequent mention. Of the rest Mlles Duclay, Fitz-James and Céleste occur from time to time in the critical reviews (for different reasons). The salaries list, in this instance, does not correspond anything like as closely with the order given (though the problem is probably exaggerated because of the dates — the extant salaries list is from April 1851 to March 1852. It is clear from the list that members of the troupe in 1851 had moved on by 1852, some of them, like the men Bache and Bardou, were highly regarded artistes).

What follows is taken in the main from the *Almanachs* and *Galéries* of the mid-nineteenth century. Exceptionally (as in the cases of Fréderick Lemaître, Arnal and Céleste and Ozy) some material is drawn from the later nineteenth-century biographies. But the intention remains to give as clear an indication as possible of the way in which the actors were seen in the early 1850s. In the men's cases the material, though patchy, allows an idea, an outline of an actor to show through. In the women's cases rather more imagination has to be exercised; the material is scarce and impressionistic. Mlle Boisgontier will remain, unfortunately, only a mere shadow of what she clearly was on stage.

THE ACTORS

i) Frédérick Lemaître (1800–1876)

Frédérick-Lemaître (usually written in the nineteenth century with the hyphen; or, more familiarly, shortened to Frédérick) was not a product of the Conservatoire. A natural, but uneven and unpredictable actor, he made his reputation in Melodrama, playing in the work of Ducange (and later, Dumas, Hugo and Vigny) in the late 1820s and early 1830s, at the Porte Saint-Martin where he worked alongside Marie Dorval.[8]

Henry Lecomte sums up what seems to have been the general opinion of Frédérick's talent:

> Les grands comédiens sont rares. Celui dont nous écrivons la vie n'a, dans le passé, que trois rivaux de gloire. Seuls, en effet, Baron, Lekain et Talma ont laissé de souvenirs comparables à ceux qu'éveille le nom de Frédérick-Lemaître.[9]

In 1852 Frédérick was in London in self-imposed exile following the *coup d'état* of Napoléon III. Rather than continue to make what was a fairly futile political gesture he returned to Paris in April 1852 in order to pick up his career. Given his reputation, it seems odd that he was not approached by one of his old theatres. It was, in fact, M. Carpier of the *Variétés* who approached Frédérick and drew up a contract for the summer and early autumn of 1852. For Carpier the prospect was simple: to increase the box-office receipts and bring in an audience during the annual period of 'les chaleurs' when attendance at overheated theatres could, and did, drop dramatically. For Frédérick the prospect was financially quite enticing [see the Chapter on finances] and it was made more so by the offer of two new *comédie-vaudevilles* to be written especially to show off his particular talents: *Le Roi des drôles*

---

[8] For background to Frédérick Lemaître see initially L.-H. Lecomte, *Frédérick Lemaître, un comédien au XIXe siècle* (2 vols, 1888, Paris, chez l'auteur). For recent mention see the work of F.W.J. Hemmings, *The Theatre Industry in nineteenth-century France* and Marie-Pierre Le Hir, *Le Romantisme aux enchères*.

[9] L.-H. Lecomte, op. cit., vol I, p.1.

which was put on in August 1852 and *Taconnet* which ran in November and December. The first mentioned was by Duvert and Lauzanne (usually associated with Arnal — and a touch unexpected as authors for Frédérick) a three-act vaudeville based loosely on Diderot's *Le Neveu de Rameau* — a bold, and in the eyes of some, an unwisely chosen model (in the sense that it could not be matched). The second was a five-act vaudeville, by Béraud and Clairville, likewise based on an eighteenth-century model. The play's full title was *Taconnet ou l'acteur des Boulevards* based on the life of Taconnet (Toussaint-Gaspard, 1730–74) an actor whose popularity related to the realism with which he played working-class roles, especially, apparently, those of cobblers and drunkards. He began his acting career in that hardest of training grounds, the *théâtre de la foire*.

In theory the idea was a good one. Frédérick was a crowd-puller. The authors were all four of them of long theatrical experience, Duvert (1795–1876), Lauzanne (1805–77), Béraud (1792–1860) and Clairville (1811–79) were no novices. Each had hundreds of *comédie-vaudevilles* to his name, some of them — those by Duvert in particular (*Les Cabinets particuliers* 1832, *Le Mari de la dame de choeurs* 1836 and *Riche d'amour* 1845 — all written for the Théâtre du Vaudeville) — had become standard repertory (and all three featured in the *Variétés'* 1852 programmes). In addition, Béraud had been director of the Ambigu for ten years, 1839–49, so should have been aware of what was, or was not, likely to succeed. *Le Roi des drôles* had its première on 3 August and ran for 25 performances. It was not picked up again. *Taconnet* was first put on on the 13 November and had 24 performances. Neither play, in terms of length of run, came into the top dozen in the year. After a disastrous July (see financial statistics) the *Roi des drôles* did improve the box-office receipts somewhat; even so, the August takings were still the second worst for the whole year (and certainly did not justify the salary Frédérick was being paid). The November takings, however, were relatively high — but that would have been expected at that season and Frédérick's presence probably did not make much difference.

The critical reaction to both plays was mixed; the *Roi des drôles* getting much the better reception. Some comments were over-optimistic to say the least: '*Le Roi des drôles* va être l'objet d'une vogue immense et durable; la pièce aura cent représentations' [A. Roch].[10] And, it would seem, the crowds were drawn: 'Aussi plus de mille personnes — et nous n'exagerons pas — n'ont pu trouver de place hier' (*L'Entr'acte*, 5.8.52). If such was indeed the case then a lot of the seats must have been given over to complementary tickets[11] because the takings were only just over 1,800 francs. Perceptions — or personal taste translated into perceptions — varied from the plainly (over)eulogistic — '*Le Roi des drôles* a obtenu un éclatant succès; c'est une de ces pièces qui sont jouées cent fois et qui décident de la fortune d'un théâtre' [Adolphe Schaeffer] — to the crassly optimistic: 'le succès ne pouvait être douteux, puisque le personnage principal, celui de Rameau, était rempli par Frédérick Lemaître. Le célèbre comédien s'y est montré digne de sa réputation et nous ne doutons pas que le théâtre des Variétés ne réalise en plein été des recettes d'hiver, — problème difficile à résoudre et qui est la pierre philosophale des directeurs de théâtres' [Louis Huart]. The reality of the situation was much harder to face — the audiences simply did not give the piece the expected (or at least the hoped for) support — the average attendance of *paying* spectators indicated a half-full theatre at best. The 'fructueuses recettes' were a mirage. The play was, or was perceived as, mediocre. Jules Janin thought the whole idea of using Diderot a mistake. The Goncourt brothers called it 'une mauvaise œuvre' and suggested it best avoided.

But everyone, including those who disliked the play, had something good to say about Frédérick — even the Goncourts: 'Frédérick a joué de tout son coeur, de tout son zèle et de toute sa voix' (though the claws are beginning to show!). 'Frédérick a tenu pendant trois heures sous le charme une assemblée unanime dans ses éloges et son admiration" [M. Listener]. Little could disguise the fact that Duvert and Lauzanne were unable to produce a work that would do Frédérick proper justice. The *Variétés* was not his natural milieu and in him the playwrights had material they were quite unused to.

The succeeding play for Frédérick, *Taconnet* (five acts — 'Vaudeville *et* cinq actes, ces deux idées ainsi accouplées hurlent

---

[10] All these references come from a collection of cuttings in the Rondel Collection at the Bibliothèque de l'Arsenal entitled *Répertoire de Frédérick Lemaître*, with the *côtes* Rt 8881 and Rt 8882.
[11] See F.W.J. Hemmings and G. d'Heilly.

comme des couleurs disparates'), was received with virtually no compliments in the press. There had apparently been some intention to make a play from George Sand's novel *Nello*, but the subject matter was thought wrong for the *Variétés* ('une scène où le flonflon, la parodie, la parade même avaient droit de cité').[12] The alternative was the 'biographie dramatique' of *Taconnet* — 'un vaudeville de faiseurs'.[13] Had it been much shorter — say an act or two at most — it might have worked. As a five-act, long drawn-out piece it clearly proved both uninteresting and, worst of all, lacking in humour. It was described variously as 'une plate bouffonnerie', a 'pièce essentiellement mauvaise ... et point du tout amusante', a 'bonbonnière de mauvais goût' full of 'flatuosités d'une prose essentiellement anti-littéraire'. 'Il n'y a seulement pas apparence de pièce dans les cinq actes'. 'Pour le seul plaisir de voir Frédérick, peu de personnes se condamneront à cinq actes ennuyeux coupés par des entr'actes de trente-huit minutes'.[14]

Frédérick himself came out of it with considerable sympathy (with the odd exception — 'Frédérick est peut-être un peu vieux pour le rôle de Taconnet: on conçoit difficilement l'amour que peut inspirer ce visage fâné').[15] The main part was long. Frédérick was considered the only actor capable of making the 'éternel monologue' even passibly entertaining (at best). 'Pendant cinq actes, il tient sous le charme la salle entière, à qui il commande à volonté le rire ou l'émotion, et qu'il passionne à son gré'. 'Frédérick a montré comment, à force de verve, de talent, de génie dramatique, on peut forcer le public à applaudir'.[16] It was about as charitable a reaction as could have been hoped for. Otherwise one was forced to talk about the 'mise en scène exacte et soignée, due à l'habileté de M. Boulé' [directeur de la scène] which 'n'est pas le moindre attrait de la pièce nouvelle'.

Carpier must have realised fairly early in the run that *Taconnet* was not going to redress the theatre's finances. Indeed, the realisation could well have come during rehearsals. One way of keeping the audiences coming (even in November when people were in any case readily

---

[12] H.L. Lecomte, op. cit., p.156.
[13] ibid, p.161.
[14] The previous quotations are taken from Rt. 8881.
[15] ibid.
[16] ibid., Rt. 8881.

inclined to spend a long evening in a warm theatre) was to vary as much as was consistent with a troupe's capabilities the evenings' programmes. No sensible director, and certainly no director who was finding it difficult to keep his financial head above water, would fail to plan well ahead — even when he knew he had a hit on his hands (and with even more reason when he could see that a new production would have difficulty pulling in a large, paying audience once word had got around about its qualities — or lack of them.) The most popular night of the week, almost without exception at any time of the year, was Sunday. Carpier, clearly deliberately, kept *Taconnet* off the Sunday slot in November (14th, 21st and 28th), off the first Sunday in December (the 5th) but allowed it on the following Sunday, the 12th, because on that night *it had its last performance.* That would be the last time for the audience to see Frédérick on stage: the idea worked. But it worked because on two of the Sundays (November 21st and 28th) Carpier put on new plays using, among others, Arnal. And on the Saturday immediately preceding 12 December he again put on new material mixed with older, proven *comédies-vaudevilles* — an evening of 4 one-act plays with an *Intermède* of music — dance, song and instrumental music. (The box-office receipts for that night were 3,137 francs; and for the Sunday, the last night of *Taconnet*, 2,708 francs, the best receipts over its whole run of 24 performances. That was intelligent planning; Carpier knew his audience.)

Hiring Frédérick Lemaître had been something of a gamble. It had not been totally unsuccessful but it had, overall, failed to turn round the theatre's finances. Frédérick had appeared on stage 49 times over the period 3 August — 12 December. Given the size of the parts he played there would have been a considerable number of rehearsals, but in terms of *performances* he was paid, on average, virtually 400 francs a night (as far as I can ascertain from the monthly accounts — and making a guess at September, for which the monthly statement is missing, of 900 francs as payment during rehearsals, the same as the October figure). This was a huge sum in 1852. And it is permitted to wonder whether such expense could really have justified the risk of 'producing' Frédérick on a stage that was basically unsuited to his particular talents. It did him no harm. The same cannot be maintained with regard to the *Variétés* itself.

ii) Etienne Arnal (1794-1872)[17]

'Quand Arnal joue, recette double, quand il se repose, il y a un peu de vide dans la salle'.[18]

It is evident from all acounts written about Arnal that he was one of the great comic actors of the nineteenth century.

'Après Brunet et Potier [also part of the *Variétés* troupe earlier in the century and, among their many talents, famous for their 'drag' roles], je ne connais pas d'acteur plus comique qu'Arnal'.[19]

There exists a letter from Arnal written about his early life as an actor (after having been a soldier in his teens)[20] that goes as follows: 'Comme je faisais beaucoup rire [in, of all things, *Mithridate*!] je pensai à prendre les rôles comiques, et l'auditoire alors devint plus sérieux. L'idée me vint de me présenter au théâtre les Variétés [in 1817]. On me répondit qu'on n'avait besoin de personne." In the event he was persuasive enough and stayed at the *Variétés* for ten years until 1827. From there he moved on to the Vaudeville. Comic genius he no doubt was, but it was a long, hard path to the consummate artist he eventually became and his early years suggested nothing more than a competent comic actor. He may well have appeared a 'natural', but it is more than once suggested that he worked hard at being a comic and that his act was meticulously prepared. It is indicated that he hardly ever risked a genuine *ad lib* and that even his most 'spontaneous' lines

---

[17] His date of birth is sometimes given as 1798 — and given very firmly: see Eugène de Mirecourt, *Arnal*, p.5 "La 31 décembre 1798 est la date de la naissance d'Etienne Arnal".
[18] J. Arago, *Foyers et coulisses*; Panorama des théâtres de Paris, 1852, p.45.
[19] *Galérie Illustrée des célébrités contemporaines*: Les Théâtres de Paris, (Paris, Martinon, 1854. 2 vols). Vol I, *Arnal*. (There is no pagination.) The writer of this particular piece, Th. Nézel, goes on, however, to complain that Arnal lives with his old repertoire and has created nothing new for a few years. 'Nous l'avons beaucoup aimé, vu qu'il nous a beaucoup amusés.'
[20] Eugène de Mirecourt, op. cit., p.14.

were the result of study and reflection.[21] And it appears to be the case that he himself had as much to say about pieces submitted to the theatre in which he was meant to have a part as had the official 'comité de lecture' (which normally decided on the acceptability of new works submitted). It also seems that he was in a position to insist on certain conditions regarding rehearsals and learning time: he required a month to learn a one-act vaudeville; six weeks for two acts and two months for three acts.[22] Given that a lot of the one-act *comédie-vaudevilles* were often no longer than 12 or so printed pages it is evident he spent a lot of time polishing his roles. And once a performance was fixed, he simply did not deviate from its details.

In itself, of course, technical perfection would never have been sufficient to create such a popular comedian. Though it is not evident from his photographs, his *physical* stage presence was on its own a source of considerable laughter. 'Il en est venu à ce point que la seule annonce de sa présence fait monter le rire du parterre jusqu'aux amphithéâtres voisins des combles'.[23] This side of Arnal had been amply documented as early as 1842 in an article by Eugène Briffault.[24] It is worth quoting at some length:

> Sa nature est fantasque, il est bizarrement construit. Au premier aspect on reconnaît en lui quelque chose de drôle, dans l'acceptation la plus singulière et la plus complète du mot, on ne se rend pas compte tout d'abord de ce que provoque le rire, mais on ne peut s'en défendre. La disgrâce de tout son être est plaisante par elle-même; ses imperfections physiques n'affligent pas, elles réjouissent et amusent. Sa voix et son regard sont en harmonie, pour ainsi dire, avec le burlesque désordre de toute sa personne; il y a en lui une caricature naturelle et bien plus divertissante que l'art des hommes n'aurait pu la faire ... Ce qui sied le mieux à Arnal, c'est la parure; elle, forme un contraste surprenant

---

[21] See comments and the collection of press cuttings and articles in the Arsenal, côte Rt. 5646.
[22] Eugène de Mirecourt, op. cit., p.75.
[23] ibid, p.25.
[24] In *Galérie des artistes dramatiques de Paris*, Vol. III (Paris, Marchant, 1842). The article is repeated word for word some 13 years (!) later in the *Nouvelle Galérie des artistes dramatiques vivants*, Vol. I (Paris, Libraire Théâtrale, 1855).

avec le désagrément de sa personne, et cette opposition manque rarement de produire une hilarité générale et instantanée.

All successful comedians need good material; they require writers who understand their particular talents and write in order best to bring them out. Duvert (and Lauzanne)[25] turned out to be the ideal team. Arnal's first real triumph was in one of their comédies: *Renaudin de Caen*.[26] Each recognized in the other the means to success; each, ultimately, had the most to do with the other's reputation. Among the most successful pieces, frequently revived, was *Les Cabinets particuliers*, first produced at the Théâtre du Vaudeville in October 1832.[27] It was still playing to full houses in 1852 at the *Variétés*. Other popular pieces were *Les Gants jaunes*[28] (Duvert and Lauzanne) and *Riche d'amour*[29] (Xavier, Duvert and Lauzanne).

The point is that once Arnal had found his particular *niche* he hardly ever ventured outside it. 'On a souvent dit de lui qu'il était partout le même: ce n'était pas un blâme, c'était un éloge. Si Arnal perdait son naturel, il perdrait tout.'[30] Roles were written expressly to suit his acting personality. For an actor who went outside the normal comic conventions (and who, in a sense, became a convention in himself) it needed a writer who was prepared to exceed the recognised limits. 'Ce vaudeville est insensé et extravagant à outrance, dans ses faits, dans ses gestes et dans son language; il contrarie à la fois les mots et les idées, il les bouleverse, les confond, et se plaît au renversement de la pensée et de la grammaire. Interprète de ces conceptions désordonnées, Arnal

---

[25] Although Duvert's name is usually linked with Lauzanne, Lauzanne was not his only collaborator; Xavier was another writer whose collaboration produced instant — and enduring— hits.

[26] It even had one performance on 4 January 1852.

[27] A one-act vaudeville by Duvert and Boniface, though E. de Mirecourt has Duvert's collaborator as Xavier (*op. cit.*, p. 32).

[28] By Bayard. First performance at the Théâtre du Vaudeville on the 6th March 1835, according to Wicks. I am much more inclined to trust Wicks than Mirecourt.

[29] Again first performed at the Vaudeville on 20th November 1845.

[30] Eugène Briffault.

est admirable.'[31] Most of the contemporary comments on Arnal follow the same lines. Mirecourt quotes a journalist (without naming him); 'il [Arnal] a trouvé un sérieux si comique et un comique si sérieux qu'il est impossible de résister à cet état de mélange, inconnu jusqu'à lui, et qui provoque toute une salle à pousser des éclats de rire à fendre une voûte. Si Arnal s'attendrit, il n'y aura plus moyen d'y tenir. Vous verrez tout le monde se tordre dans des convulsions dont rien ne peut donner l'idée. Arnal, c'est le type même de la farce. C'est une moquerie vivante; c'est la bêtise la plus complètement spirituelle'.[32] 'Il soulève de tous côtés un rire extravagant, immense, qui éclate comme une solennelle protestation contre toute raison'.[33] All this is singularly impressionistic (because nothing at all is said about acting styles; and reconstruction, particularly where it concerns an individual actor who was by all accounts exceptional, is entirely out of the question) but it all points in the same direction, namely, Arnal's rapport with the audience.

Great comedians (and there is some justification in considering Arnal as one of them) need an audience. They draw their life-blood from the spectators. And in Arnal's time there is sufficient evidence to indicate that there were moments when the audience took, as it were, an active part in the stage proceedings. The auditorium was lit during performances so there was not the modern distinction between the visible stage and the more or less invisible audience. The performer could not only hear the spectators' reactions, he could see them. Both forms of contact were essential. Like one or two other members of the Variétés troupe, Arnal took a critical interest in his craft; sufficient, at least, to the point where he was able to commit some of his thoughts to paper. Mirecourt, using some of Arnal's writing, produces two telling quotations: 'L'acteur comique doit particulièrement étudier le goût des spectateurs et y être partfaitement soumis, il doit s'attacher à deviner ce que pense le public de ce qu'il a dit';[34] and 'le suffrage du public est tout. C'est le seul dont un comédien puisse raisonnablement

---

[31] Briffault. One suspects that Briffault gets somewhat carried away — but even so the *singularity* of Arnal's playing comes through.
[32] Mirecourt, op. cit., pp.19–20.
[33] Briffault — quoted in Mirecourt, pp.28–29.
[34] Mirecourt, op. cit., p.83.

s'enorgueiller'.[35] Again, contemporary acccounts are few (and what few there are are repetitive) but agree on Arnal's ability to use, to feed on, to manipulate an audience. He may well have been extraordinarily well-prepared and well-rehearsed but complete control of his material did not mean rigid and virtually identical performances. The more a role is mastered the greater freedom it allows the performer; and in Arnal's case his total technical command freed him to react as and when and how he wanted with the spectators. He adressed them directly. He built into his performances areas of direct reaction: 'Arnal lui [the audience] adresse ... la parole en face, brusquement et sans préparation.[36] Il lui envoie tout ce qu'il veut, raillerie contre lui-même, raillerie contre la pièce qu'il joue, raillerie contre les personnages.'[37] It would seem that Arnal used the public as part of his performances. Everything was directed towards entertainment, and towards control. Audiences no doubt exercised a tyranny, but a tyranny that was always willing to concede its power to the greater tyranny of the gifted performer. 'Les applaudissements éclatent. Il [Arnal] les réduit, il les apaise, il les renouvelle, il les calme, il les précipite à son gré. Jamais on n'a tenu de la sorte les rênes du rire.'[38]

In the light of comments of this nature — and one has to assume that they contain something of the truth — it is easy to understand why Arnal disliked, hated even, the *claque*.[39] The *claque*'s rôle, in general terms, was to orchestrate the audience's response to the plays, especially during the opening nights. Theatre mangers depended on the *claque*, at least in part, in order to launch and establish a new vaudeville. Actors, too, in some instances. But Arnal must have seen the *claque*'s rôle as demeaning to his own work as a comedian. 'Ce qu'Arnal déteste le plus ce sont les claqueurs; il les poursuit sans relâche de sa haine et de ses sarcasmes.'[40] The *claque* got, or could get,

---

[35] ibid., p.57.
[36] which is, I think, how it would be made to appear, unscripted freedoms became, as it were, routine; but a routine in which the possible variations were endless.
[37] Mirecourt, op. cit., p.23.
[38] Ibid., p.24.
[39] For a full discussion of the *claque* and its place in nineteenth-century French theatre, see F.W.J. Hemmings, op. cit., Chapter 7.
[40] Briffault.

in between Arnal and his direct contact with the audience. No wonder he saw them as the enemy of his art. And no wonder the relations between him and the leaders of the *claques* were at best cold and at worst openly hostile.

Not, apparently, that he was especially easy to get on with off-stage. He had the reputation, among his fellow actors, of being prickly and quick-tempered. As far as it is possible to tell he made few, if any, friends from among them. Indeed they are rumoured to have been rather frightened of him and to have found him too authoritarian.[41]

This attitude extended to the management and affected his choice of plays and rôles (remembering that many more plays were submitted than were ever produced). Not only that, he insisted on quite a number of conditions to be added to his contract, of which two are reputed to have been the following: 'On lui payera, tous les soirs, dans sa loge, ses feux, *en or*'; and 'Tous les jours il aura droit à deux stalles de balcon numérotées.'[42] True or not in detail, there seems to be a sufficient number of indications to confirm the view of Arnal as a hardheaded individual — good at his particular trade and determined to get out of it, in material benefits, as much as he could. His annual salary at the Variétés (taking the period April 1851 to March 1852 as representative) was 24,000 francs; twice as much as Bache (who had left the troupe by the beginning of 1852) and three times as much as the best paid among the other *artistes*. In addition Arnal was paid appearance money (his *jetons*) and was guaranteed 20 francs minimum per day each day he performed. It was an arrangement that could easily earn him another 3-4,000 francs a year (to put this into perspective, the average working man's wage was, in round figures, about 100 francs a *month*).

It is not easy, at such a remove, to even attempt to reconstruct the way an actor actually acted. There are the plays (but to an untrained eye the scripts seem about as promising as a script of Frankie Howerd's). But the humour seems either obvious (and occasionally crude) or non-existent. One thing is clear: Arnal's appearance aroused laughter (not because of 'funny' dressing but simply because he appeared funny in his person — much as Frankie Howerd did or, for

---

[41] See the press cuttings etc., Rt 5646.
[42] See Mirecourt, op. cit., p.75.

that matter, Eric Morcambe: that is not to say that there was not calculation, but the calculation remained hidden). But that says nothing about an acting *style*. There are clues (and not just relating to Arnal). In yet another book of souvenirs, dating this time from the early twentieth century, Justin Bellanger wrote: 'le nom d'Arnal était pour nous synonyme de prince des acteurs comiques. Il signifiait la perfection dans celui de tous les genres de rôles qui exige le plus d'esprit et de *naturel*.'[43] The key word is 'naturel'. The actor's aim, at one level, appears to have been to copy what was true to life. Imitation served as a steady, firm base for the portrayal of a character. Humour, presumably, came from the minute distortions, exaggerations, emphases that the actor built into the rôle — never losing sight of the main 'type' the while. In an article on Numa (the son, Charles) Francisque Sarcey (one of the nineteenth-century's most eminent theatre critics) writing in May 1888 recalled Numa *père* acting with Arnal. The passage is worth quoting at length (because it also gives a clue about changes in comic acting style post-Arnal):

> C'est ainsi qu'il a joué pour nous les *Erreurs du bel âge* avec Arnal pour partenaire. Arnal a été, avec Samson, le plus correct, le plus fin et le plus spirituel diseur de notre époque. Numa ne lui était pas inférieur comme comédien. Je me souviens toujours de la scène où tous deux, devenus hommes graves, se remémorent leurs folles années de jeunesse, les erreurs de leur bel âge, et se laissent entraîner par les souvenirs à esquisser un pas du vieux temps, aujourd'hui on se livrerait à des déhanchements extraordinaires, on lèverait la jambe à la hauteur de l'œil; ce ne serait que contorsions et grimaces; le mouvement était à peine indiqué par ces deux comédiens exquis; un échange de coups d'œil, les deux corps se penchant en avant et se touchant l'épaule, les jambes comme agitées de fourmillements, cela suffisait et le public se pâmait de rire. *C'était la vérité prise sur le fait*; à cette heure où l'on parle sans cesse de naturalism sur la scène, on ne

---

[43] My underlining. J. Bellanger, *La Vie de Théâtre: souvenirs de jeunesse* (Paris, Lemerre, 1905). The author is recalling a very late appearance of Arnal on the stage in Nice (A mistake, in his view, because Arnal was then too old and should never have been tempted back).

nous y donne que de la fantaisie, et encore une fantaisie exagérée, parfois macabre.[44]

The point will crop up again in the sections on other male actors. (The qualities demanded from the women were not quite identical.) It can be expressed in a negative way: one of the terms relating to acting which occurs frequently is the term 'une charge'. It relates normally to painting: 'Se dit d'une figure dans laquelle les défauts sont exagérés' or 'représentation exagérée, imitation qui excède, ressemblance bouffonne'.[45] Inferences can again be drawn, namely, that there existed certain agreed gestures, postures, tone of voice (and so on) as being appropriate to portray certain character types; and that these gestures *etc.* were larger than life. At worst they have to be seen as crude, stereotyped movements designed to express, or at least indicate, certain types of simple emotional states or, more likely, reactions. Bad actors would, presumably, rely on them. Good actors would modify them, making them more subtle or simply dispense with them. In Arnal's time it became something of a compliment if a critic praised a performance by declaring that it did not depend on the appropriate 'charge'.[46]

Arnal remained at the Variétés until 1863. In that year a doctor Prosper Vigo produced a book: *Charges et Bustes de Dantan jeune.* In it he describes how Arnal took his leave of the Variétés: 'Voici ... le couplet par lequel Arnal a pris congé du public des Variétés ... Ce couplet, dont il est l'auteur, fut dit par lui avec une émotion à laquelle s'associa toute la salle, en l'exprimant par de longs applaudissements mêlés même de quelques larmes:

> Adieu, messieurs! je pars ... mais ma voix tremble,
> Ma gaîté fuit ... Je suis tout défaillant.
> Quand si longtemps on a fait route ensemble,

---

[44] Francisque Sarcey, from the collection of press cuttings on Numa (fils) Charles, Rt 9805(6). (My underlining.)
[45] *Dictionnaire de l'Académie française*, 15th edition, L'an VII de la République, Vol. I, p.224.
[46] The term was used to describe the small, caricatural figures that Dantan made of the famous actors, actresses, politicans, writers *etc.* of his time. There is a good display of these at the Musée Carnavalet. Among them is Arnal.

On ne peut pas se quitter en riant.
Mais je le sens, la retraite où j'aspire
Pour mon cœur seul est un sujet d'émoi,
Que votre adieu soit encore un sourire;
Que le chagrin ne reste que pour moi![47]

iii) Jean-Baptise Leclère (1802–1861)

Like many actors of his time Leclère spent years in the provinces (especially in Rouen) before making his début in Paris in 1841. And it was during John Bowes's first year as owner of the Variétés, 1848, that Leclère became a member of the troupe. He remained at the Variétés until his untimely death in 1861. One of his last notices, in Emile Abraham's *Les Acteurs et les actrices de Paris*, more or less sums him up: 'un très bon comédien; il joue avec une rondeur, une bonhomie, un naturel rares'.[48] Leclère himself provided his biographers with a longish autobiographical sketch in a letter: 'En 1841, je viens à Paris, je débutai au Vaudeville dans une mauvaise pièce ... En 1848, M. Nestor Roqueplan, qui était directeur des Variétés, me proposa un engagement pour son théâtre; alors là, je fus plus heureux encore. Les bons rôles m'arrivèrent coup sur coup ... *Paris qui dort, L'Homme* [sic.] *qui prend la mouche, Souvenirs de jeunesse, les Deux prudhommes.*'[49] (The titles were all played in 1852, two of them very successfully.)

Leclère was often Arnal's partner in the one-act vaudevilles in which the latter excelled. But he also played bigger roles, in particular in *Paris qui dort* where he was the male lead.

---

[47] Vigo, P. op. cit. (Paris, Libraire nouvelle, 1863), p.77.
[48] Abraham, op. cit. (Paris, Michel Lévy, 1861), p.55. At this date Leclère was one of only a few of the 1852 troupe left at the Variétés. Arnal was at the Palais-Royal, Numa the Théâtre-Lyrique and Mlle Page (see later p.43) at the Cirque Impérial.
[49] The first appearance of this letter was in the *Galerie Illustrée des Célébrités contemporaines, les Théâtres de Paris* in 1854. The article was signed Albert. The article and the letter are regurgitated elsewhere every time Leclère is mentioned — including the obituary in *La Patrie* on 5 November 1861.

Interestingly, however, what is written about him, in spite of its relative brevity, usually concerns his acting style. In Arnal's case it was difficult to sum up his qualities: they were touched with that shade of genius that makes them elusive to describe; in Leclère's case there was not the same problem. Jacques Arago, in 1852, puts his finger on (among others) two of the qualities that singled out Leclère's acting (they are really the two sides of the same coin): 'acteur éminent, *comique sans charge*, aventureux parfois, *toujours vrai*, toujours communicatif, toujours inspiré.'[50] What there is a hint of here are those qualities that were mentioned with regard to Arnal and Numa: the ability to act without recourse to stereotyped and over-the-top gestures: 'Jamais Leclère n'a fait une grimace, ni un geste exagéré, ni un pas de trop.'[51] And there is an interesting observation about his stagecraft: 'Il jouait sur place, les mains dans ses poches, l'œil sur le parterre, et ainsi planté il animait tout.'[52] This is a style of acting that depends on an absolute minimum of movement but equally necessitates a maximum of contact with the audience. (Especially with the *parterre* — the cheaper, unnumbered seats where people were crushed together, the volatile yet responsive heart of the theatre, the section that had to be won over if the performance was to be successful because there, more than anywhere else in the theatre where people were more 'isolated' in individual seats, the audience tended to respond *en bloc*, to act as a crowd, to interact with the stage.) The reason is clear: the interest in the plays was never in stage business (the actors moved — the indication on some of the printed scripts showed as much — but the movement was not the central point) but in the verbal exchanges. The humour was in the delivery, the nuances of comic dialogue; aided and abetted by gesture, no doubt, but gesture always subordinate to the word. The good comic actor needed a good voice and an expressive face. Leclère had both: 'Le masque de Leclère est excellent, sa voix

---

[50] Arago, J. *Foyers et Coulisses*, 1852, p.47. My italics.
[51] *Galerie Illustrée*, op. cit.; see also Rt. 8614.
[52] Ibid.

sonore et de nature à exciter le rire et les pleurs.'[53] Interestingly, the qualities of his diction are detailed in the obituary in *La Patrie*: 'une lenteur de diction, comiquement calculée, qui lui permettait d'équilibrer ses effets, de balancer ses mots et de les lancer toujours au bon moment. Par ce procédé de lenteur habile et de tatillonnement de prononciation, il nuançait tout, il détaillait tout, sans avoir l'air de toucher à rien.' It is not difficult to see, therefore, how effective a foil he was for Arnal nor to see why their partnership, in 1852, was one of the mainstays of the Variétés.

But there is also the business of 'vérité', 'naturel'. The audiences appeared to want (at least from the male parts) one of two things: either a form of stereotyped exaggeration (in the support roles — see the sections on Kopp and Lassagne) or a form of characterization built on 'real' life — types that had a recognizable, familiar identity (though with whom one never in fact identified; distance and laughing *at* were the crucial factors). This latter was Leclère's strong point: 'La qualité dominante de cet artiste, c'est d'apporter dans tous ses rôles *le type exact* du personnage qu'il a à représenter, avec lui, avant tout, la vérité. Homme d'observation, d'étude et de conscience.'[54] The quotation begs a lot of questions, but it indicates that Leclère was able to portray characters that were believable in and that the audience could consider 'real' (as characters in *Coronation Street* are 'real'). And there is no question but that Leclère was an audience favourite. 'Le verve de Leclère est intarissable. Une situation languit-elle, le public écoute-t-il avec distraction ou indifférence, Leclère entre et tout de suite l'action renaît, le public redevient attentif, il s'anime, il rit, les applaudissements se font entendre. Voilà, selon moi, ce qui constitue l'artiste, le comédien. Et ce privilège, il le possède au suprême degré.'[55]

---

[53] *Galerie Illustrée*, op. cit. The 'masque' is a theatrical term: 'On dit d'un acteur dont la physionomie a beaucoup d'expression et de jeu, surtout dans les rôles comiques, qu'*il a un bon masque*,' *Dictionnaire de l'Académie*, op. cit., Vol. II, p.76.
[54] *Galerie Illustrée*, op. cit.
[55] *Galerie Illustrée*.

Small wonder, then, that his unexpected death in 1861 was such a blow to the Variétés. With Arnal and Numa elsewhere by then Leclère was the main attraction. 'C'est aux Variétés que nous avons à constater le plus grave, le plus douloureux de tous ces sinistres et le plus irrémédiable. Leclère est mort. "Le Théâtre des Variétés perd son porte-drapeau" a dit M. Hippolyte Cogniard [the director], sur la tombe de l'excellent comédien.'[56]

iv) **Numa (Marc Beschefer) (1800–1869)**

Numa joined the Variétés in the autumn of 1852 — 22 September — and remained with them until April 1858. His début was in *Deux Gouttes d'eau* (a one-act *comédie-vaudeville* by Bourgeois and Labiche) on 22 September playing opposite Arnal. The play had 39 performances between then and the end of the year and must have been, at the very least, averagely successful.

His early career took place largely in Versailles and then he moved to the Gymnase (against his family's wishes — they were *commerçants* who wanted him to take over the family business; failing that he was meant to study medicine ...).[57]

The move to the Variétés must have come at the instigation of M. Carpier. (The salary must have been an inducement. The monthly accounts from September to December 1852 inclusive show monthly payments of 1,045; 1,155; 1,065 and 1,175 francs respectively. These sums, if continued throughout the year, would have made Numa the second highest paid actor of the troupe, after Arnal.) And Carpier, apart from wanting another well-known *comédien* on his books, seems to have sought out an actor whose qualities appear to have mirrored those of Leclère. (Are we looking at something that had become the acting fashion in the vaudevilles in the late 1840s and early 1850s? It is hardly likely that the Variétés were going out on a limb.)

---

[56] Obituary notice in *La Patrie*.
[57] For the material on Numa see the Arsenal *côte* Rt. 9805(7). (Numa (fils) has the *côte* Rt. 9805(6). It is important not to confuse the two!)

Numa had at least one approach to his work in common also with Arnal: the hard preparation and the concomitant respect for what was in the script. 'Numa s'en tenait rigoureusement au texte de l'auteur. Il appartenait à une génération de comédiens qui ne donnait rien au hasard et se méfiait de l'inspiration.'[58] Of course we see only what three or four critics have written about him; but the appreciations coincide on the salient points. (Is this another case of writers labelling an actor and being unable to see beyond the label or are the writers coming to their conclusions independently, thereby confirming that actors deliberately restricted their range to the (few?) things they knew best and which, in turn, were what the spectators paid to see?) A quotation from a M. Rolle will serve as well as anything to delineate Numa's style: 'il a deux qualités principales et qui deviennent plus rares de jour en jour: la simplicité et le naturel. Numa est sur la scène comme chez lui; nul apprêt, nulle prétention, nul effort. Son comique est facile, commode, sans façon, *les mains dans les poches*. Il a un certain laisser-aller qui inspire la confiance et plaît aisément.'[59] Like Leclère there is the same economy of gesture, the same ease and the same command. He has his own manner that works. Philoxène Boyer commented: 'Numa ... n'est pas un acteur varié. Il ne s'impose pas l'obligation de renouveler continûment ses grimaces et ses onomatopées. Il a accoutumé le parterre à sa voix et à son visage. Il s'en tient à des gestes qui ont toujours leur effet ... Quelques nuances très fines indiquées deci delà pour témoigner la spécialité d'un caractère, un peu plus de retenue, ou un peu plus d'emportement ... et pour le reste l'uniformité.'[60] Here, too, there are tantalizingly incomplete glimpses of an acting style, minimalist and, somehow, *intimiste*; as though the audience was meant to be drawn into the spectacle; *had* to be drawn in for the nuances in diction and *masque* to be appreciated. This was not exactly playing to the audience, this was playing *with* the audience. It was a style which

---

[58] Francisque Sarcey, op. cit. (19 May 1888; the piece was on Numa *fils* who had died in that month.)
[59] In Rt. 9805(7); the quotation comes in a piece by Eugène Moreau, *Les Théâtres de Paris* (Numa — Variétés). My italics. See the section on Leclère.
[60] Ibid.

was meant to give the spectators a sense of a shared experience — helped, no doubt, by the relatively cosy nature of the Variétés' auditorium.

It is noticeable that Arnal, Leclère and Numa were all 50 or over in 1852. This meant choosing pieces that were suitable and excluded the *jeune premier* rôles that were popular but in these cases would have seemed inappropriate. They were mature professionals and, given the fashion of realism, were given parts accordingly. Gérôme, writing soon after Numa's death in 1869, describes the characteristic Numa part: 'Il y eut des Numa comme il y eut des Arnal. Vous vous rappelez ce mélange de bonhomie et de brusquerie, ces vieillards bourrus, grognons, bougons, qu'il jouait avec tant de simplicité, de naturel, de laisser aller et, ainsi qu'on l'a dit, les mains dans les poches. Quel comique fin et sans prétention! quelle habileté à lancer le mot sans le souligner! Et comme il savait *écouter* et seconder les effets de ses interlocuteurs, sans tirer à lui la couverture! ... '[61]

Jacques Arago summed up Numa in a phrase that, on the surface, is derogatory. It was, on the contrary, intended as a compliment: 'la monotonie du bien'.[62] Or, as Boyer put it more colourfully (?): 'J'apprécie singulièrement ces procédés de peinture monochrome appliqués au talent dramatique.'[63]

Arnal, Leclère and Numa [discounting the exceptional six-month contract of Frédérick Lemaître] were the principal attractions of the male troupe, and in many respects their presence dictated the type of *comédie-vaudeville* that dominated the Variétés. But there were other permanent members of the troupe who became crowd favourites and who tended to specialize in certain types of comic rôle (and on occasion take the male lead). The best known were Kopp and Lassagne. In addition, there were a number of actors who were not type-cast and

---

[61] Rt. 9805(7), op. cit. The view of Numa had not changed much since 1853 when V. Darthenay wrote of 'la froideur systématique et la nazillarde diction de cet excellent comédien; il joue ses rôles en se dandinant et les mains dans ses poches', *Les Acteurs et les actrices de Paris*, p.59.
[62] Arago, J., *Foyers et coulisses*, p.44.
[63] In Rt. 9805(7).

who therefore would turn their talents to whatever was available or required. The most obvious example of this sort was Pérey.

v) Pérey (Charles) (1819–)

This is one of the infuriating cases where the information available has virtually nothing to do with his acting career. It is known that he started his professional career at the Théâtre de l'Ambigu-comique in 1838. And it was Nestor Roqueplan, the Variétés' director, who spotted potential talent and signed him up in 1843. He remained there until 1854 or 1855, without, it seems, creating a rôle with which his name became associated (the common fate of a lot of supporting actors). That particular 'reward' came in 1866 when, at the théâtre de la Gaîté, in a piece called *La Petite Pologne* (by Lambert Thiboust and Blum — a five-act *drame*) he acted *with a monkey*. He retired from the stage around 1873 and lived in isolation in a modest *mansarde* in N° 2 (bis) Boulevard du Temple. He was, apparently, well known for being very close to his *sous* – 'être étrange ... et d'une prodigieuse avarice ... cependant on lui savait une douzaine de mille francs de rente, une vraie fortune pour l'époque.'[64] (His salary at the Variétés in 1852 was 4,800 francs a year, plus *jetons* — not the 20 francs *jetons* of Arnal — much more likely to be 2 francs or 3 francs.)

What distinguished Pérey in the eyes of those writing about him was his interest in books — 'grand amateur de livres, Charles Pérey possède une très-belle et très-nombreuse bibliothèque au milieu de laquelle il s'enfouit, des jours, des semaines entières, lorsque le théâtre lui laisse ces loisirs'[65] — and the fact that he was a writer; on the one hand children's books, 'nous avons lu, signés de lui, des Contes à l'usage des enfants, qui ne manquent ni de grâce, ni de naïveté';[66] on the other

---

[64] See the Arsenal *côte* Rt. 9915 — some of this information comes from one of the many series on actors, politicians etc. — called, rather picturesquely, 'Les contemporains en pantoufles' (Pérey was N° 331!) of 26 November 1862.
[65] Op. cit., Rt. 9915.
[66] Ibid.

... plays. He evidently did not write for the Variétés but produced what were described as 'une foule de jolis vaudevilles dans les théâtres plus modestes', presumably some of the smaller theatres in the Boulevard du Temple.

Pérey must have acted because he wanted to. With a substantial private income he had no need of the much more modest salary he earned at the Variétés. His acting and his writing of vaudevilles suggests a man of solid talent whose passion was the theatre and whose personal wealth allowed him to indulge his passion fully with reasonable success.

vi) **Kopp (Jean-Laurent) (1812–1872)**

With Kopp we come to those actors — known as 'seconds comiques' — who were quickly identified with one type of role. Born in the faubourg St. Antoine, Kopp was an apprentice 'ouvrier ornementiste', a job he abandoned at the age of 15 to earn, or scratch, a living making children's toys. His first theatre was the Théâtre de Belleville (where it is said he played for no salary) and from there he moved round quite a lot: the Théâtre St. Marcel, the Beaumarchais, the Renaissance before arriving at the Variétés where he made his début in *Le Père Trinquefort*. 'Enfin, sans bruit et sans fracas, il entra aux Variétés, où son talent devait *seul* le faire connaître et lui assigner sa place, car jamais la réclame ne fut pour un artiste aussi économe de ses entrefilets louangeurs, et le public s'aperçut le premier que Kopp le faisait rire.'[67]

He became identified with one type: 'En argot de théâtre, les emplois de Kopp s'appellent les *domestiques insolents*'. The identification took place fairly quickly and is consecrated by his playing of Baptiste in *La*

---

[67] See the Arsenal *côte* Rt. 8345 — the holdings on Kopp seem to come exclusively fom the *Galerie Illustrée des célébrités contemporaines — les Théâtres de Paris*.

Vie de Bohème[68] (a five-act 'pièce mêlée de chants' by Barrière and Murger first played on 22 November 1849, but which also had thirteen performances in 1852), one of the Variétés' big successes. The problem — if problem it was — was that Kopp was labelled from virtually the start of his career at the Variétés: in 1853, in yet another compilation of 'stars', namely, *Les Acteurs et les actrices de Paris*, the author writes: 'l'emploi des valets lui est adjugé exclusivement et sans partage. Le public, content de son service, lui paye ses gages en bravos'.[69] And it was certainly the rôles of *domestique* that he played in two of the longer running plays of 1852 — *Le Puits mitoyen* and *Un Monsieur qui prend la mouche* (with Arnal and Leclère). He also played in *Trois Amours de pompier,* another successful 1852 production.

Kopp stayed at the Variétés until the end of his career (and enjoyed some of the enormous popularity attached to the operettas of Offenbach; he played Ménélas in *La Belle Hélène*, the first of the Offenbach pieces put on at the Variétés in 1864 for which the director had persuaded Hortense Schneider to play the lead.) Kopp's untimely death would, in itself, have kept him in public memory for some time: 'Kopp, l'amusant Kopp des Variétés, s'est suicidé dans la nuit de dimanche à lundi, en se tirant un coup de revolver au dessus de l'oreille droite'.[70] He had been due to appear before the 'police correctionnelle'. The writer is coy about the reason — but totally the opposite about Kopp's money: 'Kopp laisse plus de 100,000 francs. On a trouvé chez lui 12,953 francs en billets, en or et en argent, et pour 90,000 francs environ de valeurs diverses',[71] all bequeathed, in equal amounts, to the Association des artistes dramatiques; the Association des artistes musiciens; les Pauvres de Paris and the Blessés de la dernière guerre (the Franco-Prussian war of 1870-71). He was buried in Père-Lachaise.

---

[68] See E. Abraham, *Les Acteurs et les actrices de Paris*, 1861 — 'Kopp ... créa d'une façon très-drôle le rôle de Baptiste ...'

[69] V. Darthenay, *Les Acteurs et les actrices de Paris* (chez les Editeurs, rue Grange-Batelière, 13, 1853), p.58.

[70] Arsenal, Rt. 8345.

[71] Ibid.

THE TROUPE 31

vii) Lassagne[72]

Lassagne was another comic actor who specialized in, or was given, clearly defined rôles in a very narrow spectrum. He came to the Variétés after a period at the Palais-Royal and then the Folies-Dramatiques. He made his début at the Variétés in *Drin-Drin* (a one-act vaudeville by Brisebarre and Nyon) on 13 September 1851.[73] He played the rôle of a young conscript, Fritz a *dragon*, opposite the female lead played by Alice Ozy. The rôle is described simply as a 'rôle de genre'. It was considered 'un heureux cadre pour son talent, car le rôle de jeune conscrit qui lui fut confié lui permit d'utiliser un de ses meilleurs et plus sûrs types du théâtre des Folies-Dramatiques'. 'Son emploi fut nettement dessiné: les paysans grossiers, les soldats candides ou les étudiants bambocheurs'. He was also, apparently, good at drag roles. He clearly was of a striking appearance because he was the subject of cariacatures by Doré, Gavarni and others. And he provides an example of the comedian with a (or in his case, two) stock-phrases: ‹O Mon Dieu — Je!› (from *Drin-Drin*) and a 'formidable cri d'âne' from *Les Bibelots du Diable* — ‹Hi-han! ... Hi-han! ... Hi-Han!›. Not, one might think, a particulary promising utterance, but one which 'avait failli cent fois faire crouler la salle sous les bravos'.[74]

Lassagne's descent into madness must have been rapid: 'il était devenu fou aux environs de la quarantième année. Il mourut peu après avoir été enfermé'. There was one touching, pathetic incident before he died: his doctors, in an attempt to restore at least a touch of sanity, took him back to the café at the Variétés. The actor — 'une sorte de vieillard courbé et vacillant' — responded by producing his famous 'cri d'âne'. The incident became news for a day or two. The hoped-for amelioration in his condition did not happen.

---

[72] All the material in this section comes from the Arsenal *côte* Rt. 8523.
[73] It received another 22 performances in the course of 1852, mainly during the slack months of June, July and August.
[74] Op. cit., Rt. 8523.

Not all the other male actors can have been the make-weights the lack of publicity suggests, but few of them were accorded anything other than the odd lines of comment in the course of the year's production. Mutée, Danterney and Henri-Alix get the bulk of what little press notice is given to others apart from the seven mentioned above.

The situation with regard to the actresses is worse. Without any really outstanding women in its troupe (though with a number of good ones) the Variétés had to get by (perhaps that is too harsh a judgment?) with actresses who attracted attention for reasons not always related to their acting ability.

THE ACTRESSES

i) Clarisse Miroy (1820–1870)

Mlle Clarisse's appearance on the Variétés' stage in 1852 was due entirely to her relationship with Frédérick Lemaître, both professional and personal.[75] By 1852 she was a well-established actress with a good reputation. Ten years earlier she had received a largely favourable write-up in the *Galerie des artistes dramatiques de Paris*:[76] 'non contente de l'excellence de ses facultés intellectuelles, [elle] est douée d'une voix charmante, a la taille bien prise, le regard expressif, la physionomie mobile, les mains les plus mignonnes du monde. Mais ... elle paraît quelquefois oublier que de toutes les qualités du comédien, la plus précieuse, la plus essentielle, est le naturel ... Que mademoiselle Clarisse ne s'efforce pas trop violemment d'être bonne, elle sera excellente.'[77]

Her two appearances were in *Le Roi des Drôles* and *Taconnet* playing opposite Frédérick. Regardless of the general opinion that neither of these plays was anything other than a mixture of good and bad, Clarisse received good notices in both. Adolphe Schaeffer wrote of her performance in the first: 'Mlle Clarisse ... a déployé un esprit, une finesse et une verve entraînante qui ont enlevé tous les suffrages, et que les plus sincères applaudissements sont venues récompenser.'[78] Listener, in the *Revue et gazette des théâtres*, singled out Clarisse's performance as one of the best.[79] In *L'Entr'acte* it is claimed that

---

[75] See the biography of Frédérick Lemaître by Robert Baldick. Clarisse Miroy lived with him for a number of years before a notorious row — she attempted to kill him — put an end to the affair.

[76] 2 vols; (Paris, Marchant, 1842). The article comes in the second volume. (Not paginated.)

[77] Edouard Lemoine. It is interesting to note, *en passant*, the emphasis on *le naturel*. 'La taille bien prise' refers to the upper body between the shoulder and waist and means *well-made* (selon les goûts du jour).

[78] See Rt. 8882. Schaeffer was one of the few critics who thought highly of *Le Roi des drôles*.

[79] ibid.

Frédérick 'a été merveilleusement secondé par Leclère et Mlle Clarisse Miroy'.[80]

Her rôle in *Taconnet* was of a different nature. Here 'elle apparaît pour la première fois sous les traits vulgaires mais amusants d'une femme des Halles'.[81] The *Revue et gazette des théâtres* (18 November) reported that Clarisse 'porte avec entrain de bonne humeur gaillarde, un rôle en dehors jusqu'ici de ses habitudes scéniques'.[82] Two days later the *Courrier des Spectacles* carried the following brief mention: 'Clarisse Miroy a été adorable de gaieté, de bonhomie, une vraie écaillère.'[83] The interesting point is the change in the *type* of rôle she played. Whereas previously she had taken the expected female parts — the 'jeune première' — now she was tackling a 'genre' rôle: the coarse fish-wife. That she could succeed was a tribute to her acting talent; that she *had* to move to rôles of that sort was the result of an unkind cut of fate. The reason was clearly visible: 'Si Clarisse Miroy abordait les rôles comiques, ce n'était pas sans raison. La jolie femme, mignonne, d'un charme si fluet, avait été envahie vers l'âge de trente deux ans [if this is accurate then we are talking precisely about 1852] par un terrible embonpoint ‹dont l'aspect seul déterminait le rire›. Cette obésité avait pour cause, paraît-il, une maladie de cœur. Elle devint un obstacle à la carrière de l'artiste.'[84]

She does not appear to have negociated a special deal with the Variétés (as Frédérick had done) and so, presumably, was paid a salary along with the other actresses — possibly 400–500 francs a month. Her only separate mention in the accounts is on 29 October: 'un châle pour Mlle Clarisse, *Roi des drôles*, 18 francs'.

---

[80] Ibid, A. Roche, 5 August 1852.
[81] See Rt. 9500.
[82] See Rt. 8881.
[83] Ibid ('écaillère' — who sells, and opens, oysters).
[84] See Rt. 9500.

ii) Alice Ozy (née Julie-Justine Pilloy) (1820-1893)

Mlle Ozy had a number of claims to fame, not the least of which was her friendship with Théophile Gautier which is reputed to have begun in September 1843. Her biographer Louis Loviot[85] claims she was the inspiration for what he calls 'cet hymne enflammé, *Le Poème de la Femme'*.[86] He is correct about its first appearance in the *Revue des Deux Mondes* on 15 January 1849, but it is much more likely that it was inspired by La Païva because the third stanza refers to the Théâtre des Italiens.

She also stimulated Théodore de Banville to a cleverly wicked verse:

> 'Les demoiselles chez Ozy
> Menées
> Ne doivent plus songer aux hy —
> Menées!'

It was in 1840 that she made her début at the Variétés on a relatively modest salary of 1,200 francs a year (a livable but modest sum). Her initial appearances were moderately successul, but her break through came with her portrayal of the part of Louise in *Le Chevalier du Guet*. 'Elle s'y révéla bonne comédienne, lançant le mot avec assurance et sang-froid, chantant les couplets avec beaucoup d'humour. On l'applaudit et ses appointements furent aussitôt élevés à 2,000 francs.'[87] If salary increases are an indication of talent then she cannot have improved much over the next ten or eleven years because her salary for 1851/52 was only 2,500 francs (plus *jetons* — which may have boosted her income by 300-400 francs a year).

That she had her *aficionados* is beyond dispute. The genrally sober Jacques Arago writes in 1852: 'Va pour elle! la voilà lancée, gare dessous! La fusée est partie, on la suit de l'œil, on l'applaudit des

---

[85] L. Loviot, *Alice Ozy* (Paris, Les Bibliophiles fantaisistes, 1910).
[86] Ibid., p.27. The *Emaux et Camées* came out first in 1852; there were eighteen poems, of which *Le Poème de la Femme* was the third.
[87] Loviot, op. cit., p.18.

mains.'⁸⁸ Jules Janin, *Débats,* 8 August 1853, even referred to the Variétés as 'le théâtre de Mademoiselle Ozy'. There was no question but that the light entertainment in which the Variétés specialised (and still does!) suited her minor acting talents perfectly well; it also suited (and allowed her to exploit / or allowed the management to exploit) her particular physical attractions. The latter are what tended to get noticed. When she actually acted well (or more than passably) there was often a note of surprise in the reviewer's comments. Darthenay, in his *Les Acteurs et les actrices de Paris* (1853), reinforces the popular conception of her as 'une des plus jolies femmes de Paris' before suggesting (as a sort of house point) that she was now devoting herself fully to her acting and that in *Une Bonne qu'on renvoie* '[elle] vient de prouver ... un talent sincère'.⁸⁹

1852 was the year of Dumas (fils)' *La Dame aux camélias*, put on, after some difficulty, at the Théâtre du Vaudeville. It became, almost overnight, one of the great successes of the century. It started, or at least it reinforced, a certain trend in light entertainment. This piece, preceded in 1849 by *La Vie de Bohème,* 'marqua le commencement du règne des filles. Elles s'appelaient encore à cette époque, les *lorettes* ... la courtisane s'était infiltrée partout, ou plutôt toutes les classes de la société avaient vus naître les leurs ... Jules Janin, le grave prince des critiques, écrivit même, dans nous ne savons plus quelle préface: ‹Que faisait la France en 1852?› dira-t-on. ‹Elle pleurait sur les malheurs de *La Dame aux camélias*!›.'⁹⁰

Up until the late 1840s and early 1850s women from a certain *milieu* had scarcely ever been portrayed on stage. But Dumas's play changed all that: 'La pièce eut un succès fabuleux. Cela était si nouveau, si osé,

---

⁸⁸ In *Foyers et coulisses,* p.43.
⁸⁹ Darthenay, op. cit., p.60. *Une Bonne qu'on renvoie* was first performed at the Variétés on 23 February 1851. It was given twenty-one performances in 1852, but only during June, July and August — the least successful months of the year (see the section on finances).
⁹⁰ Marguerite Bellanger, *Les Courtisanes du Second Empire* (Bruxelles, Office de Publicité, 1871), pp.14-15.

si hardi!.'[91] It was a fashion quickly followed: 'On mit à la scène toutes les lorettes, toutes les grisettes, les unes pour les flétrir, les autres pour les exalter ... On éleva des autels à des drôlesses qu'on avait auparavant honnies et conspuées, et on trouva des gens pour applaudir à cette honeuse exhibition!'[92] This particular trend (encouraged by the theatre directors for obvious financial reasons) coincided with a vogue for 'fééries-revues' which were shows that depended for their success on the stage settings and the costumes.[93] In the case of the actresses, the costumes became more and more revealing and interest switched rapidly, and easily, to the figure on display: 'l'artiste ne comptait plus, il ne restait que la femme.'[94] It was not too difficult to amalgamate the taste for a measure of *déshabillé* with the vogue for the stage *lorette*. Indeed, the one seemd to necessitate the other (for reasons of realism, perhaps?).

Ozy herself appears to have gone along with the fashion, to the point where she was 'une des premières *fées* en maillot de couleur chair ... '.[95] And it is more than apparent that her reputation as an actress — 'un léger brin de talent distingua toutefois Mlle Ozy'[96] — was based largely on her attractive physique and, more importantly, her willingness to show it off. 'Mlle Ozy compta parmi ces *dames de beauté*, ces *camélias*, qui figurèrent dans des pièces destinées seulement à mettre en valeur d'agréables qualités plastiques'[97] ... 'petits rôles très anodins ou très décolletés.'[98]

Given her reputation it was understandable that the Variétés should want to use her as a crowd-puller. She appeared in many of their 1852 productions, including *Une Queue rouge*, *Déménagé d'hier*, *Le Mari de la dame de chœurs*, *Mam'zell' Rose*, *Une Bonne qu'on renvoie* and

[91] G. d'Heilly, *Le Scandale au Théâtre* (1861), p.11.
[92] Ibid., pp.11-12.
[93] See F. McCormick, op. cit.
[94] Loviot, op. cit., p.33.
[95] Loviot, op. cit., p.33.
[96] Ibid., p.11.
[97] Ibid., p.11.
[98] Loviot dates the move to the rôles 'très décolletés' to 1849 in a piece called *Les Marrons d'Inde*.

Taconnet. Of these, however, only the first named ran to thirty (or more) performances.

Totally unexpectedly, at the beginning of 1855 'le public apprend avec stupeur qu'Ozy renonce définitivement au théâtre'.[99] She was no doubt 'en pleine gloire', but the rôles in which she shone would soon have become inappropriate. In any case, her private life (which her stage life was not totally disassociated from) was finally more rewarding.

iii) **Céleste Mogador**

'Les comédies de ce siècle vivent de lorettes et de gens tarés.'[100] Céleste Mogador wrote four volumes of *Mémoires* that were published in 1858/59 (Paris, Librairie Nouvelle). As an accurate reflexion of either her life or her theatrical career they are probably very untrustworthy — full of anecdote, very self-centred, short on facts and dates and largely concerned with her, shall we say, 'emotional' life. It seems likely (to voice what is in itself only a suspicion) that she got her place at the Variétés *via* the director's couch. 'M.C. ... directeur ... promit de m'engager ... il me fit signer un engagement où il me donnait douze cents francs d'appointements, avec un dédit de vingt mille francs.'[101] She was given small parts in the end-of-year *Revue de cinquante et un*[102] and various other parts, again mainly support or incidental rôles, in some of the 1852 productions notably, if her *Mémoires* are correct, *Paris qui dort* and *Les Reines des bals*. In the former she had a small part as a guitar player (?); in the latter she was used presumably for her ability to dance. As Darthenay said of her in 1853, 'Mlle Céleste ne manque pas d'un certain talent, et qui excelle dans les rôles où elle danse'.[103] She seems to have enjoyed her time at the Variétés and to have worked hard at improving her acting skills ('Je

---

[99] Loviot, op. cit., p.106.
[100] G. d'Heilly, op. cit., p.18.
[101] Celeste, *Mémoires*, vol. 3, p.294.
[102] Its proper title was *La Course aux plaisirs*.
[103] *Les Acteurs et les actrices de Paris*, p.60.

travaillais avec ardeur à mon théâtre')[104] yet her view of herself was that she was a poor actress: 'Je débutai. J'étais toujours mauvaise[105] ... En ma qualité de mauvaise actrice, je jouais toujours au lever du rideau. Je venais de finir *Les Reines des bals.*'[106] The fact that she played 'au lever du rideau' requires some elucidation (though it does confirm her view that she did not know much about acting). 'L'acteur qui, par exemple, doit jouer dans la pièce qui commence un spectacle, quel que soit d'ailleurs le nombre d'actes qui la composent, appelle cela *balayer les planches* ... les directeurs intelligents ... font d'ordinaire balayer les planches par leur *troupe de carton*. La troupe de carton, autre mot d'argot, désigne volontiers les artistes dont le talent, l'utilité et les appointements marquent zéro au baromètre budgétaire.'[107]

Critical reaction to *Les Reines des bals* merely served to underline the point: 'L'exhibition [in a very literal sense it seems] de Mmes Boisgontier et Céleste-Mogador a fait tolérer cette folie'[108] because it was 'aussi peu spirituel que mal dit'.[109] Céleste herself came in for some strong criticism: 'Mlle Céleste joue assez mal la comédie et ne la chante pas mieux, c'est la parodie d'une comédienne exécutée par une danseuse qui ne saurait qu'un pas et qu'une figure.'[110] (but the public continued to turn up and *Les Reines des bals* had 47 performances during the year).

She illustrates what, for some commentators, was becoming a problem: quite simply the quantity of female flesh visible on stage. The objectors had a case which, merely from the acting point of view, was a strong one: 'on engage des actrices, non pas pour leur talent, mais pour leur beauté; non pas pour leur esprit, mais pour leur mollets.'[111] 'Elles ne savant ni se tenir, ni marcher, ni parler, ni chanter; mais elles

---

[104] *Mémoires*, Vol. 4, p.97.
[105] Ibid., Vol. 3, p.297.
[106] Ibid., Vol. 4, p.116.
[107] Montagne, Edouard, *Le Manteau d'Arlequin* (Paris, Lacroix, Verboeckhoven et Cie, 1866).
[108] *Le Corsaire*, 1 March 1852.
[109] *L'Eclair*, 6 March 1852.
[110] *L'Illustration*, Vol. XIX, N° 471, 4 March 1852.
[111] D'Heilly, op. cit., p.104.

sont jolies.'[112] What also caused discomfort was the fact that in a theatre where the vast majority of *comédie-vaudevilles* were supposedly realistic (i.e. 'true' to life) the vogue for pieces of the *Vie de Bohème* and *Dame aux camélias* type suggested only too clearly that public morals were fast degenerating. If prostitutes could be heroines then something was wrong with the moral focus. Theatres had always possessed this aura of 'freer' living, of places that even at the best of times were never entirely out of the shadow of dubious moral standards. But sex had been, in the Variétés and theatres like it, a matter of verbal innuendo (sometimes crude, though as often as not a matter of standard routine; good for a laugh, at any rate). Hardly ever had it become a matter of blatant exhibitionism. But that was what it was fast becoming. And the general public held a very straightforward view of the situation: 'le public juge beaucoup la vertu des actrices ... sur la longueur des robes qu'elles portent ... et le public a grandement raison.'[113] If actresses played women of easy virtue then the chances were they themselves fell into that category. If the said 'actresses' could not act then the probability was they *were* women of easy virtue. 'Elles arrivent en scène en maillot, les épaules nues, les seins à peu près au vent, le visage fardé, les yeux allongés, les lèvres rougies, les mollets arrondis ... ce ne sont plus des actrices: elles se font marchandise.'[114]

In an age when women's everyday fashion meant that they were covered from neck to toe, such *public* sights as bare shoulders and calf-length skirts (or shorter) must have been as offensive to some as they were attractive (for reasons that had little to do with acting) to others. Theatre managers had somehow to achieve a balance that would draw in an audience without offending their regular clients.

Céleste Mogador (and to a lesser degree Alice Ozy) represented a director's bid to increase box-office takings, but it stirred opposition without having much of an effect on the finances. The articulate opposition came from certain sections of the theatrical press. Céleste was more than aware of it: 'Les journaux prenaient la peine de

---

[112] Ibid., p.104.
[113] D'Heilly, op. cit, pp.98–101 in particular.
[114] Ibid., p.104.

THE TROUPE 41

m'abîmer ... le journal *Le Corsaire*, ce chien hargneux de la littérature, me mordait au sang ... J'allais jouer une nouvelle pièce, *Paris qui dort*. M.C. ... [Carpier] me dit: ‹Il faut absolument que vous alliez voir M.J. ... [Janin??], il est mal disposé pour vous.'[115] It appears that the 'visite' was successful and that the journalist in question altered his article. *Quod est demonstrandum*.

iv) Boisgontier (Elisa-Geneviève)[116]

Mlle Boisgontier was one of the regular members of the Variétés troupe. Her salary of 4,000 francs a year (plus *jetons*) says as much as anything else about her relative standing within the theatre. She could not be, and was not, confused with the Célestes (or Ozys even) of her world. 'On rit à voir Boisgontier, on rit à l'entendre; puis on sort en disant: je suis sûr que c'est une bonne fille.'[117]

She had begun her acting career in 1838 at the Porte Saint-Antoine, but had soon moved to the Variétés where she made her début in *L'Hospitalité*. Her main occupation was playing small rôles 'de genre' — fruit-sellers, flower-girls and so on, the standard stock-in-trade characters of many a *comédie-vaudeville* and the equally common servant girl. She must have been good in these sort of parts because her reputation was widespread ('une actrice que tout Paris connaît').[118] Her outstanding qualities appear to have been her 'franches allures — la gaieté, l'entrain, le gros rire long et franc'; she was 'pleine de cœur, entraînante de verve' and, a capital quality, 'si communicative, si sympathique ... la plus accorte soubrette que Paris eût applaudie'.[119] Nor was she lacking in physical charms. But in her case 'on lui passe

---

[115] Céleste Mogador, op. cit., Vol. 3, pp.297–98. Perhaps she did mean Jules Janin; but the regular dramatic critic for *Le Corsaire* was Charles de Besselièvre.
[116] Sometimes written Boisgonthier.
[117] J. Arago, *Foyers et Coulisses* (1852), p.43
[118] See the Arsenl *côte* Rt. 6057.
[119] Rt. 6057 and *Nouvelle Galerie des artistes dramatiques vivants* (1855), Vol. I.

volontiers son gentil décolleté en faveur de sa franchise.'[120] She was, it seems, a girl of ample proportions but with a 'joyeux tempérament' to accompany them.

She had lots of supporters and the press nearly always gave her a good, if brief, mention. By 1852 she was considered in some quarters as ready for rather more sophisticated rôles (those with the 'éventail' as opposed to those with the 'éventaire'). She was, in fact, not only putting on years but putting on weight — 'un beau physique ... beaucoup de rondeur' — and it was suggested that 'il lui manque les rôles à sa taille'.[121]

Her popularity was such that on the occasion of Leclère's 'bénéfice' performance on 17 April 1852 — a special one-act entertainment (among other things) was put on called *Les Tribulations de Boisgontier*.[122] And her own 'bénéfice' in December was one of the high spots of the first half of that month, a fitting tribute to one of the Variétés most popular actresses.[123]

v) Fitz-James (Clara) [or Cara]

Mlle Fitz-James illustrated, at her début in the Théâtre-Français (1841), one of the not infrequent abuses of theatrical practices. She was on stage largely because a rich 'protector' had paid the mangement to give her a part. In addition the *claque* had had instructions to applaud everything she did. Nothing, it seems, could disguise the fact that she was a bad actress — 'la nullité de Mlle F ... '[124] — and no amount of organized approval could overcome the general mood of annoyance and derision that her inept performance provoked. A certain L.F. de V ...

---

120 *Nouvelle Galerie*, op. cit.
121 See Darthenay, op. cit., p.59. Boisgontier had, in her earlier days, been the subject of a portrait by Louis Gratien, shown in the Salon of 1844.
122 Subsequently referred to as *Les Tribulations d'une actrice*.
123 Later in 1859, in *Le Foyer. Journal de littérature et de théâtre*, 7 April 1859 in the section on the Variétés, Boisgontier is briefly dismissed as 'une femme qui prend du ventre'.
124 See Arsenal *côte* Rt. 7574.

who described himself as an 'habitué, depuis 1814, du Théâtre-Français' wrote in the *Courrier des théâtres*, 3 June 1841: 'ce que j'espère, c'est que le vrai public laissera la débutante en face de ses claquetins seuls [i.e. not turn up to her performances], ou saura une autre fois exprimer son opinion de manière à ce que Mlle F. et ses adhérents ne puissent pas s'imaginer qu'il a été pris pour dupe.'[125]

After such an inauspicious start it is something of a surprise to find her still acting in 1852. She must have gained a certain amount of skill and did, on the odd occasion, receive words of praise from the theatrical press — for her rôle in the *Femmes de Gavarni*, for example.[126] But mainly she went unmentioned. That her 'bénéfice' was held on the 10 July - the *worst* month for box-office receipts — only serves to underline her lack of outstanding qualities. Yet there is an anomaly — her salary for April 1851 to March 1852 is recorded as 8,000 francs (plus *jetons*), which is a substantial figure seemingly unrelated to her perceived acting ability. One can only assume she was still 'supported'. Jacques Arago, in *Foyers et coulisses* of 1852, considered she was still lacking proper rôles. But judging by those rôles accorded her in 1852, the 'proper' ones were not forthcoming.

vii) Page (Adèle) (1822–1882 ?)

Barbey d'Aurevilly, in *Les Vieilles actrices* (1884) devotes half-a-dozen pages to Mlle Page: 'Elle était née actrice comme elle était née jolie femme, car c'est jolie qu'elle est bien plus que belle'; her voice was 'douce, reposante, savoureuse et voluptueuse'; what distinguished her acting was 'la distinction spirituelle. Elle avait le don du sourire fin, de la gaieté sobre, de la passion vraie ... '.[127]

---

[125] Op. cit. Rt. 7574.
[126] Mme Coquardeau.
[127] B. d'Aurevilly, *Les Vieilles actrices* (Paris, Librairie des Auteurs Modernes, 1884), pp.54–55. Barbey, like so many critics (of whom the worst was Banville — all flowery nothings; infuriating!) is short on fact and long on impression.

Her career began, like that of so many others, in the provinces — Lyon, Saint-Etienne, Brest. In Brest she is said to have played 'a côté de Lassagne' who was himself playing Pierrot. She made her début in Paris at the Vaudeville in 1842 (with Arnal). It was Arnal, apparently, who persuaded her to come to Paris and who got her the position at the Vaudeville. Here she was a success, receiving the customary accolades: her 'finesses du bien dire', the 'artifices de la démarche élégante' (whatever that might mean), her 'geste gracieux et sobre' and her 'coup d'œil rayonnant et doux' were all noted and approved.[128]

She disappeared from the Paris scene for three years to St. Petersburg but on 27 January 1848, 'on la revit aux Variétés' where 'un accueil plein d'effusion salua son retour' and where she made a deep impression in, among others, *La Ferme de Primerose* (premièred in June 1851, but getting 28 performances in 1852), *Paris qui dort* (the hit of 1852), *La vie de Bohème* (as Musette) and *Souvenirs de Jeunesse* (first performance 2 September 1852).[129]

Appreciations of her at this time are best left to contemporary accounts. Two will do; first Jacques Arago in 1852: 'Cette toute ravissante personne joue le drame et le rire avec un égal succès; et bien des pièces, grâce à elle, one traversé sans naufrage l'heure de la tempête ... Rien n'est plus doux et plus caressant que son organe, rien n'est plus dominateur que sa parole, et le cœur se laisse doucement bercer à cette musique ... je me fais ici l'écho de la foule, qui proclame Mademoiselle Page la plus jolie actrice de Paris; moi je soutiens qu'elle est une des meilleures.'[130] And Darthenay in 1853: Mlle Page is 'le diamant de la troupe des Variétés. Charme, élégance, distinction, sensibilité vraie et adorablement jolie, voilà Madame Page définie.'[131]

---

[128] See Arsenal *côte* Rt. 8945 (from an article by Etienne Enault).
[129] Arsenal, Rt. 9845.
[130] In *Foyers et coulisses*, pp.42–43.
[131] In *Les Acteurs et les actrices de Paris*, pp.60–61.

THE MUSIC

In all the foregoing one crucial aspect of the *comédie-vaudevilles* has been omitted: the fact that they contained *songs*. It was expected, necessary in fact, that actors and actresses could sing — and sing well enough to project to all parts of the theatre. The 'couplet' was usually an integral part of the rôle and audiences expected the performers to be able to cope at least adequately with the music.

The Variétés possessed an orchestra of around twenty-four musicians. (A band that size would produce a considerable sound and the actors would require a decent singing volume to project through even a modest accompaniment.) Its 'chef d'orchestre' was one Nargeot, a conductor and composer (of suitable 'airs') of no small reputation. Jacques Arago, in *Foyers et coulisses* has some very elogious remarks about him: 'M. Nargeot [est] imprégné de mélodies, et les motifs dont il enrichit le répertoire de son théâtre disent une éducation musicale au niveau de celles qui font les réputations.'[132] He expects that Nargeot will eventually move on to a theatre more commensurate with his talent, and suggests the Opéra-Comique. But in 1861 (as evidenced in E. Abraham's *Les Acteurs et les actrices de Paris*) he was still part of the Variétés.[133]

It is to be hoped that by that date he was earning rather more than the 3,600 francs that was his salary in 1851–52. His deputy, the *sous-chef* M. Reine, earned only 2,000 francs. Members of the orchestra were paid a mere 700 or 800 francs a year — it has to be assumed they played in more than one orchestra and gave private lessons. The members of the chorus were even worse paid — 400–600 francs seems to have been the going annual rate. The *chef des chœurs*, a M. George, was paid 1,200 francs — just about a living wage.

The music normally used in these productions was drawn from existing operettas, operas, vaudevilles, popular tunes, folk-tunes — a real, eclectic mix. Among them, however, was the occasional original *air*. Nargeot had a talent for providing these and, in 1851, produced a

---

[132] J. Arago, op. cit., p.48.
[133] E. Abraham, op. cit., p.53.

number that stuck in the popular memory: the 'gracieux couplets' from the *Ferme de Primerose* (played 28 times in 1852) and the signature tune — a genuine *hit* — from *Drin, Drin*,[134] clearly a catchy piece that was kept going over at least the next ten years (and which some critics found annoying!).

With a *chef d'orchestre* of this quality it is not surprising that the Variétés was a popular theatre. What tended to let it down was the quality of the vaudevilles. The choice of pieces was crucial — but sometimes the choice was wrong; and a number of relative failures could have a marked effect on the financial soundness of the establishment. 1852 seems to have had its share of mistakes.

---

[134] Produced 22 times in 1852. In the *Chansonnier nouveau pour 1852* there is mentioned *Le Château rouge*, ronde chantée par Mlle Flore au Théâtre des Variétés dans la pièce *Paris L'Eté* ... musique de M.J. Nargeot — chez L. Vieillot, éditeur, Paris, rue Notre Dame de Nazareth, 32. It is a bit of a puzzle — there was no *Paris L'Eté* in 1852 (or in 1851 for that matter). (Was this meant to be *Paris qui dort*?)

III

1852 — A Year at the *Variétés*

The conditions under which a popular - but not by any means a working-class theatre operated in Paris were difficult. To begin with there was an enormous amount of competition — from theatres with a similar repertoire (the Vaudeville, the Odéon, the Gaîté, the Ambigu, to name but a few of the best known), from the genuine working-class theatres in the area around the Boulevard du Temple and (certainly for a proportion of the Variétés clients) from the more 'serious' theatres (including the Comédie Française and the Théâtre des Italiens; perhaps, too, the Opéra).

Given that theatre-going was one of, if not the principal form of entertainment, given also the huge captive Parisian population, it might seem that theatre managers were not going to be too hard-pressed to put bottoms on seats. But to have filled the Variétés every night of the week for the whole year (and, in theory, that was the ideal target — the theatre only closed its doors for really unavoidable reasons: epidemic, illness or refurbishment) would have meant a *weekly* audience of some 8,500; and over the year the extraordinary number of around 440,000 spectators. Now, a lot of these would have been regulars (how many it is impossible to estimate) — but a manager would still have had to keep them coming in. There were two main methods: a regular diet of *new* vaudevilles (the theatres, long before TV, were ratings-driven; audiences voted initially with whistles and cat-calls and then with their feet; novelty was crucial) and a troupe that included some of the crowd-pulling names. Here again the managers were in competition: the number of good, successful writers of vaudevilles was limited (though there was no *shortage* of writers, one of the problems was reading through and sorting out the decent material from the mediocre; established writers tended to be preferred) and the really good ones were unlikely, at best, to produce more than seven or eight vaudevilles a year (and not all for the same theatre). Higher salaries could induce actors and actresses to change theatres — so high salaries were necessary to retain the best performers.

To put it mildly, the activity within any one theatre must have been frenetic. In 1851 the Variétés had put on 59 different works of which 37 were new. 1852 was not quite so active, but nonetheless there were 58 different works (which included some of the more successful novelties from 1851) of which 32 were new. To achieve such numbers, the theatre put on the work of as many as 55 writers usually working as a team.

Fifty-eight pieces sounds as though the theatre ran each piece for about a week. Nothing could be further from the truth. Each evening's entertainment consisted of a minimum of three vaudevilles (exceptionally sometimes two — but only if one of them was of five acts, and that in itself was uncommon). The troupe kept in its active repertoire for any given month (a month is a more accurate measure of what was put on) a minimum of 10 pieces, but more usually around 13–14. The following table gives an accurate account of the year's productions expressed as figures. (Each figure represents the number of different plays put on in the given month; plays figuring in one month might well figure in subsequent months.)

January	16	July	15
February	13	August	10
March	11	September	19
April	10	October	20
May	13	November	16
June	13	December	19

A definition of the *comédie-vaudeville* is not easy to come by (a play of anything from one to five acts of humorous dialogue with songs designed primarily to entertain) — Francisque Sarcey, in *Quarante ans de théâtre*, nonetheless manages to give a not unreasonable idea of what was required (he ignores the music):

Dans la pièce *bien faite*, on ne cherche ni l'analyse profonde des passions, ni une peinture plus ou moins exacte des caractères, ni rien de ce qui constitue le grand art; on prend pour point de départ ou un fait amusant, ou une situation curieuse, on groupe autour de ce fait ou de cette situation des événements qui en contrarient ou qui en secondent l'action. Ces événements s'en déduisent et s'y ramènent par une invincible logique, et c'est la logique encore qui doit donner la conclusion. C'est ainsi que sont faites la plupart des pièces qui, sous nom de vaudevilles, ou sous le nom de comédies de genre, ont empli notre théâtre depuis 1820 jusqu'à 1850. Scribe, Bayart, Duvert et Lauzanne ont été les maîtres de ce genre.[1]

By definition the *genre* was light; by definition also it seems that it was best suited to its shorter manifestations — i.e. one or two acts. Its prime purpose was to entertain. Given the almost insatiable demand for new pieces, it was imperative that a new vaudeville make its mark immediately in order that it be given a decent run. But a decent run in the 1850s was of a quite different order from a decent run nowadays. Today we would expect a few months as a minimum; in 1852 a run of, say, twenty consecutive nights was a success (and probably guaranteed the piece being put on again — more as a stop-gap or as a brief attempt to increase box-office receipts than as a serious, equally long revival). Anything beyond that became a genuine triumph.[2]

The 1852 figure of fifty-eight vaudevilles is explicable (and understandable) in such conditions. The quick turnover of new pieces was necessary; few would become real successes — and theatre managers were aware of that fact (and not every run of 15 or so performances meant that the play was successful — a play could be kept going simply in order to fill up the evening's entertainment; or to justify the amount of rehearsal time spent on it, or merely to plug a gap until the next novelty was ready for performance).

---

[1] Sarcey, op. cit., p.26.
[2] See M. Descotes, *Histoire de la critique dramatique en france*, p.7. His figures are 15 'représentations consécutives' as a success; 40 as 'un triomphe'. The *Variétés* figures tend to corroborate this.

It remains, now, to see how well — or how badly — the Variétés performed.

i) **January 1852**[3]

Les Deux prudhommes	2, 3, 6, 7, 8, 9, 10, 11, 12, 15, 24.
Soutiens-moi, Chatillon	2, 3, 4, 5.
La Négresse et le Pacha	2, 3, 4, 5, 6, 13, 14, 15, 18.
La Course au plaisir	2, 3, 5, 7, 8, 9, 10, 11, 12, 13, 14, 15.
Riche d'amour[4]	2, 3, 7, 8, 25.
Mignon	4, 5.
Renaudin de Caen	4.
Le Bal des Variétés	4.
Une Erreur académique	6.
Quittance de minuit*	6, 7, 8, 9, 10, 11, 12, 13, 14, 15, 18, 19, 20, 21, 22, 23.
Drinn, Drinn	9, 12, 13, 14, 20, 23, 24.
La Ferme de Primerose	10, 18, 19, 21, 22.

---

[3] The figures on the right-hand side are the *dates* on which the particular vaudeville was given. Note that for January there were no performances on the 16th. An asterisk denotes a *first* performance of a *new* piece.

[4] *Riche d'amour* was by Duvert and Lauzanne — another Arnal vehicle, commented on by Gautier in 1845: 'Arnal a joué ce désopilant vaudeville avec une verve étonnante — c'est assurément, depuis *Passé minuit*, le plus grand succès qu'il ait obtenu', *Histoire de l'art dramatique en France*, Vol. 4, p.159.

*Une Queue rouge**	17, 19, 20, 21, 22, 23, 24, 26, 27, 28, 29, 30, 31.
Le Goton de Béranger	18, 25.
*Le Puits mitoyen**	25, 26, 27, 28, 29, 30, 31.
*Trois amours de pompier**	25, 26, 27, 28, 29, 30, 31.

In all, the troupe put on *sixteen* different pieces, of which four were new. Of the remaining twelve, the *Bals des Variétés* was a one-off event (not a play), nine had had their first performance the previous year (1851) and only the remaining two were older: *Riche d'amour* dated from 1845 (first put on at the Théâtre du Vaudeville, it was written by Duvert and Lauzanne and was a vehicle for Arnal. It would be played thirteen times in 1852, mainly, one suspects as a regular, popular stand-by to fill out the evenings' entertainment) and *Renaudin de Caen*, which was even older, having first been performed at the Théâtre du Vaudeville in 1836 — again the authors were Duvert and Lauzanne and the main player was Arnal. (It was one of his early triumphs.)

Of the sixteen pieces, half exactly were *one-act comédie-vaudevilles* or vaudevilles (there does not seem to be any perceptible distinction; the designations seem interchangeable); four were *two-acts* (including the 1851 end-of-year *revue, La Course au plaisir*); one was five acts: *Le Goton de Béranger* and the remaining three were, respectively, *Le Bal des Vairiétés*, *Soutiens-moi, Chatillon*, called simply a *scène*, and *Quittance de minuit* described as an *opéra-comique* (an unexpected genre for the Variétés, given its remit).

The injection of new material was necessary to keep audiences coming in. It would be expected that a new piece (or pieces) would increase attendance figures. *Quittance de minuit* failed to do so on the 6th; *Une Queue rouge* on the 17th was a moderate success; but the performances on the 25th (with *two* new plays) produced the highest box-office receipts of the month: 2,097 francs.

On the whole the regular dramatic critics focused on a theatre when there was a new piece.[5] Occasionally there would be a much more general piece which would make a thoughtful overall résumé of a theatre's situation. One such review appeared in *L'Eclair*, 12th January 1852 (written by Charles de Villedeuil). It is worth quoting at length:

> Le directeur des Variétés poursuit le cours de ses brillants succès. Sous son heureuse influence, le théâtre a repris son aspect des anciens jours, et la caisse a retrouvé cette rotondité de bon augure dont elle semblait avoir perdu l'habitude.[6]
>
> Dances, chants, tombola, produits asiatiques, l'activité de M. Carpier n'a rien négligé. Son audace est même allée plus loin. Un homme d'esprit, un vrai poète, M. de Montheau, a fait *Mignon*,[7] et le public des Variétés s'est convaincu qu'on pouvait en conscience applaudir à autre chose qu'aux grosses balourdises d'Arnal, à ces farces concentriques [?!] qui ont le tort de ne plus avoir le mérite de la nouveauté.
>
> Arnal est sans contredit un acteur d'un grand talent ... [mais] il est grand par lui-même, voilà tout. Il est aujourd'hui ce qu'il était il y a vingt ans; il n'a pas grossi son sac d'un geste, il n'a pas étendu son répertoire d'une grimace. Arnal est toujours le même, grand acteur sans doute, mais objet d'étude pour ceux seulement qui ne l'ont jamais vu.

The piece has a section on the translations of the vaudevilles into foreign languages; but the author reassures his readers 'nos voisins peuvent bien contrefaire nos livres, mais ils ne pourraient contrefaire

---

[5] In the *Almanach des spectacles pour 1852* there is a breakdown of the previous year's performances — these include the startling figures of 534 vaudevilles, of which 337 were *reprises* and 197 *new* — i.e. the critics have about 4 *new* vaudevilles on average every week!

[6] Perhaps this was so for December 1851 — but January 1852 was a mediocre month for receipts.

[7] Put on only twice in January (and once in February) and not again during 1852.

ni Mlle Ozy, ni Mlle Page, ni aucune de toutes ces brillantes odalisques qui font les délices du public parisien'.[8]

The 'brillantes odalisques' were not to everyone's taste. As has already been pointed out, there was a reaction, largely on moral grounds, to the display of what was thought of as excessive quantitites of unadorned female flesh. The Variétés end-of-season *Course au plaisir* had one critic (A. de Bragelonne) expressing reservations about one actress in particular:

> N'est-il pas fâcheux de voir une scène qui devrait être de bonne compagnie, dégradée par la présence, même passagère, d'une célébrité empruntée aux bals publics les plus mal famés? N'est-il pas déplorable qu'une demoiselle Mogador, usurpant le titre d'artiste, vienne exhiber sur un théâtre consacré à l'art et à l'esprit l'affligeant et repoussant spectacle de ses pieds en dedans et de ses danses sans nom honorable dans aucune langue ... le public souffre pour lui-même et pour les vrais artistes condamnés à cet humiliant voisinage. En ceci nous sommes l'interprète non seulement de notre sentiment personnel, mais de l'impression générale.[9]

There follows an interesting snippet of information (which is at the same time a glimpse of attitudes common (?) at the time): the Variétés had 'leur négresse'. This is the one-and-only reference throughout the year — but was the presence in the troupe of a 'négresse' a reflexion of widespread practice or was the Variétés exceptional in this? She is not named, so there is no way of knowing which, if any, of the named actresses she was. The paragraph goes as follows:

> ce que nous pardonnons de bon cœur aux Variétés, c'est leur négresse; elle est jeune, jolie, bien faite, gracieuse comme une Parisienne, et tout juste assez noire pour ne pas démentir le sang dont elle sort. On dirait une blanche passé au chocolat. Elle chante avec verve, elle manie sa guitare à la façon d'une Andalouse, et débite

---

[8] *L'Eclair*, 12 January 1852, p.12.
[9] A. de Bragelonne in *La Chronique de Paris*, 1852, 4ème année, 11 janvier, p.22.

d'un ton fort gentil un petit baragouin qu'elle semble prendre très sérieusement pour du français: c'est une curiosité musicale très amusante à voir et à entendre.[10]

Of the new productions put on in January, the one that drew most critical attention was *Une Queue rouge*.[11] There were two main reasons for this: Arnal was in the lead rôle and the authors were Duvert and Lauzanne. That particular combination had proved highly successful on numerous occasions. But Duvert and Lauzanne had something slightly different in mind. The plot is simple: a young provincial actor is booed and whistled off-stage in the presence of the young woman he loves. Later, when he has made his reputation, he discreetly helps her out of serious (financial) difficulties and they end up by marrying. Gautier is categoric: 'MM. Duvert et Lauzanne se sont trompés, nous le croyons, en voyant dans cette donnée un rôle pour Arnal.'[12] He believes they should have chosen a younger actor — 'elegant, distingué, sérieux'. Arnal, he writes, 'ne peut être que comique; ses traits, ses gestes, ses intonations sont invinciblement risibles; l'ahurissement des imbroglios burlesques est figé sur son masque; il est capable, tout au plus, à la fin d'une folle intrigue, de faire un joyeux mariage avec une héroïne délurée ou une veuve égrillarde; mais l'amour sentimental lui est interdit.'[13]

The mis-match between rôle and actor was noted elsewhere in the press: 'Arnal joue avec beaucoup d'art un rôle qui n'est pas dans ses cordes et qui n'est plus de son âge. C'est une idée assez saugrenue que d'avoir fait de ce spirituel farceur un amoureux pour tout de bon qu'aime sérieusement une jeune et jolie personne de province.'[14] *Le Corsaire* simply noted that 'Arnal a mis le comble à sa gloire artistique

---

[10] Ibid. For those who would wish to, there is a whole series of assumptions (or prejudices) lying here waiting to be analysed. One has to assume, as a reader, that there was no deliberate intention to offend.

[11] Wicks, in *The Parisian Stage*, gives this as 2 acts. It is, in fact, a *three-act* comédie-vaudeville.

[12] *L'Art dramatique en France*, vol. 6, p.292.

[13] Ibid., p.293.

[14] In *La Chronique de Paris*, 1 February 1852.

en se révélant sous un jour tout nouveau'.[15] But that was really to sidestep the issue. *La Chronique de Paris* had further critical points to make: the piece was too long (Charles de Besselièvre in *Le Corsaire* on 21st January suggested the play should be 'quelque peu raccourcie'); but far more damning was the fact that it lacked real wit and humour ... 'la phrase qui produit le plus d'effet ... est celle-cit que débite Arnal: ‹Tous les jours je dis des bêtises au public, et pourtant je ne suis pas un homme politique›.'[16] In short, as Gautier summed it up, 'MM. Duvert et Lauzanne nous ont habitué à des triomphes plus éclatants'.[17]

Arnal's partner was Mlle Page. As the *Chronique* put it, 'Mlle Page ... est admirablement jolie, et cela suffit à l'intérêt de son rôle'; the *Corsaire* had a point to make: 'Mlle Page ... a montré une grâce et une distinction charmantes. Cette artiste a assez de talent pour qu'on ne la déshabille pas, comme on l'a fait à la fin de la pièce.'[18] Gautier, on the other hand, seemed to appreciate the sight: 'Mlle Page est admirablement jolie dans son costume de nymphe décolletée par en haut et par en bas.'[19]

The other female rôle was played by Alice Ozy. The *Chronique* thought it a shame that she should have to play a 'personnage trivial, absurde, et qui pis est, sans gaieté'; the worst of it was, though, that the rôle had originally been intended for the 'allures vulgaires de Mlle Boisgontier'.

The play was not exactly a flop. It ran for 25 [consecutive] nights until the middle of February — at which point Besselièvre wrote: 'Depuis qu'on ne donne plus la *Queue rouge*, les spectateurs font *queue* aux portes du théâtre.'[20] It appeared again five times in March and then was dropped.

The remaining novelties are not accorded anything like the same attention in the press. *Quittance de minuit* was held to have been

---

[15] *Le Corsaire*, Tuesday, 20 January 1852.
[16] Besselièvre in *Le Corsaire*, Wednesday 21 January 1982 — simply reinforcing the point in *La Chronique de Paris* (the author, I think, is A. de Bragelonne).
[17] Gautier, op. cit., p.295.
[18] Ch. de Besselièvre.
[19] Gautier, op. cit., p.295.
[20] *Le Corsaire*, 20 February 1852.

successful. The leading rôle — singing, in this instance — was taken by a *débutante*, Mlle Anaïde (sister of Mlle Duez of the Opéra-National). 'Sa voix est agréable, son physique a paru faire une vive impression sur le public. À son entrée en scène j'entendis plusieurs de mes voisins murmurer: ‹As-tu déjeûné, Jacquot?›.[21] The initial run was 16 performances. There were a further five: one in March and four in April.

The two one-act vaudevilles *Le Puits mitoyen* and *Trois Amours de pompier* were much more the standard Variétés fare. Both had their first performance on the same night, the 25th. The first was described as 'une drôlerie dans laquelle se débitent force plaisanteries et bons mots ... le public a applaudi' (the main players were Kopp and Duvernoy); the second had 'quelques bonnes grosses plaisanteries ... un dénoûment assez original, et enfin du jeu intelligent de Kopp, de Danterny et de Mlle Potel.'[22] Both plays did well in the course of the year receiving 46 and 52 performances respectively. Their appearance for the last week of January did at least succeed in improving the box-office takings for the month; that the 25th was also a Sunday meant that there was more chance that more people would turn up.

ii) February 1852

Les Deux Prudhommes	1, 2, 3, 4, 5, 6, 7, 8.
Le Puits mitoyen	1, 2, 3, 4, 5, 6, 7, 8, 9, 10, 11, 12, 13, 14, 22.
Une Queue rouge	1, 2, 3, 4, 5, 6, 7, 8, 9, 10, 13, 14, 29.
Trois Amours de pompier	1, 2, 3, 4, 5, 6, 7, 8, 9, 10, 11, 12, 13, 14, 16, 17, 18, 19, 20, 21, 22, 23, 24, 29.

---

[21] *Le Corsaire*, Friday, 9 January 1852.
[22] Ibid., Wednesday, 28 January 1852.

Mignon	9
Les Cabinets particuliers	10, 13, 14, 15, 16, 17, 18, 19, 20, 21, 22, 23, 24, 25, 26, 27, 28, 29.
Paris qui dort*	11, 12, 23, 24, 25, 26, 27, 28.
L'Ami de la maison*	15, 16, 17, 18, 19, 20, 21, 29.
Derrière le rideau	15.
Un Chef de brigands	15.
Riche d'amour	16, 17, 22.
Supplice de Tantale	18, 19, 20, 21.
Les Reines des bals publics*	22, 23, 24, 25, 26, 27, 28, 29.

February saw a reduction in the number of pieces put on: 13, of which *three* were new. Of the 13, six had been performed in January. Of the remaining seven, *Les Cabinets particuliers*, a one-act vaudeville by Duvert and Boniface, was a favourite stand-by. It was already twenty years old, having been first put on at the Théâtre du Vaudeville in October 1832. It was the perfect vehicle for Arnal.[23] *Supplice de Tantale* dated from the end of October 1850 (another one-act *comédie-vaudeville* from Duvert and Lauzanne). *Derrière le rideau* (two-act *comédie-vaudeville*) and *Un Chef de brigands* (a one-act vaudeville) both dated from 1851, July and October respectively. The other three were new: *L'Ami de la maison* a one-act *comédie-vaudeville*; *Paris qui dort* — one of the Variétés big productions — a five-act piece; and *Les Reines des bals publics*, one-act and described as a *folie-vaudeville*.

To take them in reverse order of interest, *L'Ami de la maison* had eight performances and was then dropped completely. It had originally

---

[23] It would receive 64 performances in 1852 — a tribute to its continuing popularity.

been accepted by the previous director, M. Morin, but it was quite clear that M. Carpier was reluctant to stage it because it had been ready (at least as a completed script) since 1850. It seems that the new director was obliged, legally, to put it on. According to Besselièvre[24] there was an obligation 'par autorité de justice' to stage it *thirty* times. In the event eight was sufficient.[25]

Les Reines des bals publics[26] was not met with any critical acclaim. It was put on, presumably as an attempt to draw in the uncritical, voyeuristic perhaps, theatre-goers. It certainly succeeded in that respect, because from its inception on Sunday 22nd February receipts rose noticeably. One comment will suffice. In *L'Eclair*, N°.9, 6 March 1852, we find a brief assessment, the piece is 'aussi peu spirituel que mal dit'. Then comes the reason for the success and the opprobrium: 'nous nous sommes seulement émerveillé sur le réalisme avec lequel la troupe des Variétés jouait les mœurs de la Bohème. Il y a encore du talent à reproduire, aux feux de la rampe, les intimités de sa vie privée.'[27] But *Les Reines* was not alone in drawing the crowds.

Paris qui dort had begun its run on the 11th; had managed to indicate it would continue on the 12th but had had to have that performance cancelled. It would not go into regular showings until the 23rd (the day following the start of *Les Reines* ...). Besselièvre gave the reasons in *Le Corsaire* of the 20th: 'Au théâtre des Variétés, *Paris qui dort* est toujours alité. M. Ch. Perey, qui, par un enrouement subit, avait arrêté la pièce le jour de la première représentation après le premier acte, est complètement rétabli; mais voilà que Mlle Page est tombée malade à son tour. C'est une épidémie ... qui heureusement n'a pas gagné le public qu'Arnal, avec la reprise des *Cabinets particuliers* tient dans un état de santé très satisfaisant.'

---

[24] In *Le Corsaire*, 20 February 1852.
[25] Besselièvre had one of his own vaudevilles waiting for performance — perhaps he had an axe to grind? Whatever the reason, *Le Château de Coëtaven* was put on in March.
[26] See the comments under Céleste Mogador, p.39.
[27] *L'Eclair*, op. cit., p.108.

Paris qui dort was intended to show off the whole troupe (except Arnal), and had substantial parts for Leclère (the male lead), Perey, Cachardy, Duvernoy, Dauterny and Bache[28] as well as for M$^{lles.}$ Page, Bertin, Esther, Joly and ... Céleste. Reactions to it were mixed. *L'Eclair* did not like it at all. '[Delacour et Lambert Thiboust] ne sont parvenus à produire qu'un vaudeville vulgaire ... Et certes, si l'on dort à Paris, c'est peut-être quand l'on va voir leur pièce.'[29] *La Chronique de Paris* was much more favourable: 'une pièce ... qui repose sur un donnée rebattue, à savoir que Paris n'est jamais mieux éveillé que lorsqu'on le croit endormi. Tout est donc dans l'antiphrase du titre ... [La] pièce est remplie de scènes gaies et pétille de mots heureux ... Mlle Page est comme toujours une créature ravissante. On n'est pas plus jolie qu'elle en costume de bouquetière et en petite robe à l'indienne! Et Leclère, en garde national, est bien la plus désopilante figure que vous puissiez voir ... *Paris qui dort* ... réussira et fera de l'argent.'[30] The critical article is quite long and goes on to raise the often debated issue of *realism* (which seems central to the dramatic critic's ethos of the time). It faults some of the details in terms of exactness of observation and concludes, 'Il n'y a pas de détails insignifiants dans un tableau de mœurs, qui vit surtout par l'observation. S'il n'est pas vrai absolument, il n'est pas.'

Although the *comédie-vaudevilles* were a mixture of dialogue and song, there was no concensus regarding the respective proportions of each. Authors were presumably free (within wide limits) to allow their characters to burst into song at whatever point seemed appropriate. It followed that a piece could seem to contain a relatively large number of songs for its length or vice-versa. *Drinn-Drinn*, for instance, a one-act play, had eleven songs. *Paris qui dort*, on the other hand, a five-act play, had no more than *twenty* songs — which suggests an emphasis on dialogue (situation, repartee, intrigue) to the point where songs were

---

[28] Bache was with the Variétés until March 1852 [?]. He had created Gautier's *Pierrot posthume* at the Théâtre du Vaudeville — he was described as 'long, maîgre, pâle, l'air ascétique'. See Rt. 5695(1) and Rt. 5695(2).
[29] *L'Eclair*, 6 March 1852, p.108.
[30] H. de Villemessant, 29 February 1852, pp.141-42. The financial prognostication was, for once, correct. The piece played *80* times.

introduced only when they did not unduly interrupt the plot. And *Paris qui dort,* even in its songs, did not follow the normal pattern of borrowing *all* the music from previous productions (or popular *airs* and so on); it contained *five* new songs specially composed for it: three from M. Bazile (who had composed songs for earlier vaudevilles at the Variétés — and *Les Souvenirs de jeunesse* later in 1852 would contain another of his compositions) and two from M. Nargeot (who frequently wrote the odd *air* or two for new shows). A small step, perhaps, towards the *operetta* of Offenbach and the eventual eclipse of the *comédie-vaudeville* as either the *music* dominated or, alternatively, the music was eliminated and farce became the normal fare.

iii) **March 1852**

Les Reines des bals publics	1, 2, 3, 4, 5, 6, 7, 8, 9, 10, 11, 12, 13, 14, 15, 16, 17, 18, 19, 20, 21, 22, 23, 24, 25.
Les Cabinets particuliers	1, 2, 3, 4, 5, 6, 7, 8, 9, 10, 11, 12, 13, 15, 16, 17, 18, 22, 23, 28, 29, 30, 31.
Paris qui dort	1, 2, 3, 4, 5, 6, 8, 9, 10, 11, 12, 13, 15, 16, 17, 18, 19, 20, 21, 22, 23, 24, 25, 26, 27, 28, 29, 30, 31.
Trois amours de pompier	7, 14, 18.
Une Queue rouge	7, 14, 19, 20, 21.
Drinn, Drinn	7.
Le Puits mitoyen	14, 21.
Un Chef de brigands	14.

Le Château de Coëtaven*	24, 25, 26, 27, 28, 29, 30, 31.
Un Monsieur qui prend la mouche*	26, 27, 28, 29, 30, 31.
Quittance de minuit	28.

The pattern for March was dictated by the obvious fact that the three successful productions of February continued to be box-office favourites — and indeed March turned out to have the highest takings for any month in 1852. (*60,380* francs was good by any standards; at virtually 2,000 francs a night on average it must have meant an average nightly audience of around 800 *paying* spectators. In spite of the moral strictures from some quarters regarding *Les Reines* — or, indeed, because of them — Carpier could fell well pleased with the mix of old and new). The pattern of takings shows, interestingly enough, that the absence of *Paris qui dort* on the 7th, combined with a *reprise* of *Une Queue rouge* caused a noticeable drop in takings; a drop all the more marked because the 7th was a Sunday when it would be expected that takings remained high.

Towards the end of the month the introduction of two new vaudevilles — even though the second, *Un Monsieur qui prend la mouche* (by Michel and Labiche, a combination as potent at times as Duvert and Lauzanne), had Arnal and Leclère playing opposite each other — did little to stop the slow slide towards reduced receipts, initially, that is.

The journalists had noted the popularity of *Paris qui dort*. *Le Corsaire* announced on March 4th: 'Aux Variétés le prodigieux succès de *Paris qui dort* grandit à ce point que chaque soir plus de 500 personnes ne peuvent trouver à se placer' and noted on the 16th March that the Variétés programme 'continue à attirer tous les soirs chambrée complète'.[31]

---

[31] If that was in fact the case, then there must have been a considerable number of *free* tickets in circulation; the takings, though high, do not indicate a full house of *paying* audience.

The *Château de Coëtaven* (a one-act vaudeville, one of whose authors was Ch. de Besselièvre, one of the regular drama critics on *Le Corsaire*) received a relatively favourable press — cool from *L'Illustration* which found the plot and ideas dated;[32] brief but friendly from *Le Corsaire*: 'la pièce fourmille de couplets hardis et spirituels ... la salle était nombreuse: elle a ri et applaudi';[33] and long and eventually positive from *La Chronique de Paris*: 'Cette jolie comédie, qui porte avec elle un parfum des genêts de la Bretagne ... roule sur un quiproquo aussi amusant que bien soutenu durant toute la pièce. Il s'agit d'un fiancé qui prend le château de son beau-père pour une auberge [no wonder *L'Illustration* found the plot dated; the model appears to have been *She Stoops to Conquer*]'.[34] Interestingly — especially where there was the slightest whiff of scandal of any sort — the review continues: 'La pièce de M. Besselièvre est convenablement jouée par tout le monde, à l'exception pourtant d'un comédien chargé du rôle de Gaston, et qui, assure-t-on, a été imposé aux auteurs. Cette nullité, qui répond au nom de Nanteuil (lisez Boulé), et qui n'a ni physique, ni organe, ni intelligence ... .'[35] An actor by the (stage?) name of Nanteuil is listed in the *Almanach*. But the name does not appear in the salaries' ledger. On the other hand the *directeur de la scène* was a M. Boulé (who also seems to have been the *secrétaire général*) and another M. Boulé (Gustave) is named as an *artiste* (on a salary of 1,800 francs a year; which means he was normally used for small walk-on parts). It seems to have been a case of one (influential) member of the family attempting to further the careeer of another (son? nephew?).

It was becoming customary to make complimentary noises about M. Nargeot's compositions, but unusual to hear of anyone else. In this case, however, Henri de Villemessant draws attention to the 'gracieux airs inédits' of 'le jeune maestro qui débutait ce soir-là' and whose

---

[32] See *L'Illustration*, Vol. XIX, N°· 475, 3 April 1852, p.212.
[33] *Le Corsaire*, 27 March 1852.
[34] *La Chronique de Paris*, 31 March 1852, p.190.
[35] *Le Chronique*, ibid.

name was M. Francis Morillon. (It may well have been his only claim to fame.)

With *Un Monsieur qui prend la mouche* the Variétés found another success. By far the longest review came from the pen of Gautier:[36] 'Le sublime ne s'analyse pas. Figurez-vous Arnal aux prises avec Leclère; Arnal agacé, taquinant et taqiné, ... emporté et bravache, insupportable, irrité par les contradictions comme par un invisible tétanos, démangé par de fourmillantes impatiences. Et la bonne et béate figure que Leclère! quelle placide physionomie de bourgeois! Henry Monnier et Daumier combinés, le rentier ganache surpris dans la sincérité bonhomme de son type.'[37] Gautier's impression of its reception is unequivocal: 'On a ri tout le long de l'acte d'un fou rire; on a trépigné des pieds, des mains et des cannes. Arnal était entré dans un de ces rôles qui lui sont comme une seconde peau.' Arnal and Leclère were seconded by Kopp in one of his familiar rôles of valet, 'une manière d'animal domestique qui mange ou plutôt qui broute dans les mains de ses maîtres, tyran en livrée, bête et sournois.'[38] No other writer could out-do Gautier in this form — but all were of the same opinion: 'Ceci est mieux qu'un rôle pour Arnal, c'est une comédie du genre bouffon ou fiabesque, vertement menée, et follement bourée des plus divertissants coq-à-l'âne. Le jeu de maître d'Arnal et de ses disciples Kopp et Leclère a fait rire la salle entière comme un seul homme.'[39] *Le Corsaire* was fulsome in its praise, writing of 'un succès de gros rire' where Arnal revealed himself 'd'une jeunesse, d'un comique et d'une distinction dont rien n'approche. Je ne sais quel phénomène s'était accompli en lui; mais c'était Arnal d'il y a quinze ans. Il a joué avec une verdure et un entrain extraordinaires ... En somme, c'est une bien désopilante folie.'[40]

---

[36] See *L'Histoire de l'art dramatique*, Vol. 6, 7 April 1852, pp.325-27. A summary of the plot takes up about two-thirds of the account, but it is done in a most readable fashion.
[37] Gautier, op. cit., Vol. 6, p.326.
[38] Ibid., p.327.
[39] Philippe Busoni in *L'Illustration*, Vol.XIX, N°.475, 3 April 1852, p.212.
[40] *Le Corsaire*, 28 March 1852.

There was one other snippet of news that the *Corsaire* mentioned, namely, that a new production called *Les Femmes de Gavarni* was having some pre-première problems: 'La censure retient dans ses griffes *Les Femmes de Gavarni*, et il paraît qu'elles n'en sortiront que bien déchirées ... si elles en sortent.'[41]

March, having made a good start, had made an equally good finish. The problem now was how to maintain momentum.

iv) **April 1852.**

Le Château de Coëtaven	1, 2, 3, 4, 5, 6, 11, 12, 13, 14, 15, 16, 17, 18, 19, 20, 21, 28.
Un Monsieur qui prend la mouche	1, 2, 3, 5, 6, 7, 8, 10, 11, 12, 13, 14, 15, 16, 17, 18, 19, 20, 21, 22, 23, 24, 25, 26, 27.
Les Cabinets particuliers	1, 4, 8, 10, 17, 25, 26.
Paris qui dort	1, 2, 3, 4, 5, 6, 7, 8, 10, 11, 12, 13, 14, 15, 16, 18, 19, 20, 21, 22, 23, 24, 25, 26.
Quittance de minuit	4, 25, 26, 27.
Le Puits mitoyen	7, 11, 22, 23, 29, 30.
Il faut qu'une porte soit ouverte ou fermée	17.
Tribulations de Boisgonthier* (*plus* Intermèdes and danseurs espagnols)	17.
Trois Amours de pompier	18, 24.

[41] Ibid., 21 March 1852.

La Vie de Bohème   27, 28, 29, 30.

April, along with August, was the month with the least number of shows running — *ten* in all, of which only *Tribulations de Boisgonthier*[42] (sometimes referred to as the *Tribulations d'une actrice*) was new; and that was put on only the once on the 17th as part of the special benefit performance for Leclère. The prices of some of the seats were increased for this 'représentation extraordinaire' and the theatre took 3,222 francs. Leclère himself, according to the accounts for April, benefited to the tune of 2,500 francs — a generous payment by standards of the time.

Not that, at this stage, it was necessary for Carpier to put on new pieces with the continuing run of March's successful shows. But audiences quickly tire of the same fare, no matter how good and by the end of the month the receipts showed a 33% drop when compared with March.

The press appeared to think all was going well; but on the 20th *Le Corsaire* signalled the imminent closure of *Paris qui dort*: 'cette pièce, dont la vogue paraît intarissable, n'aura plus que quelques représentations, plusieurs artistes étant à la veille de prendre leur congé.' The press's interest in things pecuniary produced the following comment: '*Un Monsieur qui prend la mouche* ... fera encaisser, comme chaque soir, 2,500 francs, grâce au talent d'Arnal et de Leclère.'[43] But the press was wrong; on only *nine* evenings throughout April did the takings exceed 2,000 francs — and only *twice* (including Leclère's benefit) did they go above 2,500 francs.

On 25th April *Le Corsaire* announced 'la dernière représentation de *Paris qui dort*, et Arnal dans deux pièces ... La salle sera comble'. Perhaps the paper got it wrong (or was in league with Carpier in an effort to boost takings?) but the same announcement appeared the following day, the 26th. This time they were correct. *Paris qui dort*

---

[42] There is a brief mention in *L'Eclair* where C. Holff refers to the 'lascives pétulances de cette folle et capricieuse gaieté', 24 April 1852, p.192.

[43] *Le Corsaire*, 23 April 1852.

came off after 61 virtually consecutive performances, but it remained in the repertoire for the rest of the year and would receive another nineteen outings.

The only other feature of note was the *reprise* of *La Vie de Bohème* on the 27th, described as 'des plus brillantes: les créateurs ont été parfaits, comme jadis, jamais succès n'a été plus complet que celui obtenu par Mlle Favart.'[44]

Theatre thrived not only on popular vaudevilles but on gossip; tit-bits of news were constantly being purveyed by the press. There were mainly two varieties: the scandalous or the virtuous. One notable absentee from all the press notices was Mlle Delorme. But she had her supporters, none more loyal than *L'Eclair*. A report on the 10th April will bear quoting:

> Tous les journaux ont cité un trait de bienfaisance de Mlle Page, qui a généreusement fourni à tous les frais d'une longue et douloureuse maladie à laquelle vient enfin de succomber Mlle Danse, son habilleuse. Mais ce que les journaux n'ont pas dit — et c'est une suite des préventions de certains organes de la presse contre la spirituelle artiste — c'est que Mlle Delorme, prévenue trop tard de l'état de Mlle Danse pour l'aider de sa bourse et de ses soins, a voulu satisfaire le dernier vœu de la morte en lui évitant la promiscuité de la fosse commune, et lui a acheté une concession à perpétuité. Ce trait de générosité n'étonnera du reste aucun de ceux qui, comme nous, ont pu apprécier l'excellent cœur de Mlle Delorme.[45]

She had for some time now refrained from appearing on stage (though *L'Eclair* carried a note to the effect that she was going to reappear in *Sophie Arnoud* 'une pièce écrite pour elle et sous son inspiration')[46] — even though she was in the list of *artistes* receiving salaries up to 31st March 1852. Perhaps her forthcoming marriage to

---

[44] *Le Corsaire*, 28 April 1852. Mlle Favart played the leading female rôle of Mimi.

[45] The piece is signed J. Planté.

[46] J. Planté, *L'Eclair*, N$^{o.}$15, 17 April 1852, p.180. The play was not performed in 1852.

1852 — A YEAR AT THE *VARIÉTÉS*

John Bowes (23rd August 1852) meant she had other things on her mind. Whatever the reason, she had really ceased being an actress — perhaps wisely, given some of the hostile criticism she had faced in the late 1840s.

By this point in the season — for all theatre directors — the best months were over (September to April as a rule). One of the difficulties of the summer months was not of their making; it was simply the heat. The theatres had no means of staying tolerably cool. And the fact that the lighting was either candles (vast quantities on huge chandeliers — permanently lit during the performances and generating a lot of heat) or oil-lamps or, more recently, gas, simply made the problem worse. Theatre managements feared a hot summer. In addition, some of the stars (and these included Arnal) took long periods of *congé* during the summer, leaving the theatres without some of their sure drawing power. All of which goes a long way to explaining the brief note in *Le Corsaire* at the end of January:

> Frédérick Lemaître et Mlle Clarisse Muroy sont engagés pour quatre mois, à partier du 1er mai. Avec eux, M. Carpier espère conjurer les chaleurs! ... Pourquoi pas?'

v) **May 1852.**

Le Puits mitoyen	1, 4, 8, 10, 12.
La Vie de Bohème	1, 3, 4, 5, 6, 7, 8, 11, 30.
Les Reines des bals publics	2, 3, 6, 7, 9.
Paris qui dort	2, 9, 10, 13, 14, 15, 16.
Un Monsieur qui prend la mouche	2, 3, 4, 5, 6, 7, 8, 9, 10, 11, 12, 19, 20, 21, 22, 23, 24.
Les Cabinets particuliers	2, 9, 14, 15, 16, 25, 26, 27, 28, 29, 31.

Le Château de Coëtaven	5, 11.
Une Vengeance*	12, 13, 14, 15, 16, 17, 18, 19, 20, 21, 22, 23, 24.
Canadar, père et fils*	12, 13, 14, 15, 16, 17, 18, 19, 20, 21, 22, 23, 24, 25, 26, 27, 28, 29, 30, 31.
Déménagé d'hier*	17, 18, 19, 20, 21, 22, 23, 24, 25, 26, 27, 28, 29, 30, 31.
La Perruquière de Meudon	17, 18, 25, 26, 27, 28, 29.
Madame Diogène*	31.
Intermèdes: *Danses*: Mlle Rosa Espert *Musique*: Giovanni Filippa	19, 20, 21, 22, 23, 24, 25, 26, 27, 28, 29, 31.

The 29th July 1851 had seen the *début* of the *danseurs espagnols* with Mlle Rosa Espert. Something must have caused a problem (moral outrage, perhaps? or merely the lack of a work-permit?) because on the 31st the 'autorité fait suspendre les représentations des danses espagnoles' only for the minister to authorise their act again on 5th August. The act ran until 28th August. The dancers — or, at the very least, Mlle Rosa Espert — must have been reasonably popular because on the 7th November, Mlle Rosa Espert was accorded a 'représentation extraordinaire' as her benefit (the evening included the 'célèbre Bosco, le prestidigitateur ... ').[47]

Some journalists remained extraordinarily optimistic about Carpier's ability to make a financial success of a season that, having peaked in March, was beginning visibly to slip out of control. It was all very well for *Le Corsaire* to announce on the 24th May that 'M. Carpier, avec

---

[47] See the *Almanach des Spectacles pour 1852* (which is really the information for 1851).

une affiche ainsi composée, lutte facilement contre les chaleurs'; but the facts were quite different. May turned out marginally worse than April, with a total month's receipts of 42,632 francs — but with only five nights in the month grossing more than 2,000 francs, the signs were bad, not good.

The interesting feature is an analysis of those particular five nights. Two were Sundays: the 2nd (2,612 francs) and the 30th (2,296 francs). The contributing factors were the normal expectation that Sunday audiences would be more numerous than other nights plus the adroit programming to ensure that this would be so: the 2nd saw a programme of favourite shows, two Arnal vaudevilles (*Un Monsieur qui prend la mouche* and *Les Cabinets particuliers*) along with the popular *Paris qui dort* and the titillating *Reines des bals publics*; the 30th included two of the month's new productions — *Canadar, père et fils* and *Déménagé d'hier* (also Arnal) along with a performance of *La Vie de Bohème* (its last outing in 1852). The 11th of May (a Tuesday — 2,060 francs) had seen *La Vie de Bohème*, *Un Monsieur qui prend la mouche* and the second of two performances of *Le Château de Coëtaven*. The 12th (2,191 francs) offered a performance of *Le Puits mitoyen*, *Un Monsieur qui prend la mouche* and two new pieces, *Une Vengeance* and *Canadar, père et fils*. The following Wednesday, the 19th (2,082 francs), had the last two mentioned, plus *Déménagé d'hier* (lauded on the 17th) and Rosa Espert's dance group, as well as yet another performance of *Un Monsieur qui prend la mouche*.

The relation of receipts to titles shows fairly convincingly that the audiences were turning up in a manner that, to a considerable extent, was predictable; and because it was, then the director could manipulate the plays at his disposal for the month and take decisions about which ones to put on at relatively short notice (probably no more than 48 hours in advance). But even so there were limits; and the quality of the new vaudevilles every month was a crucial but unpredictable factor.

The new vaudevilles on offer were no more than passably well received. It is clear from the comments that there was nothing particularly outstanding. *Une vengeance* gets an anodine sentence from *L'Eclair*: 'la vengeance reste à l'état de projet: le vengeur a le bon sens de se laisser désarmer par deux beaux yeux.'⁴⁸ *Déménagé d'hier* is treated with some reservation by the same paper on account of the rôle given Alice Ozy: 'Mlle Ozy [joue] un rôle d'ingénue ... mais j'aime mieux la voir dans ses rôles carrément grivois, où elle se complaît et où le public se complaît à l'applaudir.'⁴⁹

La Chronique de Paris does not mention *Déménagé d'hier* until June 16th when, in a longish piece devoted to another play, it gives a couple of lines: 'Arnal, entre deux femmes et entre deux vins, avait fait beaucoup rire dans un seul acte qui s'appelait ... '⁵⁰

The vaudeville which caused the most controversy was *Canadar, père et fils*. Both parts were played by Lassagne, 'et Lassagne se donne à lui-même pardons et bénédictions, que les spectateurs lui rendent en rires et en applaudisements.'⁵¹ Such was the verdict of Cornélius Holff. But *Le Corsaire* was much less charitable and on the 16th May carried a few lines that contained just a touch of vitriol: 'Passable dans le rôle de Canadar père, M. Lassagne a été pitoyable dans le personnage de Canadar fils. Nous l'avons déjà dit, et nous ne cessons de le répéter, M. Lassagne est un comique commun et trivial tout-à-fait déplacé sur la scène des Variétés.'

In a month where the new plays were not helped by the press, it must have been reassuring to read the largely favourable comments on the *reprise* of *La Vie de Bohème*. Henri de Villemessant, in the *Chronique de Paris* of 1st May, p.238, commented that the play 'représente bien des mœurs détestables; mais le spectateur rit devant les tableaux qui sont déroulés sous ses yeux et n'y cherche pas de leçon ... Kopp et Charles Perey sont toujours excellents dans les rôles de Baptiste et de Schanor. Mlle Favart, qui a succédé à Mlle Thuillier,⁵² psalmodie tristement le sien. Quand à Mlle Ozy-Musette, elle dit le mot

---

[48] *L'Eclair*, N^{o.}20, 22 May 1852, p.240.
[49] Ibid., N^{o.}21, 29 May 1852, p.252.
[50] The writer was Louis Énault.
[51] *L'Eclair*, N^{o.}20, 22 May 1852, p.240.
[52] Mlle Favart was on a salary of 8,000 francs for April 1851–March 1852, which would seem to indicate an *artiste* of some standing.

avec une voix incisive et qui porte bien, et joue avec autant d'esprit que de naturel.'

The signs for the summer were not good. The only ace that M. Carpier could command was Frédérick Lemaître. But there were two drawbacks even there: June and July would have to be endured without him to allow adequate rehearsal time for what would be two long leading rôles; and Lemaître was not exactly an actor suited to the type of rôle the Variétés' audience was used to seeing. That, in itself, would not prevent the regular patrons from turning up to begin with, but it would strain their loyalty if the plays themselves were not up to the *standard of entertainment* required and expected.

vi) June 1852

Madame Diogène	1, 2, 3, 4, 5, 6, 7, 8, 9, 10, 11, 12, 15, 16, 17, 19, 20, 22, 25, 30.
Déménagé d'hier	1, 2, 6.
Intermèdes — Rosa Espert danses	1, 2, 6.
Les Cabinets particuliers	1.
Drinn, Drinn	2, 25, 26, 29.
Les Femmes de Gavarni*	3, 4, 5, 7, 8, 9, 10, 11, 12, 13, 14, 15, 16, 17, 18, 19, 20, 21, 22, 23, 24, 25, 26.
Un Monsieur qui prend la mouche	6.
Le Château de Coëtaven	13, 14.
Une Vengeance	18, 20, 21, 24, 26.

Le Puits mitoyen	13, 23, 27, 28, 30.
Les Reines des bals publics	27, 28, 29.
Paris qui dort	27, 28, 29, 30.

With only one new production (admittedly one that had been promised for some time — and quite substantial with three acts) the Variétés managed to hold a reasonable number of its customers until the 16th. Sunday the 13th saw box-office receipts top the 2,000 franc mark for the only time during the whole month (2,106 francs). But beginning on the 17th (900 francs) the receipts would remain in three figures for the rest of the month (apart from Sunday 20th), dropping to as little as 341 francs on the 30th — which, even allowing for a number of free tickets, only represents about 12%-15% of the seats occupied.

The press comments were confined to *Les Femmes de Gavarni*. *Le Corsaire* opened the critical reaction with its review in the 6th June: 'une pièce où l'intrigue est nulle, où les scènes se succèdent dans liaison, sans motif ... ' Some of the actors receive warm praise for their efforts in dealing with a bad script; Leclère and Mlles Ozy, Fitzjames and Duclay are mentioned. *L'Eclair* and *L'Illustration* followed on 12th June. In the former the Goncourts were concise: 'le public a sifflé'.[53] In the latter, the play was described as 'un travestissement complet ... je vous laisse à penser la stupéfaction du public et sa colère mêlée de sifflets ... '[54]

It was left to the *Chronique de Paris* and its critic, Louis Enault, to spell out the objections to the piece. For him the morality of the enterprise was where the main offence lay:

> Autrefois on se cachait pour faire le mal: c'était le dernier hommage rendu à la vertu, — c'est un moraliste qui l'a dit; maintenant on ne se cache plus. Nous n'avons plus le déshabillé, nous avons le nu; Diderot prétend que c'est moins indécent.

---

[53] *L'Eclair*, N^o·23, p.276.
[54] *L'Illustration*, Vol.XIX, N^o·485, p.388.

Ces réflexions chagrines me viennent à l'esprit quand je jette les yeux sur les affiches de nos théâtres, et quand je me rappelle la série d'actes malsains qu'on vient de nous présenter depuis quelques mois. *Les Femmes de Gavarni* sont le chef d'œuvre du genre: on n'ira pas plus loin ... Le public en a fait le premier soir une justice cruelle. Le rideau est tombé au milieu d'un ouragan de sifflets, qui a dispersé les noms des auteurs. Nous ne serons pas plus sévères que les spectateurs, qui n'ont pas voulu les entendre; nous ne les dirons pas.[55]

With such a poor critical reception, the additional problem of the long spell of hot weather was one the Variétés could have done without. 'Hier, dans la soirée, il y avait 35 degrés de chaleur au théâtre des Variétés.'[56]

vii) July 1852

Le Puits mitoyen	1, 2, 18, 26.
Comment l'esprit vient aux garçons	1, 2, 3, 4, 5, 6, 9, 12, 13, 19, 25.
Les Musiciens hongrois*	1, 2, 3, 4, 5, 6, 7, 8, 9, 27, 28, 30.
Drinn, Drinn	1, 2, 3, 4, 5, 12, 13.
Les Reines des bals publics	3, 4.
Trois amours de pompier	4, 8, 14, 15, 16, 18, 20, 23.
Canadar, père et fils	5, 6, 7.

---

[55] *La Chronique de Paris*, 16 June 1852, pp.316-17.
[56] *L'Eclair*, N°.25, 26 June 1852, p.300.

Une Bonne qu'on renvoie	5, 6, 7, 8, 9, 10,12, 13, 19, 22, 24, 25, 26.
Madame Diogène	7.
Le Château de Coëtaven	8.
Un Homme de cinquante ans*	9, 10, 12, 13, 14, 15, 16, 18, 19, 20, 22, 23, 24, 25, 26, 27, 28, 30.
Il faut qu'une porte soit ouverte ou fermée	10.
Intermèdes (chants et danses)	10.
Les Femmes de Gavarni	14, 15, 16, 18, 19, 20, 22, 23, 24, 25, 26, 27, 28, 30.
L'Enfant gâté*	27, 28, 30.

July was virtually unmitigated disaster. With a number of its principal actors on their annual *congé* (notably Arnal); with the Lemaître play not ready to be staged and with the continued heat-wave, the Variétés ran into grave financial difficulties (though it cannot have been alone in this); the *Chronique de Paris* reported on the 16th July: 'Les théâtres, depuis quinze jours, sont asphyxiés par la chaleur sénégambienne qui règne à Paris. Le Vaudeville a encaissé les plus fortes recettes; il a fait 6,000 francs du 1er au 15 ... '[57] By any standards that was awful. But the Variétés managed to take only 9,116 francs for the *whole* of July. On the 13th, for example, only *93 francs 25 centimes* came in through the box-office (29 paying customers!) and there were five nights without performances at all (the 11th, 17th, 21st, 29th and 31st).

---

[57] p.53. The writer was Charles de Besselièvre.

The Variétés' response to the crisis was hardly calculated to remedy the situation. The two new plays received mixed reviews — *L'Homme de cinquante ans* being the most (the term is relative in the circumstances — one would have assumed that critics too would have stayed away from the theatres in the prevailing conditions) commented on. Charles de Villedeuil in *L'Eclair* remarked that it was 'aussi ennuyeuse que faiblement écrite, et que les caractères sont tracés de main d'écolier'.[58] The *Chronique de Paris*, however, took (as usual) the moral line: 'M. Gaston de Montheau a fait représenter aux Variétés une petite pièce que tous les spectateurs honnêtes pourront voir et montrer à leurs femmes et à leurs filles ... les détails de l'ouvrage sont agréables. De l'esprit et de la gaieté dans le dialogue, de jolis couplets, et un rôle de femme joué par Mlle Virginie Duclay, ont valu à cette pièce un succès complet. Encore trois actes comme celui-ci sur l'affliche, et M. Carpier, pourrait bien amortir les feux de l'été.'[59]

The only other novelty during the month was the *Musiciens hongrois*. *L'Eclair* considered them a total failure. The heat was to blame in part, but the act itself was considered no better than 'médiocre'.[60] That the musicians had been signed up to provide an attractive novelty was no doubt true, but their twelve appearances in July and three in August proved a costly exercise; 1,458 francs went on remuneration; 200 francs on a hotel bill; 45 francs for an interpreter and, in addition, a M. Savigny had had to travel to Boulogne to collect them (they had come from London) at a cost of 425 francs. It was a sign of the desperate measures that M. Carpier (and other theatre directors) were having to resort to. As *L'Illustration* put it: 'Les lamentations

---

[58] *L'Eclair*, N$^{o.}$28, 17 July 1852, p.23. (The July issues begin numbering from p.1 again.)

[59] Charles de Besselièvre, 16 July 1852, p.53. It was a fact that *L'Homme de 50 ans* had (coincidentally ?), 50 performances. But with 33 of them coming in July and August it is debatable whether the play could be termed a success. Had the runs been in February–March or October–November then the claim would have had more substance.

[60] See *L'Eclair*, N$^{o.}$27, 10 July 1852, p.12.

continuent; le ciel est trop pur et le soleil trop radieux; faute de quelques nuages cette belle saison va manquer son effect.'[61]

viii) **August 1852**

L'Homme de cinquante ans	1, 2, 5, 7, 8, 9, 11, 13, 15, 16, 18, 20, 22, 24, 29.
L'Enfant gâté	1, 2, 4, 6, 8, 10, 12, 14, 15, 17, 19, 23, 28.
Musiciens hongrois	1, 2, 8.
Les Femmes de Gavarni	1, 2.
Le Puits mitoyen	3, 30.
Le Roi des Drôles*	3, 4, 5, 6, 7, 9, 10, 11, 12, 13, 14, 16, 17, 18, 19, 20, 21, 22, 23, 24, 25, 27, 28, 29, 30.
Trois amours de pompier	8, 15, 24, 25, 27, 30.
Drinn, Drinn	8, 27, 28.
Madame Diogène	15, 18, 21, 25.
Une Bonne qu'on renvoie	17, 19, 20, 21, 22, 23, 29.

---

[61] *L'Illustration*, N°·490, 17 July 1852, p.35. *L'Homme de 50 ans* was thought 'bien conduite ... intéressante et spirituelle ... digne des applaudissements qu'on lui a donnés', p.35.

1852 — A YEAR AT THE *VARIÉTÉS*

The event for August was the appearance of Frédérick Lemaître in *Le Roi des Drôles*.[62] The heat, however, remained a problem: 'les grandes chaleurs ne diminuent en rien l'activité des théâtres; au contraire, ils cherchent à combattre l'inflence d'une atmosphere brûlante en multipliant les nouveautés.'[63] But it was not the heat that preoccupied the *Chronique de Paris* (in the shape of Besselièvre), it was Frédérick himself. On 1st August the *Chronique* carried a long piece on the impending creation of *Le Roi des Drôles* — but it was basically an attack on Frédérick, not even thinly disguised. There was a mention of *L'Enfant gâté*, 'petite pièce anodine que les habitués du théâtre Beaumarchais reverront sans doute avec plaisir.'[64] It was suggested that the piece was merely a pleasant stop-gap — as, indeed, was its mention within the article. What mattered was the appearance of *Le Roi des Drôles* — 'apparition dont on commence à douter, surtout lorsqu'on connaît Frédérick Lemaître'.[65] There may well have been some truth in the matter; but then the article becomes more offensive: 'Frédérick-Lemaître, reconnu pour ainsi dire impossible par toutes les directions de Paris, est engagé aux Variétés pour la saison d'été, c'est-à-dire pour les mois de juin, juillet, août, septembre. Frédérick-Lemaître doit jouer trois pièces pendant la durée de son engagement ... Nous voici au mois d'août et Frédérick-Lemaître touche ses appointements depuis deux mois, seulement pour avoir répété ... il avait été engagé *pour combattre l'influence des chaleurs sur les recettes* ... Chaque jour de retard est un coup de poignard qu'il enfonce dans la caisse de M. Carpier ... le comédien qui, ne remplissant pas ses engagements ou les remplissant mal, fait perdre 2 à 3,000 francs par jour à un théâtre, et finit par devenir la cause de sa ruine.'[66] That acid piece had preceded by only

---

[62] For some reactions see the previous chapter and the section on Frédérick, pp.10-11.
[63] *La Chronique de Paris*, 1 August 1852, p.78.
[64] *La Chronique de Paris*, 1 August 1852, p.80.
[65] Ibid., p.80.
[66] *La Chronique de Paris*, 1 August 1852, p.81. Besselièvre may be wrong in what he assumes the Variétés would take; but he was correct about how much Frédérick was costing the theatre — around *400 francs per performance* (i.e. c.20,000 francs *in toto* as salary).

two days the first performance of *Le Roi des Drôles*. On the 6th August the critical review came out; and while in all fairness Frédérick Lemaître received equitable treatment for his acting, the play itself was thought poor — because Duvert and Lauzanne were unable to produce material suitable for such an actor. The play was un-funny: 'le moidre défaut est de ne pas être drôle ... L'esprit est bien clairsemé dans ce vaudeville. La verve habituelle des auteurs a été etouffée sous la casaque de l'acteur dont ils n'avaient pas la mesure.'[67] And if Besselièvre is correct (and is not just grinding an axe) the reception by the audiences those first nights was hostile: 'On a sifflé le premier jour, et l'on siffle encore; quand on ne sifflera plus, tout sera fini.'[68]

Given the costs of the production — fees, salaries, extra rehearsal time — M. Carpier had little option but to persist with the scheduled number of performances simply in order to recoup what he could. After the financial catastrophe of July, August could only be an improvement. Even so, monthly takings of 30,448 francs was the second worst figure for the year. No individual evening produced 2,000 francs, and one evening — of all days a Sunday, the 15th — seeing only 89.25 francs as box-office takings (though *Le Roi des Drôles* was not playing on that particular date).

The experiment with Frédérick Lemaître was not a financial success; nor was it a total artistic success. The risk element was too great. And yet it could be argued that his presence did keep a modest amount of money coming into the theatre, money that might not otherwise have materialised (given the heat — and given what he was costing).

But with August behind him, M. Carpier *had* to regain his regular *seasonal* audience. As high summer slipped away, the theatres would come into their own again — such was the hope if not the expectation.

---

[67] Ibid., 6 August 1852, pp.108–9.
[68] Ibid., p.109.

ix) September 1852

Un Homme de cinquante ans	2, 4, 5, 6, 8, 19, 26.
Souvenirs de jeunesse*	2, 3, 4, 6, 7, 8, 9, 10, 11, 12, 13, 14, 15, 16, 17, 18, 19, 20, 21.
L'Enfant gâté	3, 7.
Madame Diogène	5, 10, 15.
Les Femmes de Gavarni	5.
Une Bonne qu'on renvoie	5.
Canadar, père et fils	9, 11, 17, 28.
Déménagé d'hier	9, 10, 11, 14, 20, 21, 24.
Les Reines des bals publics	12, 13, 16, 18.
Riche d'amour	12, 13, 15, 26, 28.
Trois amours de pompier	14, 27.
Un Monsieur qui prend la mouche	16, 17, 18, 19, 22, 23, 25, 27.
Soutiens-moi, Chatillon	20, 21, 22.
En Ballon*	20, 21, 22, 23, 24, 25.
La Ferme de Primerose	22, 23, 24, 25, 28, 29, 30.
Deux gouttes d'eau*	22, 23, 24, 25, 26, 27, 28, 29, 30.
Paris qui dort	26, 27.

Un Vieux de la vieille roche*   29, 30.

Les Cabinets particuliers   29, 30.

What is immediately noticeable about the September bill of fare is the number of vaudevilles put on: 19, of which four were new. Equally noticeable is the return to the tried formula: the one-act *comédie-vaudeville* dependent for its success on the male actors: Arnal, Leclère and Lassagne. Indeed the main point about September was the return of Arnal after his (long) summer *congé*. *La Chronique de Paris* commented simply that the main September attraction was the 'Souvenirs' ... 'Les Variétés vivent de leurs *Souvenirs* ... *de jeunesse*, nouvelle édition de la *Vie de Bohème*, revue et corrigée par la censure'.[69] But there was a warm welcome for Arnal in the *Illustration*:

> la rentrée d'Arnal avec tous ses agréments; l'excellent comédien et même quel comédien nouveau après trente ans d'exercice et de succès! Au rebours de tant d'autres conquérants que leurs conquêtes ont affaiblis, Arnal a grandi par les siennes. C'est le comique le plus réfléchi et à la fois le plus expansif qui nous reste. Le jour de la retraite d'Arnal ... Paris aura perdu la meilleure pinte de sa gaieté ... Arnal appartient à une grande race éteinte, race essentiellement comique, dont il est peut-être le dernier représentant ... L'absence d'Arnal aura duré trois mois.[70]

Financially the pick-up was beginning. The month grossed 40,314 francs through the box office — not a huge amount, but sufficient to suggest a move back towards the high spots in February and March.

The other main point about September was the appearance at the Variétés of Numa (see previous chapter) alongside Arnal in *Deux gouttes d'eau*. *L'Illustration* got round to mentioning him in early October:

---

[69] *Chronique de Paris*, 16 September 1852, p.168.
[70] *L'Illustration*, XX, N⁰·499, 18 september 1852, p.179.

Puisque nous passons à d'autres nouveautés, comment ne pas remarquer les *débuts* de Numa dans le voisinage d'Arnal? ... Aux Variétés Numa le père représente un M. Tourillon (*Deux gouttes d'eau*) avec une verve, une grâce et un entrain ... mais ici le mot de Médée convient à cet excellent Numa: ‹Moi, seul, et c'est assez ... pour le succès›.[71]

x) October 1852

La Ferme de Primerose	1, 2, 5, 6, 12, 13, 15, 18, 22, 24.
Deux gouttes d'eau	1, 2, 3, 4, 5, 6, 7, 8, 9, 10, 11, 12, 13, 14, 15, 16, 17, 18.
Un Vieux de la vieille roche	1, 2, 3, 4, 5, 6, 7, 8, 9, 14, 16, 17, 20, 25, 27.
Déménagé d'hier	1, 3, 4.
Un Monsieur qui prend la mouche	2, 6.
Paris qui dort	3, 4.
Les Cabinets particuliers	5, 10.
Compagnie hongroise (musiciens)	7, 8, 9, 11, 12, 13, 14, 16, 17.
Le Mari de la dame de chœurs	7, 8, 9, 11, 12, 13, 14, 15, 16, 17, 18, 19, 20, 21, 22, 23, 24, 25, 26, 27.
En Ballon	10, 11, 15, 17, 18, 21, 26.

[71] *L'Illustration*, XX, N°·501, 2 October 1852, pp.211-12.

Souvenirs de jeunesse	10, 28.
L'Enfant gâté	19.
L'Ami François*	19, 20, 21, 22, 23, 24, 25, 26, 27, 28, <u>29</u>, <u>29</u>, 30, 31.
Un Monsieur qui ne veut pas s'en aller*	19, 20, 21, 22, 23, 24, 25, 26, 27, 28, <u>29</u>, <u>29</u>, 31.
Madame Diogène	23.
Soutiens-moi, Chatillon	24, 28.
Mam'zelle Rose*	<u>29</u>, <u>29</u>, 30, 31.
Les Gants jaunes*[72]	<u>29</u>, <u>29</u>, 30, 31.
Flambart l'exterminateur*	<u>29</u>, <u>29</u>, 30, 31.
Intermèdes de chants	30.

This month the formula worked. The box-office receipts went up to 53,407 francs. Twice, the nightly takings exceeded 3,000 francs — the 29th and the 31st. The seeming 'double' performance on the 29th needs some explaining. There were *not* two performances. The evening's entries on the nightly accounts sheet had been put in as usual — but a second set of entries was added when it was realised that the prices of some of the seats had in fact been put up because the evening was a benefit evening for Charles Perey. The evening was clearly a success — though M. Perey was not paid his *bénéfice* until December 31st — a modest enough sum of 600 francs.

---

[72] This was the first performance in the Variétés. The play itself was quite old, having been first put on at the Théâtre du Vaudeville, 6 March 1835.

xi) November 1952

L'Ami François	1, 2, 3, 4, 5, 6, 7, 8, 9, 10, 11, 12, 14.
Mam'zelle Rose	1, 2, 3, 4, 5, 6, 7, 8, 16, 17, 18, 19, 20, 21, 28.
Les Gants jaunes	1, 2, 3, 5, 9, 10, 11, 12, 14.
Flambart l'exterminateur	1, 2, 3, 14.
Un Monsieur qui ne veut pas s'en aller	1, 4, 5, 6, 7, 9, 10, 11, 12, 14, 21.
Compagnie hongroise[73]	2.
Les Frères Lionnet (intermède)	2, 3, 4, 5, 6, 7.
Le Mari de la Dame de chœurs	4, 6, 7, 8, 14.
La Ferme de Primerose	8, 9, 10, 11, 12, 21.
À Bas les maris (intermède)	8, 9, 10, 11.
Un Homme de cinquante ans	13, 15, 28.
Taconnet, ou l'acteur des Boulevards*	13, 15, 16, 17, 18, 19, 20, 22, 23, 24, 25, 26, 27, 29, 30.
Danse espagnole	21.
Ce que vivent les roses*	21, 22, 23, 24, 25, 26, 27, 28, 29, 30.

[73] Carpier had persisted with the Hungarian musicians even though they had been so poorly received in the early summer — they had had *nine* appearances in October. It is clear from the programming in October, November and December that *intermèdes* of various sorts were becoming an accepted (and expected?) part of an evening's entertainment.

Les Deux gouttes d'eau   21, 28.

Les Deux inséparables*   28, 29, 30.

This was Frédérick Lemaître's second show. Like the first it was neither outright success nor total failure. And the faults and virtues were similar: '*Taconnet*, pièce un peu trop longue [5 acts] et passablement prétentieuse, faite pour M. Frédérick Lemaître, et où l'excellent comédien n'a réussi qu'à moitié ... On a cependant remarqué et beaucoup applaudi deux ou trois scènes bien posées et encore mieux faites ... L'acteur soutient la pièce, et il l'écrase. A supposer qu'elle offre d'autres rôles que le sien, personne n'a été tenté de s'en apercevoir.'[74] Carpier was clearly aware of Frédérick's basic unsuitability for the vaudeville. But he had a contract to honour. He could honour the contract and protect the box-office receipts by keeping *Taconnet* off the Sunday programmes — which he did; Sunday being the most popular day in every sense. It had not escaped his notice that the most financially successful night in November had been Monday 1st — a night given over to *five* one-act *comédie-vaudevilles* which belonged to the main troupe: Arnal, Leclère, Ozy, Boisgontier, Page. The Variétés' audience liked its favourite actors — just as it liked 'new' vaudevilles written to the old formulae. The combination — profoundly conservative — was what worked best.

xii) December 1852

Les Deux inséparables   1, 3, 5, 8, 10, 13, 16, 18, 23, 28.

Deux gouttes d'eau   1, 2, 3, 4, 5, 7, 8, 10, 16, 18.

Taconnet   1, 2, 3, 4, 6, 7, 9, 10, 12.

---

[74] *L'Illustration*, XX, N⁰·509, 27 November 1852, p.338.

Ce que vivent les roses	2, 4, 7, 9, 12, 18.
Mam'zelle Rose	5, 16, 18, 19, 29, 30.
Intermèdes de danse (Mlles Dabbas)	5.
Paris qui dort	5, 6, 8, 19.
Soutiens-moi, Chatillon	6.
Un Vieux de la vieille roche	8, 9, 14.
Un Homme de cinquante ans	11, 15, 17, 19, 20, 21, 31.
Ah, vous dirai-je Maman*[75]	11, 13, 14, 15, 16, 17, 18, 19, 22, 24, 25, 26.
Intermède — concert vocal et instrumental, danses	11.
Le Pour et le contre[76]	11.
Les Frères féroces	11.
L'Ami François	12, 16.
Intermède (M. Lassagne)	13, 14, 15.
Souvenirs de jeunesse	13, 14, 15, 17.
Les Variétés en 1852*	20, 21, 22, 23, 24, 25, 26, 27, 28, 29, 30, 31.
Madame Diogène	27.

---

[75] Wicks gives the first performance as 14 December 1852. Assuming the Variétés account sheets are correct, then the 11th was the first performance of this *one-act* vaudeville.

[76] First put on at the Théâtre Français, 22 January 1852.

The awaited highlight of the month was the end-of-year revue, *Les Variétés en 1852* (3 acts and 12 *tableaux*, by MM. Guénée, Lambert Thiboust and Delacour). The previous year's revue, *La Course aux plaisirs*, had been a success, but of more modest proportions (2 acts and 3 *tableaux*). The 1852 version was deliberately intended as a spectacular finish to the year. Interestingly, one of the writers, Delacour, had gone through the script with the *artistes* on the 18th November — presumably to test their reactions and possibly (?) to suggest the distribution of rôles.

The end-of-year revue would become an established feature of the Variétés' programme, particularly after Hippolyte Cogniard took over as Director in 1855.[77] In 1856 Auguste Vacquerie brought out a book on the theatre called *Profiles et grimaces*.[78] His account of the revue gives a clear enough indication of what was involved: 'Une forme excellente, c'est celle des ‹revues de l'année› ... Résumer dans une action aussi chimérique qu'on voudra la somme des inventions et des renouvellements d'une année ... un genre auquel le public permet tout ce qu'il défend aux autres, la hardiesse, la témérité, extravagance, le pêle-mêle, le chant et la parole, la strophe et le calembour, la charge à outrance et l'acclamation enthousiaste, la féerie et la critique, le coup d'aile et le coup de pied ... '[79] Whatever precise form these 'extravagances' took, it is manifestly the case that the primary purpose of the revue was sheer entertainment, by whatever means available. And the revue itself constituted the bulk of the evening's programme. The curtain-raiser consisted of one of the current *one-act comédie-vaudevilles* (a rôle switched among five of the available plays for the period 20–31 December), and the rest of the evening was the revue itself. Interestingly, the best box-office takings for the month, 3,158 francs, came on Christmas Day.

As a *cadeau de Noël* it could not have been bettered.

---

[77] See J. Long, op. cit.
[78] Published by Michel Lévy frères, Paris.
[79] *Profiles et grimaces*, p.100.

IV
A Financial Overview

The one thing guaranteed to arouse the interest of all parties — directly involved or not — was money. Who was earning what; who was the recipient of free tickets; how much was the theatre taking and, more to the point, how much of a personal fortune was the director making? It was assumed, probably correctly, that theatre directors were only in the business to make money. Speculation about the sums involved was rife — but speculation was all it was. A tiny number of directors no doubt did make money, but had probably been lucky enough — or perhaps shrewd enough — to have popular actors on their books, a good supply of genuinely entertaining plays to put on and a summer season that was not so hot so as to discourage theatre-goers during the three (worst, financially) summer months. Most directors would have willingly settled for two out of the three factors to turn out favourably. There were other elements to consider. Directors had to buy themselves into their posts in the sense that they were obliged, by their contracts, to put an agreed sum into the theatre each year — in Carpier's case this was 100,000 francs (£4,000). Their (supposedly) lucrative gains had to be set against sums of that order.

Theatres were not simply a matter of actors and writers. An establishment such as the Variétés employed a small army of people. Including the *artistes* (but excluding the writers) there were between 160 and 170 on the payroll at any given time; and there was a limit to the absolute minimum needed to run the theatre reasonably efficiently; my own guess would be about 145-50. In addition there would be the ongoing costs of materials for scenery, costumes and lighting. If, on top of that, was added the money needed for the 'droit des auteurs' and the tax levied for the 'indigents', plus the nightly sums for the 'garde impériale' and the 'pompiers' then the costs of a theatre the size of the Variétés were not inconsiderable.

In such conditions the business of making a fortune was at best difficult. It is likely that most directors struggled to keep the income and expenditure balanced let alone make enough profit to pay themselves a monthly allowance that guaranteed them the return of their 100,000 francs (or whatever the sum was) plus a decent income (say 20,000 francs? — comfortable, but no more than that). That did not stop the speculation, the work, largely, of journalists and, in the case of those who wrote reviews of the *comédie-vaudevilles* put on at the Variétés, journalists who should have known better. The point was that they were not simply journalists — a significant percentage of them were also playwrights; and it was this fact that coloured their opinion about a theatre's income. They, as writers of plays, would receive their due financial return; but their perception of a play's success led some of them to believe that large queues at the theatre's box-office meant large income for the director — too large, perhaps, when seen against their own modest fees (because in, say, an evening's performance of three or more *pièces* there could be involved six or more writers — so that the individual's share of the 'droit des auteurs' might appear small beer indeed beside what he surmised the theatre was taking).

Sums were exaggerated. Nestor Roqueplan was said to have had 700,000 francs through the box-office of the Variétés annually. It may well have been true for a year or two and it would certainly have made him some money, but not a fortune. Nor could he sustain such an income. But the high figures were the ones that took hold of the imagination, or, rather, fuelled the prejudices.

The reality was, as a rule, rather different. The previous section on the year's productions showed a theatre having a struggle to maintain its financial viability. *Ipso facto* the director would not be making any profit let alone covering the amount he put into the theatre.

The following represent only the main costs to the theatre (for a fuller picture see the appendices).

FINANCES AND SALARIES

SALARIES[1]

(a) The Actors

The striking feature of the actor's salaries is the huge gap between what was paid to Arnal (Frédérick Lemaître's salary was paid only during the few months he was the special guest actor — though had he been a permanent member of the troupe his salary would no doubt have been at least as high as Arnal's) and what was paid to the rest of the men.[2] Arnal received 24,000 francs a year and his contract allowed him three months' leave (as well as giving him a considerable supplementary income from his assured *jetons* and *feux* — rising to around an extra 5,000 francs some years). It has to be assumed that the salary reflected his real acting ability and, what was crucial, his ability to pull in the paying spectators. In terms of the Variétés average nightly income of 1,400 francs over 1852, Arnal (if his *jetons* and *feux* are included) required a minimum of 20 nights box-office income just to service his salary.[3] No other actor came anywhere near that.[4] The most highly paid men were, in descending order of salary, Bardou (fr.7,200); Leclère (fr.6,000); Perey (fr.4,800); Cachardy (fr.4,600); Kopp and Laba (fr.4,000) and Danterny (fr.3,000). While such amounts pale in comparison with Arnal's income, they were, none the less, *good* incomes. Even Danterny's represented two-and-a-half times the basic necessary income.

The remaining actors received salaries ranging from 2,000 francs down to 1,200. The walk-on parts, however, ranged from 900 francs to 600 francs. In such cases the individual would have needed other

---

[1] As a rough guide a livable salary — but right at the bottom of the scale and really providing little more than tolerable subsistence — was 1,200 francs per annum (in English money more or less £1 a week).
[2] *Basic* salary, that is, i.e. not counting the *jetons* or *feux* — for these details see the full salaries list.
[3] In a rough approximation he was earning £22 a week (in 1852!) — a small fortune.
[4] Hoffmann had been with the Variétés until 1 May 1851 and had received a salary of 12,000 francs per annum.

members of the family to work or for he himself to have held another job — which would have been possible, given that he would not have appeared on stage very often and when he did he would not have had much to learn (or many rehearsals to attend).

A couple of the men had no salary as such. They were guaranteed a certain minimum sum (Jeault, for instance, was paid at 5 francs *feux par pièce.*); or were simply paid 5 francs per *pièce* — as in the case of Mutée; though he was given enough work to more or less guarantee him a monthly income of 150 francs.

Contracts were drawn up for a specific period (Arnal's, for example, was to end on 1 March 1856) and in some cases the *engagement* was *résiliable* at a specific date annually.

b) **The Actresses**

Only the rare acknowledged star could expect to be able to negotiate a salary that could compare with the male stars. At the Variétés that had meant Déjazet (until the late 1840s — she received an annual salary of 20,000 francs and, in addition, a minimum of 50 francs an *act* with at least 20 acts guaranteed) and would, later, mean Hortense Schneider during the Offenbach period. In 1852 the Variétés possessed no actress of comparable ability or reputation. But it did possess a number of well-known and popular female *artistes* whom the direction must have considered the equals of their male counterparts. Reading the critical reviews it is fairly easy to discern two main areas of interest; first the male stars (Arnal and Lemaître with frequent enough mention of Leclère); secondly, the female rôles. It is equally clear that what was wanted from the actresses was not the male humour of an Arnal or a Numa, but the ability to speak clearly and naturally, to sing competently and to flatter the eye. The actresses draw the audiences as much and as successfully as the Kopps, the Pereys or the Cachardys. They were therefore paid accordingly. Mlle Delorme (the eventual Mrs Bowes) drew an annual salary of 8,000 francs (plus *jetons*) until her effective retirement from the stage at the end of 1851. An identical salary went to Mlle Fitzjames and Mlle Favart.[5] The remaining main salaries were more modest, but still represented a decent living: 4,800 francs for Mlle Chevalier, 4,000 for Boisgontier and Page; 2,500 for Alice Ozy and then down to a basic 1,200 francs. Boisgontier, Fitzjames, Jolivet and Ozy were also the recipients of *jetons* (though not quite so generously treated as the men).

Both men and women could be, and were, granted *bénéfices*, special evenings when they would receive an agreed percentage of the evening's box-office receipts. Again, the system favoured the big names because in certain cases a minimum sum was guaranteed (say 1,500 francs); and also, in some cases, there would be an *annual bénéfice* written into the contract. (Mlle Fitzjames, for example, was due 1,200 francs by this means.)

Given the strength of the *troupe* — as far as can be seen never less than 40 salaried actors/actresses — the annual salaries bill for them alone would run at around *150,000 francs* minimum.

c) **Orchestra and Chorus**

Merely reading the numerous *comédie-vaudevilles* gives virtually no indication at all of the vital rôle played by the music (and, probably, by some form of dancing?) — but the number of songs that even the short one-act pieces contained indicate that in any given evening anything between 30 and 50 songs would have been played. That, in terms of time, represents a good percentage of an evening's performance. The orchestra was made up of 25–27 players; the chorus (male and female) of around 30 singers.

The *chef d'orchestre*, Nargeot, was paid 3,000 francs in 1851 and in 1852 this was raised to 3,600. The *sous-chef d'orchestre*, M. Reine, received 2,000 francs, while the *chef des chœurs*, M. George, earned 1,200. It had to be assumed that the members of the orchestra and the singers/dancers had other employment of a similar nature.

---

[5] In English terms almost £6 a week; a very comfortable sum by the prevalent standards.

Orchestral players received a salary of anything from 600 francs per annum up to a maximum of 900 francs, the majority appearing to earn 800 francs.

Chorus members were less well paid — the standard salary was 400 francs, though some individuals received 500 and the occasional one 600 (a certain M. Barbier whose salary went up from 500 francs to 600 on 1 January 1851).[6]

For the Variétés this represented — orchestra and chorus — a minimum annual outlay of 30,000 francs. In addition the theatre employed a M. Verrier who was the *bibliothécaire de la musique* for which he was paid an honorarium of 200 francs annually, but whose income was really made from copying out instrumental parts for the various sections of the orchestra. In 1851 he earned 2,235 francs. He had no fixed salary — but presumably was kept quite busy.

d) **Others**

The remaining important functions (importance in this instance equating with salary) were the following: M. Cuillier, *chief machiniste*, on an annual salary of 12,000 francs (of which 500 was for the safety 'inspection du matériel'); M. Boulé, *directeur de la scène*, on 4,800 francs; M. Poussin (any relation?) *peintre des décors* on 3,600 francs; M. Marage, *costumier*, 3,200 francs; M. Baudouin, *caissier, teneur de livres*, 3,000 francs; and M. Veyron, *régisseur général*, 2,700 francs.

To set against these were the humble jobs of *habilleuse*, twelve in all, receiving each the extraordinarily small salary of 180 francs a year; the *garçons de théâtre* (of whom the *chef* received 700 francs) and the individuals who formed part of what was simply called the *contrôle*, most of whom received 300–400 francs; the *chef de contrôle*, a M. Tony, was paid 1,500 francs.[7]

---

[6] A member of the chorus who joined in October 1850 was Mlle Céleste — she was not long, it seems, in rising from the ranks!
[7] For a complete list, see the following pages.

FINANCES AND SALARIES 93

e) **Recurrent major costs**

i. Because John Bowes was the owner the theatre was *let* to the director so a monthly amount was paid to Bowes as *loyer*. The figures varied considerably from month to month and the payment was sometimes late or made in instalments. The figures that I have found for 1852 are the following: April, 10,282.50; May, 8,568.75; June, 5,481.50; July, 3,425.00; August, no payment; September, accounts missing; October, 8,910.00; November, 8,911.50; December, 8,568.75. In all, seven recorded payments amounting to 54,148.00 francs. In approximate round figures Bowes would have been paid for the whole of 1852 some 80,000 francs.
ii. Theatres had obligations towards various groups of people— most of the obligations were legal requirements. The main ones for any theatre were the Droits des Auteurs at 12% *sur la recette brute* and the Droits des Indigents (or des Hospices) at *11% sur la recette brute*. These were considerable sums in relative terms regardless of how much was actually taken at the box-office and over the year 1852 would have amounted to (in round figures) 60,000 francs for the former and 55,000 francs for the latter.

There was also the obligation to have men from the Garde de Paris on hand at every performance (in case of disturbance or riot) and from the Sapeurs Pompiers because of the real risk of fire. The former cost around 250 francs a month, the latter double that amount.
iii. Heating and lighting was done originally with oil-lamps, and even in the 1850–51 period the majority of the lighting was still oil. The use of gas, however, was gaining ground. In the March 1850 to March 1851 accounts the gas lighting was confined to the *lustre du vestibule* (at 21 francs 24 centimes a day) and the *foyer* (at 2 francs 97 a day). The main theatre was still oil-lit — 4 *becs par jour* at 40 centimes each, and a further 277 at 18 centimes each — a daily total of 51 francs 46. However, there was a period of refurbishment in the summer of 1851 and it must have been at that point that a

decision was taken to replace the oil lamps with gas(?). M. Melon, who had the oil contract, was still being paid in May 1852 (for April) — the sum of 1,362.55. But after this date he does not figure again on the accounts sheet. Instead there is only a regular monthly payment to M$^{r.}$ Marguerite et Cie, *éclairage au gaz courant* (In May this amounted to 1050 francs and a much smaller amount, 138 fr.60 for *éclairage au gaz, compteur*). The average monthly gas bill was somewhat over 1,000 francs for the summer months (even given the extraordinarily hot summer of 1852; but it was *lighting the auditorium* that the gas was used for — it was intended that the heat should be removed by an improved ventilation system), and around 1,200 monthly for the winter months.

iv. Publicity was done by posters, printed by the firm of Mme Veuve Dondey-Dupré. The average monthly costs were between 700 and 800 francs.

v. In addition to these recurrent costs the Theatre had to sustain a considerable number of claims on its income (for details see the examples of the monthly accounts in the Appendices) from individuals on one-off jobs; on acts that ran for a few weeks and then went elsewhere (the Danseurs espagnols, for example) and on incidental expenditure incurred by employees of the Theatre in the course of their normal work. But even without these incidentals (some of which were quite considerable) the Variétés was committed to a regular expenditure well in excess of 400,000 francs a year. With the incidentals the cost would most certainly be in the region of 500,000 to 550,000 francs annually. If, as was the case in 1852, the box-office receipts amounted to some 505,000 francs, then the theatre was close to, if not actually, sustaining an annual loss. And what appeared (this is assuming that the accounts were honest records of what transactions did take place — an assumption that must be held only with some degree of scepticism given the eventual demise of Carpier as director and the problems that ensued) to sustain the theatre was what Carpier himself (?) contributed each month.

* * *

FINANCES AND SALARIES

The extant ledgers are fuller for the period 1st April 1850 to 31st March 1851 than for the year following, 1st April 1851 to 31st March 1852. I have therefore used the information for 1850–51 as the basis for the salaries' list but have put in as much information for 1851–52 as I have managed to find. Given that salaries tended, for the most part, to remain static there is not too much of a problem. The fact that a number of names — especially members of the chorus and the orchestra — have no salary against them for 1851–52 must not be taken to mean that they no longer worked at the *Variétés*; it simply means that I cannot find those particular figures.

There are quite a number of ledgers for the late 1840s. The main salaries ledger has a spine notice: *Paye des appointements No.2* and begins with the November salaries 1849 (paid 3/12/49) ending with the February 1853 salaries (paid in March '53). There also exists a *Paye des appointements No.1* ledger which began in March 1842 and goes right up to the October salaries for 1849. Even a cursory glance shows that salaries remained relatively static throughout that period. I have made no attempt to transcribe the *monthly* pay. My sole concern here is the *annual* salary.

What has to be pointed out is that some of the salaries — paid monthly in areas — were not paid in identical monthly amounts, especially where the *artistes* were concerned. The variations could relate to the number of appearances in any given month where those appearances carried *feux* (or *jetons*).

Interestingly, a number of the *employés*, of whatever sort, have a small deduction made from their monthly salaries (in the range of 1fr. to 4 frs). These are *fines* - imposed for what? absence? lateness? misbehaviour? M. His and M. Kolb, both members of the orchestra, seem to appear fairly frequently in this category.

NAME	FUNCTION	annual salary (fr.)	
		1850–51	1851–52
Mme Alexis	habilleuse	180	180
Mr Alexandre	chœurs	-	400
Mlle Alice Ozy	artiste	2,000	2,500 (with *jetons*)
Mr Anton	chœurs	-	400
Mr Arnal	artiste	24,000 plus: 15fr. *jetons* for 1 play; 35fr. *jetons* for 2 plays — 15fr a day *assuré*	24,000 plus *jetons* as previously: 20fr a day *assuré*
Mr Augez	chœurs	400	-
Mlle Aurélie	chœurs	400	400
Mme Avissé	habilleuse	180	-
Mr Bache	artiste	1,200	1,200
Mlle Cécile Barbé	artiste	2,000	-
Mr Bagnères	orchestre	-	800
Mr Barbier	chœurs	500	600
Mr Bardou	artiste	7,200 (plus: 15 fr par pièce quand il joue)	7,200 (plus: *jetons*)
Mr Baudouin	caissier, teneur de livres	3,000	3,000
Mr Belmance	chœurs	-	400
Mr Bernard	chœurs	400	500

FINANCES AND SALARIES

NAME	FUNCTION	1850-51	1851-52
Mme Barnard	chœurs	400	400
Mr Bernhardt	orchestre	700	700
Mlle Bertin	artiste	-	3,000
Mr Bidot	Garçon de théâtre	200	800
Mme Blanche	habilleuse	180	-
Mme Blonval	artiste	3,600	3,600
Mlle Boisgontier	artiste	4,000	4,000 (plus: *jetons*)
Mr Boituzen	chœurs	500	-
Mr Borelly	orchestre	700	700
Mr Boudeville	armurier	400	400
Mr Boulé (Gustave)	artiste	1,500	1,800
Mr Boulé	directeur de la scène	4,800	4,800
Mr Boulé	secretaire-général	-	3,000
Mr Brullé	abonnements musicaux	-	60
Mr Burguy	artiste	-	1,800
Mr Cachardy	artiste	4,600	4,600
Mlle Castellan	artiste	3,600	-
Mr Caudron	orchestre	800	800
Mr Cauvin	orchestre	700	800

NAME	FUNCTION	1850-51	1851-52
Mlle Céleste	chœurs	400	-
Mr Celliez	conseil du théâtre	600	600
Mlle Cénau	artiste	900	1,200
Mr Charier	artiste	900	900
Mr Charles	chœurs	400	-
Mlle Chevalier	artiste	-	4,800
Mr Chevrier	concierge du théâtre côté du Boulevard	800	800
Mlle Chevrier	contrôle bureau des suppléments	300	300
Mr Chollet	accessoires de la scène	180	180
Mr Clairac	contrôle, 1er placeur	400	-
Mlle Clémence	chœurs	400	-
Mlle Coblentz	artiste	1,000	1,000
Mr Cuillier	chef machiniste	11,500 (plus 500 for 'inspection du matériel')	11,500
Mme Danse	habilleuse	180	180
Mlle Danse	habilleuse	180	180
Mr Danterny	artiste	3,000 (plus: *jetons* 7 fr. pour pièce)	3,000 (plus: *jetons*)
Mr Debure (fils)	chœurs	400	-

FINANCES AND SALARIES

NAME	FUNCTION	1850–51	1851–52
Mr Debure (père)	garçon de théâtre	700	700
Mlle Déjazet	artiste	20,000 (plus: 20 pièces à 50 fr. la pièce)	-
Mr Delière	artiste	no salary — *jetons* 2 fr. la pièce	1,200 (plus: *jetons* 2 fr)
Mlle Delorme	artiste	7,000 (plus: *jetons* at 5fr la pièce)	8,000 (plus: *jetons* at 5fr la pièce)
Mme Desforges	habilleuse	180	Her *last* salary was made on 3 Déc 1851
Mr Donjon	contrôle, 2e placeur	352	600
Mr Dondeuil	contrôle	120	252
Mr Duchaussoy	chœurs	400	-
Mr Duffand	souffleur	1,500	1,500
Mr Dussert	artiste	4,800	-
Mr Dusseuil	orchestre	900	-
Mr Duval	tapissier	1,500	-
Mr Duvernoy	artiste	1,200	1,500
Mr Elena	orchestre	700	700
Mr Ernest	chœurs	600	-
Mlle Esther	artiste	1,500	2,000
Mr Eugène	chœurs	500	-
Mlle Favart	artiste	-	8,000

NAME	FUNCTION	1850-51	1851-52
Mme Felicité	habilleuse	180	180
Mr Ferdinand	chœurs	400	500
Mme Ferrey	blanchisseuse	1,080	1,080
Mlle Fitz-James	artiste	8,000 (15 *feux* assurés par mois, 5 fr la pièce; 10fr pour chansonette)	8,000 (plus: *jetons* as before)
Mlle Flore	artiste	6,000 (5fr la pièce; 3 fr la chansonette)	1,200
Mr Fournez	orchestre	800	800
Mr Gabriel	chœurs	400	500
Mme Gaillet	costumière	1,500	1,800
Mr Gallin	artiste	1,200	-
Mr George	chef des chœurs	1,200	1,200
Mme Vve Girard	contrôle, 2e bureau	300	300
Mr Gras	orchestre	900	900
Mr Graves	orchestre	700	-
Mr Grimbert	artiste	600	-
Mr Gustave	chœurs	500	-
Mlle Hélène	chœurs	400	400
Mr Hemet	orchestre	800	800
Mr Henry Alix	artiste	-	3,000 (plus *jetons*)

FINANCES AND SALARIES

NAME	FUNCTION	1850-51	1851-52
Mr Hetzel	orchestre	800	800
Mr His	orchestre	800	900
Mr Hoffmann	artiste	12,000	-
Mme Hortense	habilleuse	180	180
Mr Jeanly	artiste	-	1,200
Mr Jeault	artiste	no salary: 5 fr la pièce	1,200
Mlle Jolivet	artiste	2,400 (plus: *jetons* 4 fr. la pièce)	2,400 (plus: *jetons*)
Mr Jolly	artiste	2,000	-
Mme Vve Juty	contrôle, 1er bureau	300	300
Mr Kolb	orchestre	900	900
Mr Kopp	artiste	4,000	4,000
Mr Laba	artiste	5,000 (plus: *jetons* 5 fr. la pièce)	5,000 (plus: *jetons*)
Mr Lahaye	contrôle	120	-
Mr Lamotte	plombier	300	300
Mr Lassagne	artiste	-	2,400 (plus: *jetons*)
Mlle Laure	chœurs	400	400
Mr Lebrun	orchestre	800	800

NAME	FUNCTION	1850-51	1851-52
Mr Leclère	artiste	6,000 (plus: *jetons* 5 fr. la pièce)	6,000 (plus: *jetons*)
Mr Lemarre	chœurs	400	400
Mr Léon	chœurs	400	-
Mlle Léonie	artiste	144	-
Mr Léopold	chœurs	400	500
Mr Leroux	garçon de théâtre	360	360
Mlle Lorry	artiste	1,200	1,500
Mr Louis	chœurs	500	-
Mme Louis	habilleuse	180	180
Mlle Louisa	chœurs	400	-
Mr Loyé	contrôle	600	-
Mr Marguerite	éclairage au gaz	24.21 (par jour)	-
Mr Marage	costumier	3,200	3,200
Mr Marconnot	orchestre	900	900
Mme Marguerite	habilleuse	180	180
Mlle Maria	chœurs	400	400
Mlle Marie	chœurs	400	400
Mlle Marquet	artiste	5,000 (plus: *jetons* 5 fr la pièce; 15 *feux* assurés)	-

FINANCES AND SALARIES 103

NAME	FUNCTION	1850–51	1851–52
Mlle Martinez	chœurs	400	400
Mr Massart	orchestre	900	900
Mr Massola	balayage, frottage, entretien	1,120	1,120
Mr Mathieu	orchestre	1,200	1,200
Mr Melon	éclairage à l'huile 4 becs @ 40 centimes 277 becs @ 18 centimes	51,46 (par jour)	?
Mlle Merentine	chœurs	400	400
Mlle Michaux	artiste	600	1,800
Mr Miconin	couvreur	310	310
Mr Miscot	orchestre	600	600
Mr Molist	orchestre	700	700
Mr Moniot	orchestre	700	700
Mr Moreau-Sainti	artiste	-	4,000
Mlle Morel	artiste	2,400	3,000
Mr Muller	chœurs	400	400
Mme Muller	habilleuse	180	-
Mr Mutée	artiste	no salary; 5 fr. la pièce 150 fr. assurés par mois (2,790)	variable, as previous year, but a minimum of 200 fr. a month
Mr Margeot	chef d'orchestre	3,000	3,600
Mr Neuville	artiste	2,400	-

NAME	FUNCTION	1850-51	1851-52
Mlle Page	artiste	6,000	7,000 (?)
Mr Passerat	concierge du côté des artistes	1,100	1,100
Mr Paviot	contrôle	120	-
Mlle Pélagie	artiste	2,400	2,400
Mr Pellerin	chœurs	400	400
Mr Perey	artiste	4,800 (plus: *jetons* 10 fr. la pièce)	4,800 (plus: *jetons*)
Mr Perret	contrôle	180	180
Mr Pœncet	orchestre	700	700
Mlle Potel	artiste	1,200	1,500
Mr Poussin	peintre des décors	3,600	3,600
Mr Poylo	contrôle	400	400
Mr Pujo	aide-costumier	900	900
Mr Quéru	contrôle, bureau des billets	200	-
Mr Rambour	chœurs	400	-
Mr Reine	sous-chef d'orchestre	2,000	2,000
Mme Requiener	habilleuse	180	180
Mr Rhéal	artiste	600	600
Mr Robert	contrôle	252	-
Mr Ropiquet	chœurs	400	-

FINANCES AND SALARIES

NAME	FUNCTION	1850–51	1851–52
Mr Rougier	aide-costumier	700	700
Mr Sagot	ustensillier	1,000	1,000
Mme Sagot	habilleuse	180	180
Mr Savigny	inspecteur	2,000	2,000
Mr Savigny	mémoire de l'inspecteur	2,447	-
Mlle Ségur	artiste	180	-
Mme Summeret	contrôle, bureau de location	600	800
Mr Taite	orchestre	800	800
Mr Thibaudeau	directeur	6,000 (jusqu'a la fin déc. 1850)	-
Mr Thibout	luthier	200	200
Mr Thomas	orcheste	800	-
Mr Thomas	perruquier	1,700	1,700
Mlle Thuillier	artiste	6,000 (plus: *jetons* 5 fr. la pièce)	-
Mr Tony	chef de contrôle	1,500	1,500
Mr Touzan	tapissier	1,500	1,500
Mr Trouillebert	contrôle	180	252
Mlle Valérie	artiste	600 > 1,200 (1.12.50)	-
Mr Weidinger	orchestre	700	800

NAME	FUNCTION	1850-51	1851-52
Mr Verrier	orchestre	800	800
Mr Veyron	régisseur général	2,700	2,700
Mlle Vistorine	chœurs l'inspecteur	400	-
Mlle Virginie	artiste	1,800	2,400

V

Index of Plays and Playwrights in 1852

Title and 'genre'
Author(s)
Date of first performance (at the Variétés, unless stated otherwise)

1. *À bas les maris*   *intermède*
   (I cannot trace this piece. it was clearly no more than a filler and may well have been produced in-house?)

2. *Ah, vous-dirai-je maman*   1 act, vaudeville
   M. Leprévost, Duprat and Boyer
   14 December 1852

3. *Ami de la maison, L'*   1 act, *comédie-vaudeville*
   E. Colliot and E. Lefèbvre
   15 February 1852

4. *Ami François, L'*   1 act, *comédie-vaudeville*
   Bourgois and E. Colliot.
   19 October 1852

5. *Bal des Variétés, Le*

6. *Bonne qu'on renvoie, Une*   1 act, vaudeville
   La Rounat and H. Berthoud
   23 February 1851

7. *Cabinets particuliers, Les*   1 act, vaudeville
   Boniface and Duvert
   23 October 1832, Théâtre du Vaudeville

8. *Canadar, père et fils*   1 act, vaudeville
   Chapelle, Labiche and Michel
   12 May 1852

9. *Ce que vivent les roses* 1 act, *comédie-vaudeville*
   Martin and Monnier
   21 November 1852

10. *Chateau de Coëtaven, Le* 1 act, *comédie-vaudeville*
    d'Artois, Besselièvre and d'Onquaire
    24 March 1852

11. *Chef de brigands, Un* 1 act, vaudeville
    Marchais and Varin
    10 November 1851

12. *Comment l'esprit vient aux garçons* 1 act, *comédie-vaudeville*
    Martin and Monnier
    28 April 1851

13. *Course au plaisir, La* 2 acts, revue
    Delaporte, de Montheau and Muret (This was the end of year
    11 December 1851 revue)

14. *Déménagé d'hier* 1 act, *comédie-vaudeville*
    Narrey, Royez and Vaëz
    17 May 1852

15. *Derrière le rideau* 2 acts, *comédie-vaudeville*
    Laurençot and Nus
    12 July 1851

16. *Deux gouttes d'eau* 1 act, *comédie-vaudeville*
    Bourgeois and Labiche
    22 September 1852

17. *Deux Inséparables, Les* 1 act, *comédie-vaudeville*
    Faulquemont and Lelarge
    28 November 1852

18. *Deux Prudhommes, Les* 1 act, *comédie-vaudeville*
    Deslandes
    27 December 1851

19. *Drinn, Drinn* 1 act, vaudeville
    Brisebarre, Labie and Nyon
    13 September 1851

20. *En Ballon* 1 act, vaudeville
    Alhoy, Bourgeois and Langlois
    20 September 1852

21. *Enfant gâté, L'* 1 act, vaudeville
    Arago
    27 July 1852

22. *Erreur académique, Une* 1 act, vaudeville
    Bergenet and Jouslin de la Salle
    29 November 1851

23. *Femmes de Gavarni, Les* 3 acts
    Barrière, Beauvallet and Decourcelle
    3 June 1852

24. *Ferme de Primerose, La* 1 act, *comédie-vaudeville*
    Corman and Dutertre
    27 June 1851

25. *Flambart l'exterminateur* 1 act
    Clairville and Pérey
    29 October 1852

26. *Frères féroces, Les* 1 act, *mélodrame*
    Rougement, Jouslin de la Salle and Carmouche
    21 September 1819, Théâtre de la Porte-Saint-Martin.

27. *Frères Lionnet, Les* (an *intermède* — acrobats, jugglers or, possibly singers?)

28. *Gants jeunes, Les*   1 act, vaudeville
    Bayard
    6 March 1835, Théâtre du Vaudeville

29. *Goton de Béranger, Le*   5 acts, vaudeville
    Cormon, Dutertre, Grangé
    12 August 1851

30. *Homme de 50 ans, Un*   1 act, *comédie-vaudeville*
    de Montheau
    9 July 1852

31. *Il faut qu'une porte soit*   1 act, *proverbe*
    ouverte ou fermée
    de Musset
    7 April 1848, Théâtre Français

32. *Mme Diogène*   1 act, vaudeville
    Battu and Desarbres
    31 May 1852

33. *Mam'zell' Rose*   1 act, vaudeville
    Bercioux and Decourcelle
    29 October 1852

34. *Mari de la dame de chœurs, Le*   2 acts, vaudeville
    Bayard and Duvert
    12 december 1836, Théâtre du Vaudeville

35. *Mignon*   2 acts, *comédie-vaudeville*
    de Montheau
    15 November 1851

INDEX OF PLAYS AND PLAYWRIGHTS IN 1852

36. *Monsieur qui prend la mouche, Un* 1 act, comédie-vaudeville
    Labiche and Michel
    25 March 1852

37. *Monsieur qui ne veut pas s'en aller, Un* 1 act, vaudeville
    Clairville and Thiboust
    19 October 1852

38. *Négresse et le Pacha, La* 1 act, vaudeville
    Gautier and La Rounat
    27 December 1851

39. *Paris qui dort* 5 acts
    Delacour and Thiboust
    21 February 1852

40. *Perruquière de Meudon, La* 1 act, *comédie-vaudeville*
    Bourgeois and Dennery
    22 July 1843

41. *Pour et le contre, Le* 1 act, *comédie*
    Lafitte and Nyon
    22 January 1852, Théâtre Français

42. *Puits mitoyen, Le* 1 act, *folie-vaudeville*
    Duvert and Lauzanne
    25 January 1852

43. *Queue Rouge, Une* 2 acts, *comédie-vaudeville*
    Duvert and Lauzanne
    17 January 1852

44. *Quittance de minuit* *opéra-comique*
    Commerson and Deslandes
    (Music by Varney)
    6 January 1852

45. *Reines des bals publics, Les*　　　1 act, *folie-vaudeville*
    Delaporte and de Montheau
    22 February 1852

46. *Renaudin de Caen*　　　2 acts, *comédie-vaudeville*
    Duvert and Lauzanne
    24 March 1836, Théâtre du Vaudeville

47. *Riche d'amour*　　　1 act, vaudeville
    Duvert and Lauzanne
    20 November 1845, Théâtre du Vaudeville

48. *Roi des Drôles, Le*　　　3 acts
    Duvert and Lauzanne
    3 August 1852

49. *Soutiens-moi Chatillon*　　　Scène
    29 November 1851

50. *Souvenirs de Jeunesse*　　　4 acts, *comédie-vaudeville*
    Delacour and Thiboust
    2 September 1852

51. *Supplice de Tantale, Le*　　　1 act, *comédie-vaudeville*
    Duvert and Lauzanne
    31 October 1850

52. *Taconnet*　　　5 acts, vaudeville
    Béraud and Clairville
    13 November 1852

53. *Tribulations de Boisgontier*　　　1 act, vaudeville
    (or *d'une actrice*)
    Carré and Narrey
    17 April 1852

INDEX OF PLAYS AND PLAYWRIGHTS IN 1852

54. *Trois Amours de pompier* 1 act, vaudeville
    Delacour, Lemoine-Moreau and Siraudin
    25 January 1852

55. *Variétés en 1852, Les* 4 acts, revue
    Delacour, Guénée and Thiboust
    20 December 1852

56. *Vengeance, Une* 1 act, *comédie-vaudeville*
    Barrière and Decourcelle
    12 May 1852

57. *Vie de Bohème, La* 5 acts, *pièce mêlée de*
    Barrière and Murger *chants*
    22 November 1849

58. *Vieux de la vieille roche, Un* 1 act, *comédie-vaudeville*
    Dupeuty and Grangé
    29 September 1852

Of the 58 productions put on during 1852 (and that figure includes 4 which were not strictly speaking *comédie-vaudevilles*) *32 were new* and a further 13 had been new in 1851. 39 were *one-act* pieces.

If one accepts the figure of *30* performances (not necessarily consecutive) as an indication of popular success, then the following pieces met that criterion:

1. Paris qui dort 80
2. Les cabinets particuliers 64
3. Un Monsieur qui prend la mouche 59
4. Trois Amours de pompier 52
5. Un Homme de 50 ans 50
6. Les Reines des bals publics 47
7. Le Puits mitoyen 46
8. Les Femmes de Gavarni 40
9. Deux gouttes d'eau 39

10.	Une Queue rouge	31
=	Le Château de Coëtaven	31
=	Madame Diogène	31

What is noticeable is that apart from the perennially popular *Les Cabinets particuliers* (with Arnal) all the successes were new productions in 1852.

The other obvious point to make is that virtually all of the plays were written in collaboration. Only 5 put on in 1852 had a single author. Perhaps, when there was such a huge demand for new work and such a rapid turnover, two (or three) heads were better, or quicker, than one.

VI

Monthly distribution of Performances in 1852

TITLE	TOTAL	Jan	Feb	Mar	Apr	May	Jun	Jul	Aug	Sep	Oct	Nov	Dec
Les Deux Prudhommes	19	11	8	-	-	-	-	-	-	-	-	-	-
Soutiens-moi Chatillon	10	4	-	-	-	-	-	-	-	3	2	1	-
La Négresse et le Pacha	9	9	-	-	-	-	-	-	-	-	-	-	-
La Course au plaisir	12	12	\multicolumn{11}{c}{This was the end of the year 1851 Revue}
Riche d'amour	13	5	3	-	-	-	-	-	-	5	-	-	-
Mignon	3	2	1	-	-	-	-	-	-	-	-	-	-
Renaudin de Caen	1	1	-	-	-	-	-	-	-	-	-	-	-
Le Bal des Variétés	1	1	-	-	-	-	-	-	-	-	-	-	-
Une Erreur académique	1	1	-	-	-	-	-	-	-	-	-	-	-
Quittance de minuit	21	16	-	1	4	-	-	-	-	-	-	-	-

TITLE	TOTAL	Jan	Feb	Mar	Apr	May	Jun	Jul	Aug	Sep	Oct	Nov	Dec
Drinn, Drinn	22	7	-	1	-	-	4	7	3	-	-	-	-
La Ferme de Primerose	28	5	-	-	-	-	-	-	-	7	10	6	-
Une Queue Rouge	31	13	13	5	-	-	-	-	-	-	-	-	-
Le Goton de Bérenger	2	2	-	-	-	-	-	-	-	-	-	-	-
Le Puits mitoyen	46	7	15	2	6	5	5	4	2	-	-	-	-
Trois Amours de pompier	52	7	24	3	2	-	-	8	6	2	-	-	-
Les Cabinets particuliers	64	-	18	23	7	11	1	-	-	2	2	-	-
Paris qui dort	80	-	8	29	24	7	4	-	-	2	2	-	4
L'Ami de la maison	8	-	8	-	-	-	-	-	-	-	-	-	-
Derrière le rideau	1	-	1	-	-	-	-	-	-	-	-	-	-
Un Chef de brigands	2	-	1	1	-	-	-	-	-	-	-	-	-
Le Supplice de Tantale	4	-	4	-	-	-	-	-	-	-	-	-	-

MONTHLY DISTRIBUTION OF PERFORMANCES IN 1852

TITLE	TOTAL	Jan	Feb	Mar	Apr	May	Jun	Jul	Aug	Sep	Oct	Nov	Dec
Les Reines des bals publics	47	–	8	25	–	5	3	2	–	4	–	–	–
Le Chateau de Coëtaven	31	–	–	8	18	2	2	1	–	–	–	–	–
Un Monsieur qui prend la mouche	59	–	–	6	25	17	1	–	–	8	2	–	–
Il faut qu'une porte soit ouverte ou fermée	2	–	–	–	1	–	–	1	–	–	–	–	–
Tribulations de Boisgontier (ou d'une actrice)	1	–	–	–	1	–	–	–	–	–	–	–	–
La Vie de Bohême	13	–	–	–	4	9	–	–	–	–	–	–	–
Une Vengeance	18	–	–	–	–	13	5	–	–	–	–	–	–
Canadar, père et fils	30	–	–	–	–	20	3	3	4	–	–	–	–
Déménagé d'hier	28	–	–	–	–	15	3	–	7	–	3	–	–
La Perruquière de Meudon	7	–	–	–	–	7	–	–	–	–	–	–	–

TITLE	TOTAL	Jan	Feb	Mar	Apr	May	Jun	Jul	Aug	Sep	Oct	Nov	Dec
Intermèdes (Danses)	23	-	-	-	-	12	3	1	-	-	1	1	1,1,3
Mme Diogène	31	-	-	-	-	1	20	1	4	3	1	-	1
Les Femmes de Gavarni	40	-	-	-	-	-	23	14	2	1	-	-	-
Comment l'esprit vient aux garçons	11	-	-	-	-	-	-	11	-	-	-	-	-
Musiciens Hongrois	25	-	-	-	-	-	-	12	3	-	9	1	-
Une Bonne qu'on renvoie	21	-	-	-	-	-	-	13	7	1	-	-	-
Un Homme de 50 ans	50	-	-	-	-	-	-	18	15	7	-	3	7
L'Enfant gâté	19	-	-	-	-	-	-	3	13	2	1	-	-
Le Roi des Drôles	25	-	-	-	-	-	-	-	25	-	-	-	-
Souvenirs de Jeunesse	25	-	-	-	-	-	-	-	-	19	2	-	4
En Ballon	13	-	-	-	-	-	-	-	-	6	7	-	-
Deux gouttes d'eau	39	-	-	-	-	-	-	-	-	9	18	2	10

MONTHLY DISTRIBUTION OF PERFORMANCES IN 1852

TITLE	TOTAL	Jan	Feb	Mar	Apr	May	Jun	Jul	Aug	Sep	Oct	Nov	Dec
Un Vieux de la vieille roche	20	–	–	–	–	–	–	–	–	2	15	.	3
Le Mari de la dame de chœurs	25	–	–	–	–	–	–	–	–	–	20	5	–
L'Ami François	28	–	–	–	–	–	–	–	–	–	13	13	2
Un Monsieur qui ne veut pas s'en aller	23	–	–	–	–	–	–	–	–	–	12	11	–
Mam'zell' Rose	24	–	–	–	–	–	–	–	–	–	3	15	6
Les Gants jeunes	12	–	–	–	–	–	–	–	–	–	3	9	–
Flambart l'exterminateur	7	–	–	–	–	–	–	–	–	–	3	4	–
Les Frères Lionnet	6	–	–	–	–	–	–	–	–	–	–	6	–
À bas les maris	4	–	–	–	–	–	–	–	–	–	–	4	–
Taconnet	24	–	–	–	–	–	–	–	–	–	–	15	9
Ce que vivent les roses	16	–	–	–	–	–	–	–	–	–	–	10	6

TITLE	TOTAL	Jan	Feb	Mar	Apr	May	Jun	Jul	Aug	Sep	Oct	Nov	Dec
Les Deux Inséparables	13	-	-	-	-	-	-	-	-	-	-	3	10
Ah, vous-dirai-je maman	12	-	-	-	-	-	-	-	-	-	-	-	12
Le Pour et le contre	1	-	-	-	-	-	-	-	-	-	-	-	1
Les Frères féroces	1	-	-	-	-	-	-	-	-	-	-	-	1
Les Variétés en 1852	12	-	-	-	-	-	-	-	-	-	-	-	12

VII
Monthly accounts April – December, 1852

Accounts — April 1852

i) Dépenses

DATE	DETAILS	AMOUNT Francs	Centimes
avril			
8	payé à Mr. Carpier avec reçu	3,000	
11	payé à Mr. Jollivet — avance sur sa représentation à bénéfice	300	
12	payé à Mr. Jollivet pour 11 jours d'appointements	123	90
12	payé à Mme. Flore pour avance sur ses appointements	50	
12	payé à Mr. Chereau marchand de fleurs avec reçu	40	
12	payé à Mr. Maurec ses appointements du mois de mars, feuille	75	
13	payé à Mr. Baulé pour acompte, feuille	500	
13	payé à Mr. Lavigny, feuille	41	25
13	payé à l'association des musiciens et artistes	35	50
13	payé à Mr. Carpier, avec reçu	200	
13	payé à l'enterprise générale de balayage	6	
14	payé à Mr. Lehman une facture de rubans	1	20
14	payé à Mr. Lavigny mémoire d'inspecteur	131	70
15	payé à Mr. Lavigny accessoires, feuille	97	65
15	payé à l'ordre de Mr. Brès une traite de	500	
19	payé Pou^r frais de voitures, représentation de Mr. Leclère	12	50

DATE	DETAILS	Francs	Centimes
20	payé à l'ordre de M^r· Poucet une traite	614	
20	payé à M^r· Leclère son bénéfice	2,500	
20	payé à l'ordre de M^r· Couzan, une traite de	1,000	
20	payé à l'ordre de M^r· Fregère une traite de	300	
22	payé pour les impositions de la patente	300	
23	payé à la Comp^{ie} du Soleil, assurance contre l'incendie	150	
24	payé à M^r· Rheims, Bonnetier	36	
24	payé à M^r· Belin graveur tombola	64	
25	payé à M^r· Lavigny acompte	10	
26	payé à l'ordre de M^r· Couzan une traite de	600	
26	payé à l'ordre de M^r· Couzan une traite de	432	
26	payé à M^r· Bevestorf [?] oppositions de M^r· Colb	135	
27	payé à la Compagnie du Gaz pour le mois de mars, sur feuille	1,135	60
27	payé à M^r· Poussin pour décors de *Paris qui dort*	386	
27	payé à M^r· Carpier, avec reçu	200	
28	payé pour le loyer du magazin de décors	500	
28	payé dans le courant du mois aux auteurs en trois fois différentes	6,488	10
28	payé pour le loyer en cinq parts	10,282	50
28	payé à deux factures de Bougies	20	
28	payé à M^r· Arnal acompte	500	
28	payé à M^r· Semen avoué	2,250	

MONTHLY ACCOUNTS APRIL - DECEMBER 1852

DATE	DETAILS	Francs	Centimes
28	payé à Mr Carpier, avec reçu	3,900	
28	payé à Mlle Fitz James	875	
28	payé à M^{our} Aulansky*	1,403	75
28	payé pour la garde et les pompiers depuis le 8	525	80
28	payé pour le droit des indigents depuis le 8 avril	3,645	80
28	payé pour le droit des indigents reçu chaque jour	212	49
28	payé pour le droit des indigents une fois par mois	66	66
28	payé pour visite du matériel reçu chaque jour	15	30
28	payé à Mlle Bodimot (?) blanchisseuse	25	00
		43,707	70
	approuvé E. Carpier	43,687	70
	Erreur d'addition portée au compte suivant	13	98

* The name is HOLINSKY — whoever was doing these accounts was clearly unfamiliar with one of the Variétés' patrons.

ii) Recettes — April

DATE	DETAILS	AMOUNT Francs	Centimes
avril			
8	Reçu de M^r· Baudouin	3,098	35
8	Recette	1,412	25
10	Reçu de M^r· Maurice Loyer de M^d de Cannes	33	35
10	Recette	1,514	75
11	Recette	1,747	
12	Recette	2,276	
13	Recette	2,060	25
14	Recette	2,396	25
15	Recette	1,578	75
16	Recette	2,153	75
17	Recette	3,222	75
18	Recette	2,840	75
19	Recette	1,931	75
20	Recette	1,708	50
21	Recette	1,651	25
22	Recette	1,371	50
23	Recette	1,148	75
24	Recette	1,268	
25	Recette	2,133	25

DATE	DETAILS	Francs	Centimes
26	Recette	1,485	75
27	Recette	1,573	50
28	Recette	1,404	50
29	Recette	1,802	50
29	Reçu de M^r· Marguin, Loyer du café	250	
30	Recette	1,777	75
		43,844	71(?)
	Dépense	43,707	70
	reste à la caisse	137	01
	La recette est de	43,840	70
	La Dépense est de	43,687	70
	reste en caisse	153	

Accounts — May 1852

i) Dépenses

DATE		AMOUNT	
mai	DETAILS	Francs	Centimes
2	facture Bellangé, fournitures de bureaux	10	
6	M^r· Caron, sur son reçu	50	
11	M^r· Painblanc sur son mémoire de ferrurerie et sur reçu	300	
11	Loyer du Magazin de Décors (le 28 avril 500 fr.) sur reçu de 1,500 fr.	1,000	
11	M^r· Larivière & Cie, facture d'Etoffes pour costumes	178	
15	M^r· Semen, pour compte de M^r· Ch^e Potier et sur reçu	300	
17	M^r· Marest Petit, facture Bas pour costumes	28	50
17	M^r· Melon, éclairage à l'huile (avril) reçu sur feuille d'émargement	1,362	55
19	M^r· Marguerite & Cie, éclairage au gaz courant (avril) reçu sur feuille d'émargement	1,050	10
20	Traité Carpier, pour Poucet, au 20	400	
22	M^r· Marguerite & Cie, Eclairage au gaz compteur (avril) sur reçu	138	60
22	M^r· Lassagne: avance sur ses appointemens de mai	150	
22	M^r· Deldruel, à valoir sur son mémoire de Peinture et sur reçu	200	
25	Danseurs Espagnols à valoir sur leurs représentations et sur reçu	500	
25	M^r· Giovani [sic] Filippa, pour 3 cachets de représentations, à 25fr et sur reçu	75	

mai	DETAILS	Francs	Centimes
27	M$^{r.}$ Moraye, sur facture	52	50
27	M$^{r.}$ Bienfait, sur facture	25	
28	M$^{r.}$ Parmentier, sa facture vannerie	82	
28	M$^{me.}$ Vve Dondey Dupré, affiches de mars, reçu sur feuille d'émargement	1,088	
28	M$^{r.}$ Lan, avoué, 2 notes du 25 sept 1851 au 17 mars 1852	97	
30	M$^{r.}$ Chantepie, sur facture	32	
30	M$^{r.}$ Brie, sur facture	24	55
30	M$^{r.}$ Ménard, sur facture	38	
31	Danseurs Espagnols, à valoir sur leurs représentations et sur reçu	300	
31	Appointemens des Artistes et Employés du Théâtre (avril)	18,915	75
31	Droits d'auteurs du 1er au 31 mai inclus sur reçu	5,115	55
31	Droits des Indigens du 1er au 31 mai inclus sur reçu	4,170	79
31	Garde municipal du 1er au 31 mai inclus sur reçu	232	50
31	Sapeurs pompiers du 1er au 31 mai inclus sur reçu	516	05
31	Loyer de al Salle du 1er au 31 mai inclus sur reçu	8,568	75
31	M$^{r.}$ Holinsky du 1er au 31 mai inclus sur feuille d'émargement	850	95
31	Monsieur Carpier, espèces comptées du 1er au 31 mai inclus et sur reçu	4,545	
	Dépenses f^{rs}	50,397	14

ii) Recettes — May

DATE		AMOUNT	
mai	DETAILS	Francs	Centimes
1er	En Caisse ce jour	137	01
3	Reçu de Mr Lallemant, pour loyer du vestiaire du théâtre (avril)	50	
3	reçu de Mr Duffaud à titre de retenue pour opposition	25	
3	reçu de Monsieur Carpier, espèces	12,000	
15	reçu de Mr Maurice pour loyer de la devanture du théâtre (mars et avril)	66	70
22	reçu de l'administration du Noirciarama pour le mois d'avril	200	
27	reçu de Monsieur Carpier, espèces	3,200	
28	reçu de Monsieur Carpier, par les mains de la personne du Commerce	1,000	
31	Recettes du théâtre du 1er au 31 mai inclusivement	42,632	25
31	Change de pièces d'or du 1er au 31 mai inclus	5	90
	Recettes	59,316	86
	Approuvé A. Carpier Dépenses	50,397	14
	En Caisse au 31 mai	8,919	72

Accounts — June 1852

i) Dépenses

DATE		AMOUNT	
juin	DETAILS	Francs	Centimes
1er	Monsieur Gombert, affaire Lambquin	455	
3	facture, du Cain [?] de Rue	30	20
3	facture, de M$^{r.}$ Vièz, fab^n de chaises	15	
3	facture, de M$^{r.}$ Tourneur, chaussures pour les *Femmes de Gavarni*	41	50
4	facture, Arnaud, papéterie et un timbre	5	50
7	M$^{r.}$ Parard, sur note	5	55
8	M$^{r.}$ Dieudonné sur facture 27 mai	20	00
8	M$^{r.}$ Millon, facture du 1er janvier au 26 mai 1851, compte de M$^{r.}$ Bowes	143	
8	voiture, par [?] M$^{r.}$ Zoghel	1	50
9	M$^{r.}$ Roger, note du 27 février au 15 octobre 1850, compte de M$^{r.}$ Bowes	18	75
10	Danseurs Espagnols. Solde de 16 rep^{ons} à 150 f.	1,600	
12	M$^{r.}$ Taillefer, facture de bois de constructions	50	
14	M$^{me.}$ Dondey Dupré, affiches d'avril, reçu sur feuille d'émargement	962	75
14	Caisse des Dépots et Consignations, app^t sur Mlle Boisgontier	750	
15	Abonneme^{nt}, 3 mois Journal le Corsaire	102	
15	Mr Béraud, sur indemnité de 300 fr avec reçu	70	

juin	DETAILS	Francs	Centimes
18	Mr Marguerite et Cie, éclairage au gaz courant, mai, feuille d'émargement	1,122	50
18	Marguerite et Cie, éclairage au gaz compteur, mai, sur reçu	177	75
19	Mr Marest Petit, facture de juillet à 9bre 1850, compte de Mr Bowes	761	
19	Mr Blonval, solde de sa facture, 9bre 1851 (sur 278 fr.)	78	
22	Mr Semen, solde de l'indemnité de M. Béraud	230	
23	Mr Gagnet, facture du 3 janvier au 19 février 1852	75	85
23	Mr Gagnet, facture du 28 juin au 5 sept, 1851	128	15
23	M. Leleux & Cottignies, 2 d ... tuiles pour décorations	187	
24	Réparation à la Borne fontaine du Boulevard (Ville de Paris)	32	10
26	Mr Burdin, affaire Lambquin	180	30
28	Mr Lamotte, mémoire du 26 oct, 1849 compte de M. Bowes	167	
29	Mr Lemaire, note chapellerie du 25 mai	12	
29	Mr Devoir à valoir sur travaux d'écriture et sur reçu	500	
30	Mr Klozdy, hongrois, à valoir sur des représentations et sur reçu	121	55
30	voyage à Bologne, au compte de l'administration	50	
30	appointements des artistes et employés, mai	19,532	05
30	appointements des figurans supplémentaires pour les *Femmes de Gavarni*	727	50
30	Droits des auteurs du 21 mai au 20 juin inclus	3,007	37
30	Droits des hospices du 1er au 30 juin inclus	3,116	19

juin	DETAILS	Francs	Centimes
30	Monsieur Carpier, espèces sur reçu	2,450	
30	Loyer de la Salle	5,481	50
30	Monsieur Holinsky, reçu sur livre d'émargement du 1er au 30 inclus	823	50
30	La Garde Républicaine du 1er au 30 inclus	321	50
30	Sapeurs pompiers du 1er au 30 inclus	514	95
	Dépenses fs	43,978	01

ii) Recettes — June

DATE		AMOUNT	
juin	DETAILS	Francs	Centimes
1er	En Caisse ce jour	8,919	72
2	reçu de Monsieur Carpier, espèces	3,900	
3	reçu de l'administration du Noirciarama	200	
4	reçu de M$^{r.}$ Lallemant, pour loyer du vestiaire du théâtre (mai)	50	
8	reçu de M$^{r.}$ Grimaldé (pour Danseurs Espagnols) des mains de M$^{r.}$ Carpier	650	
9	reçu de M$^{r.}$ Roger entrep^{r} contre billets de spectacle (compensation de sa note)	18	75
30	Recettes journalières du 1er au 30 inclus	31,115	25
	Recettes fr.	44,853	72
	Approuvé A. Carpier Dépenses fr.	43,978	01
	En Caisse au 30 juin	875	71

Accounts — July 1852

i) Dépenses

DATE juillet	DETAILS	Francs	Centimes
1er	voyage Monsieur Savigny à Boulogne pour les Hongrois	425	95
2	Droits des auteurs du 21 au 30 juin inclus	726	35
2	M$^{r.}$ Gibier, notes du 1er Juin 1851 au 22 mars 1852	147	50
2	Télégraphe électrique, pour les Hongrois	35	70
3	Hongrois à valoir, et sur reçu de 300 fr. (200 fr. à payer le 8 à M$^{r.}$ Simon)	100	
4	Hongrois sur reçu	60	
4	Hongrois, pour l'interprète et sur reçu de Mr Kalosdy	45	
8	M$^{r.}$ Simon, hôtelier des Hongrois (sur reçu daté du 3)	200	
12	Droits des auteurs du 1er au 10 inclus	435	55
13	M$^{r.}$ Vicq, ses factures du 10.7.1851 au 15 janvier 1852	50	
14	M$^{r.}$ Martignon, pour M$^{r.}$ Danterny	60	
14	note de l'Académie de Musique, rep^{lon} au bénéfice de Mlle Fitz James	40	
14	Balayage du magazin des Décors 2me trimestre	6	
14	Impositions	400	

juillet	DETAILS	Francs	Centimes
15	note du Théâtre français, rep[ion] au bénéfice de Mlle Fitz James	20	
15	M[r.] Chantepie, 3 factures du Bougier, du 3 au 22 juin	70	
17	M[r.] Furchs, note de nettoyage de gants	23	
19	facture Leleux et Cottignies, toile pour décoration du *Roi des Drôles*	35	
19	Note de voitures pour la Rep[on] de Mlle Fitz James	12	
21	facture Chevreux et Aubertot, costumes pour *Le Roi des Drôles*	16	
23	facture Marienval pleur pour costumes pour *Le Roi des Drôles*	40	
24	M[r.] Allard les retenues faites à Mlle Bertin et contre main levée	200	
27	facture Naugeois et Truchy, passementeries	45	
27	C[pt] Carpier, ou Hinfray (?) ce jour cap.[al] 500f int[rt] 8f	508	
27	Hongrois pour la Rep[n] de ce jour 27	100	
28	Hongrois pour la Rep[n] de ce jour 28	100	
29	Vve Gauetier et Charmont pour costumes du *Roi des Drôles*	115	
29	Mr Marguerite et Cie, Gaz courant (juin)	1,086	30
29	Mr Marguerite et Cie, Gaz au compteur (juin)	149	60
30	factures Parmentier du 12.8.1851 au 18 mars 1852	83	
30	Hongrois pour la rep[on] de ce jour	75	
30	Droits des auteurs du 11 au 20 inclus	228	95

juillet	DETAILS	Francs	Centimes
30	Appointemens, payés en juillet, reçu sur feuille d'émargement	14,276	95
30	Monsieur Holinsky, du 1er au 31 juillet inclus	850	95
30	Monsieur Bowes pour loyer de la Salle, jusqu'au 20 juillet inclus	3,425	
30	Mr Carpier, espèces sur reçu	481	
30	Droits des Indigens sur reçu	961	02
30	La Garde Républicaine sur reçu	195	
30	Sapeurs pompiers sur reçu	414	95
	Dépenses fs	26,243	77

ii) Recettes — July

DATE		AMOUNT	
juillet	DETAILS	Francs	Centimes
1er	En Caisse ce jour	875	71
3	reçu de Mr. Lallemant, pour la location du vestiaire (juin)	50	
3	reçu de Mr. Alexandre pour la vente des lorgnettes 1er semestre 1852	75	
3	reçu de Monsieur Carpier, espèces	11,600	
3	reçu de Mr. Maurice, Mr. Pannes [Cannes?] devanture du théâtre (mai)	33	50
5	reçu de l'administration du Noirciorama	200	
5	reçu de Monsieur Carpier, espèces	800	
10	change d'or du 1er juin au 10 juillet	5	45
10	reçu de Monsieur Carpier, par l'intermédiaire d'une Dame	2,000	
17	reçu de Monsieur Carpier, espèces	600	
21	reçu de Monsieur Carpier, espèces	1,000	
28	reçu de Mr. Maurice, Mr. Cannes devanture du théâtre (juin)	33	35
28	recettes journalières du 1er au 31 inclus	9,116	75
	Recettes, espèces reçues	26,389	56
	Approuvé A. Carpier Dépenses fr.	26,243	77
	En Caisse	145	79

Accounts — August 1852

i) Dépenses

DATE août	DETAILS	AMOUNT Francs	Centimes
7	Mr. Vallin, rachat des billets d'auteurs et concessions pour la représentation du 3 août (*Roi des Drôles*)	112	50
9	Mr. Lhopital sur facture bijoux faux (boucles pour souliers)	10	
12	Mlle. Flore, à titre de secours	50	
13	Traite Carpier ou Hinfray [?], au 13 (courant) et 500f. intérêts 8^f	508	
13	Mr. Colliot sa note, frais de procédure	62	50
13	Mr. Passerat, concierge, sa note de juillet	18	50
16	Traite Carpier ou Hinfray, au 14 et 500f. intérêts 8^f	508	
17	Mr. Gibier, cordonnier, cinq notes du 29 avril 1851 au 18 juin 1852	125	
20	Mr. Poussin à valoir sur ses travaux de Peinture (*Femmes de Gavarni*)	200	
21	2ème semestre des Eaux de la ville de Paris	87	85
23	T^{te} (Traite) Hinfray au 24 ct	500	
27	T^{te} (Traite) Hinfray au 27 ct	500	
28	Mr. Chavré, accompany^t au piano, Bénéfice de Mlle Fiz-James, 10 juillet	20	
30	Mr Marguerite et Cie, éclairage au gaz courant (juillet)	1,013	70

août	DETAILS	Francs	Centimes
30	M' Marguerite et Cie, éclairage au gaz au compteur (juillet)	148	70
31	Hongrois, pendant le mois d'août. Diverses représentations et espèces avancées	1,183	
31	Monsieur Carpier, espèces en août avec reçu	997	50
31	Droits des auteurs du 21 juillet au 20 août inclus	3,220	35
31	Monsieur Holinsky, du 1er au 31 août inclus	850	95
31	Mme Dondey, Dupré, affiches de juin	702	
31	Mr Frédérick Lemaître sur ses représentations en août	7,613	85
31	Mr Frédérick Lemaître sur sa créance en août	2,200	
31	Appointemens des Artistes et Employés	18,695	10
31	Indigens pendant le mois d'août	3,117	56
31	La Garde Républicaine le mois d'août	210	
31	Sapeurs pompiers le mois d'août	507	30
	Dépenses f^{s}	43,162	36
	Approuvé A. Carpier		

ii) Recettes — August

DATE août	DETAILS	AMOUNT Francs	Centimes
1er	En Caisse à nouveau	145	79
3	reçu de Monsieur Carpier, espèces	12,000	
3	reçu de M$^{r.}$ Lallemant, location du vestiaire (juillet)	50	
4	reçu de M$^{r.}$ Marguin, location du Café du Foyer, 2ème trimestre de 1852	250	
12	reçu de la C$^{ie.}$ Hongroise, espèces avancées par M$^{r.}$ Ste Marie, à Londres	308	
12	reçu de Monsieur Carpier	900	
16	Retenues faites sur les appointemens des Dames Artistes par le Coiffeur	85	
17	reçu de M$^{me.}$ Vve Maurice, locataire de la devanture du théâtre (juillet)	33	25
19	reçu de l'Administration des Noircioramas (juillet et août)	400	
31	recettes journalières du 1er au 31 ct. inclus	30,448	50
	Recettes journalières et encaissemens divers frs.	44,620	64
	Dépenses d'autre part frs.	43,162	36
	En caisse ce jour frs.	1,458	28

Accounts — October 1852

i) Dépenses

DATE		AMOUNT	
octobre	DETAILS	Francs	Centimes
8	un châle long, pour la *Dame de Chœurs*	7	
9	Entreprise de balayage, mag^{in} de Décors, 3ème trimestre	6	
9	M$^{me.}$ Renaud, ouvreuse, remboursement de son cautionnement	100	
9	M$^{r.}$ Poussin, 2 mois de fourniture d'eau	5	
13	M$^{me.}$ Dondey, Dupré, affiches de juillet	826	75
13	M$^{r.}$ Taillefer, sa note du 21 juillet (bois de construction)	181	
13	M$^{r.}$ Pirodon, sa note du 15 mars (peinture)	40	
18	B^{ce} Carpier, ordre Devoir au 18	300	
18	M$^{r.}$ Ricco, tailleur, à valoir	150	
18	B^{ce} Carpier, ordre (?) Touzan au 25	1,000	
26	facture Verreaux, un petit chien (*Mari de la Dame de Chœurs*)	25	
27	M$^{r.}$ Cuillier, note de M$^{r.}$ Langlois	9	90
27	M$^{r.}$ Poussin, note du *Roi des Drôles* (peinture)	343	
29	B^{ce} Carpier ou Marest-Petit au 28	739	90
29	facture du Coin de Rue (costumes)	2	
29	une veste drap. pour Fréd. Lemaître	22	
29	une presse à timbres pour le contrôle	30	

octobre	DETAILS	Francs	Centimes
29	Décorations du *Roi des Drôles*	27	60
29	Notes de Mr Passerat (juin et septembre)	32	30
29	un chale pour Mlle Clarisse, *Roi des Drôles*	18	
30	loyer du Magazin de Décors, 2ème trimestre 1852	1,500	
30	Impositions, à valoir	800	
30	M$^{r.}$ Michie, à valoir sur son prêt de 1,000 frs.	600	
30	M$^{r.}$ Lapie, traites et reçus à valoir	4,850	
30	M$^{r.}$ Hinfray, 3 traites à son ordre	1,500	
30	Assurances contre l'incendie	450	
30	Compagnie Hongroise sur reçus et pour solde	625	
30	M$^{r.}$ Fréd Lemaître, sur sa créance et pour solde	900	
30	Propriétaire, loyer de la Salle du 16 septembre au 20 octobre inclus	8,910	
30	M$^{r.}$ Carpier, espèces sur reçu	3,517	50
30	Appointemens des Artistes et employés	19,394	45
30	M$^{r.}$ Holinsky du 26 septembre au 25 octobre inclus	1,541	
30	Droits des auteurs du 21 septembre au 20 octobre inclus	5,206	80
30	Droits des Indigens, du 1er au 31 inclus	5,130	31
30	La Garde Républicaine, du 1er au 31 inclus	232	50
30	Sapeurs pompiers, du 1er au 31 inclus	516	05
	Dépenses f^s	59,539	06

ii) Recettes — October

DATE		AMOUNT	
octobre	DETAILS	Francs	Centimes
1er	En Caisse	2,040	76
2	reçu de l'Administration des Noircioramas (septembre)	200	
2	reçu de M$^{r.}$ Marguin, loyer du café du Foyer, 3ème trimestre	250	
4	reçu de Monsieur Carpier, espèces	10,000	
4	reçu de M$^{r.}$ Lallemant (vestiaire) septembre	50	
5	reçu de M$^{r.}$ Michie à titre de prêt	1,000	
6	reçu de M$^{me.}$ Lépine, Devanture (droite) du théâtre (lingerie) octobre	16	65
8	reçu de M$^{me.}$ Maurice (gauche) papeteries spetembre	33	35
29	reçu de M$^{r.}$ Laroussini, Laitier, devant du théâtre 6 mois du 1er novembre au 31 avril	100	
30	reçu de M$^{r.}$ Lallemant (vestiaire) octobre	50	

octobre	DETAILS	Francs	Centimes
30	Retenues faites aux Dames artistes, pour le Coiffeur	120	
30	Change d'or	20	25
31	recettes journalières du 1er au 31 inclus	53,407	75
	Recettes journalières et encaissemens divers frs.	67,288	76
	Dépenses	59,539	06
	En Caisse	7,749	70
	Approuvée l'écriture A. Carpier		

Accounts — November 1852

i) Dépenses

DATE		AMOUNT	
novembre	DETAILS	Francs	Centimes
1	Mme Goblin, ouvreuse, remboursement de son cautionnement, Décédée	100	
2	Mr Choller, espèces, pour la pièce intitulée *Le Mari d'une Jolie Femme*	118	
3	Hongrois et pour solde de tous comptes	496	
5	Frères Lionnet, cachets pour les chansonnettes qu'ils ont chantées	350	
6	Mr Desseuil, accord d'un piano	10	
6	Mr Alfred Albert, dessins de costumes (*Le Roi des Drôles*)	50	
9	facture de la Ville de Paris, etoffes pour costumes	7	60
9	facture Hallé, vases pour les accessoires	12	
15	location d'une Baignoire (pièce, *Un M^r qui ne veut pas d'en aller*)	7	75
15	Mme Dondey Dupré, affiches du mois d'août	871	25
16	Rempailleur	2	50
19	d'Avril [Davril?] et Cie, soie et velours pour costumes	18	50
20	Mr Eaisé [?] à valoir sur sa note chapellerie — Cte de Mr Carpier	50	
20	Mr Richer et Cie — à valoir sur sa note de Vidanges de février	100	

novembre	DETAILS	Francs	Centimes
22	M'· Ballu. Dessins de costumes, *Taconnet*	55	
24	Danseurs Espagnols, pour la Rep^on du 21	50	
25	M'· Painblanc, à valoir sur son mémoire serrierier	200	
26	M'· Henricks. Droits d'auteurs et frais pour chansonnettes	77	05
29	Impositions, à valoir	300	
29	M'· Rieu[?] tailleur, à valoir Cte de M' Carpier	100	
29	facture Lelièvre, bas et jabots pour *Taconnet*	53	
29	facture Chantepie, bougies pour le Bal	165	
29	Philippe, Léon et Frédérick pour la nuit du bal	10	
29	M'· Fleury Gérard sur son reçu	1,750	
29	Droits des auteurs, du 21 octobre au 20 novembre inclus	7,037	20
29	M' Marguerite et Cie, Gaz de septembre et d'octobre	2,605	75
29	M'· Fréd^kk Lemaître, du 13 au 30 novembre inclus	4,839	40
29	Proproétaire, loyer de la Salle du 21 octobre [?!] au 15.9. inclus	8,911	50
29	M'· Carpier, espèces	2,332	50
29	M'· Carpier, versées à M' Lapie	5,600	
29	Appointemens des Artistes et employés	19,406	95
30	M'· Holinsky du 26.8 au 25.9 inclus	1,740	65
30	Cinq traites sur [?] Fressard, ensemble	2,500	

novembre	DETAILS	Francs	Centimes
30	Deux traites sur Guillaume	1,000	
30	Une traite sur Couzan	500	
30	Une traite sur Dubief	400	
30	Une traite sur Hainfray	200	
30	Droits des Indigens du 1er au 30 inclus	4,893	93
30	Droits des Indigens pour le Bal du 27 sur 4480 + 8me	560	
30	Garde de Paris du 1er au 30 inclus	225	
30	Sapeurs pompiers, du 1er au 30 inclus	499	65
30	Garde de Paris, sapeurs pompiers et Police pour le Bal du 27	81	50
	Dépenses f^{rs}	67,787	68
	Approuvée Carpier		

ii) Recettes — November

DATE		AMOUNT	
novembre	DETAILS	Francs	Centimes
1er	espèces en caisse	7,749	70
2	reçu de M^r· Lallemant, vestiaire 9bre	66	65
2	reçu de l'Ad^{ion} du [?J^{al}] l'entr'acte 8bre et 9bre	100	
2	reçu de Mme· Lépine, lingerie devant le théâtre 9bre	16	65
3	reçu de Monsieur Carpier	19,500	
4	reçu de M^r· Maréchal, d^r des Noirciaramas 8bre	200	
4	reçu de M^r· et Vve Maurice, papéterie devant le théâtre	33	35
8	reçu de M^r· Pradié, loyer de sa chambre au théâtre 8bre	12	50
23	Retenues faites aux Dames artistes, pour le Coiffeur	200	
30	reçu de M^r· Albany, à valoir sur les bals du théâtre, café du foyer	200	
30	reçu de M^r· Neckmann pour le vestiaire du Bal du 27	69	70
30	recettes journalières du 1er au 30 inclus	50,146	

novembre	DETAILS	Francs	Centimes
30	recettes du bal donné le 27	4,340	
	Recettes et encaissemens divers	72,554	75
	Dépenses	67,787	68
	En Caisse	4,767	07
	Approuvée Carpier		

Accounts — December 1852

i) Dépenses

DATE décembre	DETAILS	AMOUNT Francs	Centimes
3	facture de la ville de Paris, costumes	6	75
3	facture des villes de France, costumes	5	70
3	Mr Poussin, note du porteur d'eau et fournitures diverses	6	60
3	Garçon de Recette du Changeur	1	
6	Mr Painblanc, à valoir sur son mémoire de serrurerie	100	
6	Mr Passerat, sa note d'octobre	13	25
8	facture du Coin de Rue, 21 oct. au 6 nov. Etoffes pour costumes	245	
8	Mr Forester, huissier, pour offres réelles à Mme Deshayes	380	
10	Demoiselles Dabbas, danseuses, cachet pour la représentation du 5	50	
11	Feuille des Comparses (*Taconnet*) 13 nov. au 4 déc. inclus	146	50
13	facture, Ville de Paris, costumes	5	
13	facture, Vial, Robe pour Fréd. Lemaître, costumes	75	
13	Mr Laporte, tapissier à valoir sur le Bal du 27 nov.	300	
13	Mr Mangin, tambour, figurant dans *Taconnet*	7	
14	facture, Vatin et Cie, Gaz argentine, costumes	16	80

décembre	DETAILS	Francs	Centimes
15	Note de la Comédie Française, représentation du 11 déc.	43	25
15	Note de l'Opéra, représentation du 11 déc.	41	85
15	M^r· Ménard, facture Lampions	37	60
15	M^r· Guillmard, cordonnier, sa note	13	
15	Mlle· Boisgontier sa part de la Repréesntation du 11 déc à son bénéfice	388	71
16	Sapeurs pompiers, gardes et Police pour le Bal du 15	84	30
17	M^r· Dusseuil, accord d'un piano	5	
17	Philippe et Frédéric pour la Nuit du Bal du 15	5	
17	facture des Villes de France, costumes	13	15
18	facture de la Ville de Paris, [costumes]	9	45
18	facture Monjal, teinturier, du 8 mars au 14 déc	49	
18	M^r· His. orchestre pour les Bals du 27 nov et 15 déc	390	
18	M^r· Brossonneau à valoir sur le chauffage	700	
18	M^r· Langlois, note de Bois de construction [Décors]	13	
18	M^r· Beaugrand, note de souliers et pardessus caoutchouc (costumes)	19	50
22	feuille des Comparses, de 6 au 12 solde	25	

décembre		DETAILS	Francs	Centimes
	22	facture des Villes de France	11	60
	22	payé à Mr Leroy, accompagnateur, rep^{on} du 11 déc	10	
	23	payé à Mr Ricco, tailleur, à valoir compte de Mr Carpier	150	
	24	facture, Ville de Paris, costumes	5	
	27	Mme Dondey-Dupré, affiches de septembre	925	75
	27	voiture à Mr Auguste Veyron, chez Mlle Page	2	
	27	Mr Marguerite et Cie, Gaz courant 1086,30, au compteur 174,70	1,261	
	28	Impositions, solde de 1852	940	15
	29	Mr Micheé, à valoir sur son prêt de 1000^{fr} (800)	200	
	29	Mr Taillefer, note de Bois (Décors) à valoir	200	
	30	facture Farray, drap bleu	40	
	30	facture Reime et C^{ier}, Boutons & Boucles, costumes	17	50
	30	Mr Eaiéé [?], Chapelier, à valoir sur sa note chapellerie, Cte de Mr Carpier	50	
	30	facteur, étrennes	2	
	31	M. Roger, maçon, à valoir sur son mémoire	50	
	31	M^r Ch. Perrey, à valoir sur son bénéfice du 29 oct	600	
	31	3 Brochures — les Frères féroces	4	50

décembre	DETAILS	Francs	Centimes
31	M$^{r.}$ Carpier, espèces et traites	4,329	50
31	Trois traites, Fressard de 1,000^{fr} chaque	3,000	
31	Six traites, Fressard de 500^{fr} chaque	3,000	
31	Deux traites, Mirault de 500^{fr} chaque	1,000	
31	Une traite au Porteur	100	
31	Propriétaire, loyer de la salle du 16 nov. au 10 déc. inclus	8,568	75
31	Droits des auteurs du 21 nov. au 20 déc, inclus	5,672	30
31	Droits des auteurs pour Chansonnettes	35	
31	M. Holinsky du 26 nov. au 25 déc inclus	1,684	50
31	M. Carpier, espèces versées à Mr Lapie	2,800	
31	Appointemens des Artistes et employés (compris Mlle Clarisse Miroy)	18,282	95
31	Droits des Indigens du 1er au 31 inclus	5,205	28
31	Droits des Indigens pour le Bal du 15 déc, le 8eme	92	50
31	Garde de Paris du 1er au 31 inclus	248	50
31	Sapeurs pompiers du 1er au 31 inclus	565	55
31	Mr Fréd.^{ic} Lemaître du 1er au 12 déc. inclus	2,247	70
	Total des Dépenses f^{s}	64,496	44

ii) Recettes — December

DATE décembre	DETAILS	AMOUNT Francs	Centimes
1er	En caisse	4,767	07
1er	reçu de M$^{r.}$ Lallemant, location du vestiaire [déc]	66	65
1er	reçu de Mme Lépine, location de la lingerie [déc]	16	65
3	reçu de M$^{r.}$ Carpier, espéces	11,000	
3	Retenue faite à Monsieur Lassagne	10	
4	reçu de M$^{r.}$ Maréchal, directeur du Noirciaramas [nov.]	200	
6	reçu de M$^{me.}$ Vve Maurice, location papéterie, nov	33	35
9	reçu de Mr Foresta, Huissier, offres réelles refusées par Mr Deshayes	380	
9	reçu de M$^{r.}$ Pradié, loyer de sa chambre qu'il occupe au théâtre, nov	12	50
13	reçu de M$^{r.}$ Flamant pour deux tableaux d'annonces au foyer	400	
18	reçu de l'Ad^{ion} du [?Jal] l'entr'acte, déc	50	
18	recette du Bal, donné au foyer le 15 ct	740	
18	reçu de M$^{r.}$ Bernard, pour le vestiaire du dit Bal	13	20
30	Retenues faites aux Dames artistes pour le Coiffeur	100	

décembre	DETAILS	Francs	Centimes
30	recettes journalières du 1er au 31 inclus	54,395	50
	Recettes Journalières et encaissemens divers fr.	72,184	92
	Dépenses	64,496	44
	En Caisse fr.	7,688	48
	[Approuvée Carpier?]		

VIII
Nightly Box-office Takings
9 April – 31 December 1852

Explanatory Note

The figure in the extreme left-hand column is the price per place in francs.

The figures in the remaining columns represent: on the left the number of tickets sold; on the right the amount taken. On the night of Sunday 11 April, for example, 51 tickets bringing in 255 francs were sold for the Stalles d'orchestre (5 francs a place).

NIGHTLY BOX-OFFICE TAKINGS 1852

	Avril 1852	Vendredi 9		Samedi 10		Dimanche 11		Lundi 12		Mardi 13		Mercredi 14		Jeudi 15	
6	Billets à toutes places	5	30	19	114	13	78	19	114	8	48	12	72	11	66
5	Loges de la galerie	27	135	7	35	22	110	24	120	17	85	22	110	24	120
5	Stalles d'orchestre	49	245	74	370	51	255	58	290	76	380	74	370	48	240
5	Stalles de balcon	10	50	11	55	12	60	11	55	19	95	13	65	19	95
4	Deuxièmes loges de face	5	20	8	32	10	40	9	36	7	28	23	92	–	–
4	Stalles de première galerie	10	40	20	80	32	128	39	156	35	140	41	164	37	148
4	Orchestre	23	92	31	124	15	60	29	116	27	108	25	100	26	104
3	Loges intermédiaires	9	27	6	18	21	63	20	60	35	105	12	36	7	21
2½	Deuxièmes loges de côté	6	15	6	15	12	30	27	67.5	7	17.5	31	77.5	13	32.5
2½	Pourtour	29	72.5	18	45	44	110	54	135	24	60	34	85	17	42.5
2	Parterre	100	200	90	180	68	136	78	156	79	158	107	214	55	110

	Avril 1852	Vendredi 9		Samedi 10		Dimanche 11		Lundi 12		Mardi 13		Mercredi 14		Jeudi 15	
2	Deuxième galerie	22	44	10	20	47	94	40	80	17	34	24	54	37	74
2	Troisièmes loges	-		-		6	12	5	10	3	6	-		-	
1½	Deuxième balcon	8	12	1	1.5	41	61.5	40	60	17	25.5	12	18	7	10.5
1¼	Premier amphithéâtre	14	17.5	14	17.5	32	40	40	50	10	12.5	19	23.75	24	30
¾	Deuxième amphithéâtre	21	15.75	15	11.25	60	45	41	30.75	33	24.75	26	19.5	18	13.5
	Location suivant la feuille	310		341.50		378		671		659		816.50		413	
	Supplémens	37.50		31.50		24		48		35.50		40.50		19	
	Billets vendus la veille après la recette	41		14.50		22.50		4.50		34.00		11.75		27.25	
	Billets d'administration avec droit	8		9		-		16.25		4.50		12.00		12.50	
	Billets d'auteur en sus du droit	-		-		-		-		-		14.75		-	

NIGHTLY BOX-OFFICE TAKINGS 1852

	Avril 1852	Vendredi 16		Samedi * 17		Dimanche 18		Lundi 19		Mardi 20		Mercredi 21		Jeudi 22	
6	Billets à toutes places	–	–	–	–	10	60	16	96	10	60	14	84	20	120
5	Loges de la galerie	43	215	–	–	31	155	40	200	14	70	32	160	23	115
5	Stalles d'orchestre	70	350	45	270	50	250	70	350	45	225	68	340	41	205
5	Stalles de balcon	30	150	12	72	16	80	28	140	10	50	25	125	7	35
4	Deuxièmes loges de face	12	48	30	120	16	64	14	56	6	24	15	60	11	44
4	Stalles de première galerie	42	168	–	–	30	120	38	152	43	172	21	84	23	92
4	Orchestre	29	116	32	160	31	124	27	108	21	84	20	80	13	52
3	Loges intermédiaires	13	39	18	54	41	123	10	30	13	39	12	36	19	57
2½	Deuxièmes loges de côté	16	40	14	35	35	87.5	14	35	23	57.5	18	45	10	25
2½	Pourtour	35	87.5	31	77.5	68	170	39	97.50	24	60	25	62.50	17	42.5
2	Parterre	50	100	116	232	112	224	73	146	45	90	65	130	40	80
2	Deuxième galerie	21	42	27	54	62	124	35	70	15	30	8	16	22	44

	Avril 1852	Vendredi 16		Samedi * 17		Dimanche 18		Lundi 19		Mardi 20		Mercredi 21		Jeudi 22	
2	Troisièmes loges	2	4	-		3	6	4	8	-		3	6	2	4
1½	Deuxième balcon	9	13.5	19	28.5	58	87	18	27	6	9	1	1.50	13	19.5
1¼	Premier amphithéâtre	10	12.5	18	22.25	64	80	7	8.75	7	8.75	6	7.5	8	10
¾	Deuxième amphithéâtre	23	17.25	56	42	145	108.75	41	30.75	13	9.75	21	15.75	30	22.5
	Location suivant la feuille	707		2026.50		813		317		615		351		359	
	Supplémens	14.75		27.00		93		17.50		38.25		20.50		25.50	
	Billets vendus la veille après la recette	11.50		-		71		20.25		50.00		19		9.75	
	Billets d'administration avec droit	16.25		2		-		18.25		16.25		7.50		9.75	
	Billets d'auteur en sus du droit	1.50		-		-		2.50		-		-		-	

* 17th April 1852 extra price performance.

NIGHTLY BOX-OFFICE TAKINGS 1852

	Avril 1852	Vendredi 23		Samedi 24		Dimanche 25		Lundi 26		Mardi 27		Mercredi 28		Jeudi 29	
6	Billets à toutes places	13	78	7	42	19	114	16	96	3	18	6	36	12	72
5	Loges de la galerie	21	105	43	215	41	205	28	140	16	80	16	80	17	85
5	Stalles d'orchestre	36	180	37	185	47	235	28	140	53	265	78	390	94	470
5	Stalles de balcon	9	45	17	85	24	120	14	70	–		12	60	8	40
4	Deuxièmes loges de face	5	20	–		3	12	11	44	7	28	10	40	4	16
4	Stalles de première galerie	21	84	16	64	32	128	24	96	–		7	28	19	76
4	Orchestre	14	56	13	52	14	56	21	84	26	104	19	76	27	108
3	Loges intermédiaires	8	24	13	39	29	87	14	42	10	30	13	39	16	48
2½	Deuxièmes loges de côté	5	12.50	16	40	22	55	11	27.5	11	27.5	14	35	4	10
2½	Pourtour	9	22.5	24	60	53	132.5	35	87.5	20	50	15	37.5	24	60
2	Parterre	59	118	40	80	92	184	46	92	41	82	53	106	73	146
2	Deuxième galerie	3	6	8	16	45	90	18	36	8	16	6	12	12	24

	Avril 1852	Vendredi 23	Samedi 24	Dimanche 25		Lundi 26		Mardi 27		Mercredi 28		Jeudi 29	
2	Troisièmes loges	-	-	5	10	-	-	1	2	-	-	2	4
1½	Deuxième balcon	7	10.5	4	6	56	84	13	19.5	12	18	9	13.5	2	3
1¼	Premier amphithéâtre	5	6.25	1	1.25	46	57.50	2	2.5	3	3.75	7	8.75	12	15
¾	Deuxième amphithéâtre	26	19.5	21	15.75	70	52.50	29	21.75	29	21.75	27	20.25	28	21
	Location suivant la feuille	338	341	453		469		769		390		576	
	Supplémens	6.50	11.50	36.35		6		20.50		19.50		11.25	
	Billets vendus la veille après la recette	11.25	4.75	21.25		10.50		33		1.50		7.75	
	Billets d'administration avec droit	5.75	9.50	-		1.50		5		4		9.50	
	Billets d'auteur en sus du droit	-	0.25	0.25		-		-		7.50		-	

NIGHTLY BOX-OFFICE TAKINGS 1852

	Avril–Mai 1852	Vendredi 30		Samedi 1er		Dimanche 2		Lundi 3		Mardi 4		Mercredi 5	
6	Billets à toutes places	7	42	17	102	24	144	10	60	25	150	25	150
5	Loges de la galerie	33	165	32	160	14	70	28	140	13	65	26	130
5	Stalles d'orchestre	88	440	82	410	71	355	78	390	82	410	61	305
5	Stalles de balcon	22	110	27	135	6	30	16	80	15	75	10	50
4	Deuxièmes loges de face	16	64	6	24	16	64	7	28	4	16	9	36
4	Stalles de première galerie	18	72	15	60	41	164	32	128	23	92	24	96
4	Orchestre	17	68	26	104	28	112	19	76	13	52	22	88
3	Loges intermédiaires	10	30	7	21	30	90	11	33	13	39	15	45
2½	Deuxièmes loges de côté	7	17.5	1	2.5	45	112.5	10	25	16	40	8	20
2½	Pourtour	20	50	32	80	77	192.5	35	87.5	18	45	25	62.5
2	Parterre	56	112	76	152	118	236	58	116	58	116	64	128
2	Deuxième galerie	9	18	15	30	57	114	21	42	18	36	10	20

	Avril–Mai 1852	Vendredi 30		Samedi 1er		Dimanche 2		Lundi 3		Mardi 4		Mercredi 5	
2	Troisièmes loges	2	4	2	4	2	4	2	4	–		–	
1½	Deuxième balcon	7	10.5	16	24	58	87	16	24	20	30	5	7.5
1¼	Premier amphithéâtre	4	5	10	12.5	46	57.50	20	25	10	12.50	8	10
¾	Deuxième amphithéâtre	19	14.25	24	18	134	100.5	58	43.50	24	18	27	20.25
	Location suivant la feuille	528		342		593		441		373		586	
	Supplémens	10.50		21		76.75		22.50		23		17.75	
	Billets vendus la veille après la recette	13.75		25.25		9		48.25		28.75		14	
	Billets d'administration avec droit	3.25		2		–		10		8		6	
	Billets d'auteur en sus du droit			0.75		0.25		4.50		0.50		–	

NIGHTLY BOX-OFFICE TAKINGS 1852

	Mai 1852	Jeudi 6		Vendredi 7		Samedi 8		Dimanche 9		Lundi 10		Mardi 11		Mercredi 12	
6	Billets à toutes places	12	72	14	84	9	54	8	48	–	–	21	126	–	–
5	Loges de la galerie	15	75	18	90	13	65	14	70	31	155	28	140	–	–
5	Stalles d'orchestre	33	165	58	290	44	220	33	165	29	145	39	195	61	305
5	Stalles de balcon	16	80	19	95	15	75	8	40	11	55	6	30	5	25
4	Deuxièmes loges de face	6	24	8	32	7	28	–	–	4	16	10	40	16	64
4	Stalles de première galerie	20	80	33	132	22	88	32	128	23	92	37	148	4	16
4	Orchestre	8	32	16	64	9	36	21	84	19	76	26	104	16	64
3	Loges intermédiaires	13	39	16	48	14	42	17	51	31	93	24	72	11	33
2½	Deuxièmes loges de côté	4	10	25	62.5	10	25	20	50	34	85	37	92.5	11	27.5
2½	Pourtour	40	100	28	70	18	45	21	52.5	50	125	72	180	39	97.5
2	Parterre	57	114	76	152	70	140	103	206	150	300	101	202	112	224
2	Deuxième galerie	17	34	19	38	26	52	44	88	76	152	77	154	72	144

	Mai 1852	Jeudi 6	Vendredi 7	Samedi 8	Dimanche 9	Lundi 10	Mardi 11	Mercredi 12
2	Troisièmes loges	1 2	–	2 4	–	6 12	7 14	1 2
1½	Deuxième balcon	9 13.5	9 13.5	8 12	11 16.5	42 63	52 78	44 66
1¼	Premier amphithéâtre	9 11.25	9 11.25	8 10	15 18.75	26 32.5	53 66.25	46 57.5
¾	Deuxième amphithéâtre	16 12	14 10.5	17 12.75	29 21.75	52 39	34 25.5	35 26.25
	Location suivant la feuille	358	322	316	429	192	284	992.50
	Supplémens	12.25	14.50	17.25	26	46	40	27.50
	Billets vendus la veille après la recette	12.75	31.25	3	10	19.50	57.50	19.75
	Billets d'administration avec droit	10.50	2.50	–	–	–	12	–
	Billets d'auteur en sus du droit	–	–	–	–	–	–	–

NIGHTLY BOX-OFFICE TAKINGS 1852

	Mai 1852	Jeudi 13		Vendredi 14		Samedi 15		Dimanche 16		Lundi 17		Mardi 18		Mercredi 19	
6	Billets à toutes places	7	42	14	84	8	48	6	36	–	–	8	48	4	24
5	Loges de la galerie	8	40	25	125	18	90	18	90	–	–	9	45	14	70
5	Stalles d'orchestre	11	55	33	165	28	140	11	55	18	90	61	305	66	330
5	Stalles de balcon	12	60	14	70	19	95	8	40	–	–	9	45	24	120
4	Deuxièmes loges de face	–	–	13	52	4	16	10	40	4	16	7	28	4	16
4	Stalles de première galerie	7	28	28	112	27	108	21	84	9	36	22	88	28	112

	Mai 1852	Jeudi 13		Vendredi 14		Samedi 15		Dimanche 16		Lundi 17		Mardi 18		Mercredi 19	
4	Orchestre	6	24	28	112	14	56	4	16	6	24	13	52	28	112
3	Loges intermédiaires	2	6	27	81	8	24	10	30	4	12	9	27	15	45
2½	Deuxièmes loges de côté	7	17.5	18	45	13	32.5	11	27.50	4	10	6	15	12	30
2½	Pourtour	9	22.5	26	65	13	32.5	16	40	7	17.5	13	32.5	22	55
2	Parterre	8	16	81	162	55	110	25	50	20	40	38	76	69	138
2	Deuxième galerie	2	4	53	106	15	30	27	54	5	10	8	16	16	32
2	Troisièmes loges	–		8	16	–		2	4	–		–		2	4
1½	Deuxième balcon	3	4.5	11	16.5	7	10.5	25	37.5	–		9	13.5	6	9
1¼	Premier amphithéâtre	6	7.5	22	27.5	11	13.75	8	10	6	7.5	9	11.25	8	10
¾	Deuxième amphithéâtre	7	5.25	13	9.75	7	5.25	63	47.25	8	6	30	22.5	26	19.5
	Location suivant la feuille	118		308		235		269		342.50		542.50		929.50	

Mai 1852	Jeudi 13	Vendredi 14	Samedi 15	Dimanche 16	Lundi 17	Mardi 18	Mercredi 19
Supplémens	2	14	6	15.50	1	9.50	16.50
Billets vendus la veille après la recette	–	19.50	39	36.25	9	8.75	9.50
Billets d'administration avec droit	–	11.50	15	3	–	4	–
Billets d'auteur en sus du droit	–	–	–	–	–	–	–

	Mai 1852	Jeudi 20		Vendredi 21		Samedi 22		Dimanche 23		Lundi 24		Mardi 25		Mercredi 26	
6	Billets à toutes places	14	84	2	12	12	72	14	84	2	12	14	84	8	48
5	Loges de la galerie	17	85	13	65	11	55	-		9	45	19	95	9	45
5	Stalles d'orchestre	13	155	33	165	34	170	14	70	30	150	28	140	34	170
5	Stalles de balcon	5	25	8	40	6	30	14	70	6	30	10	50	9	45
4	Deuxièmes loges de face	5	20	4	16	1	4	6	24	3	12	9	36	4	16
4	Stalles de première galerie	33	132	22	88	17	68	16	64	12	48	13	52	6	64
4	Orchestre	19	76	7	28	7	28	5	20	10	40	6	24	7	28
3	Loges intermédiaires	14	42	6	18	9	27	6	18	16	48	12	36	1	3
2½	Deuxièmes loges de côté	11	27.5	5	12.5	10	25	-		9	22.5	19	47.5	14	35

NIGHTLY BOX-OFFICE TAKINGS 1852

	Mai 1852	Jeudi 20		Vendredi 21		Samedi 22		Dimanche 23		Lundi 24		Mardi 25		Mercredi 26	
2½	Pourtour	30	75	23	57.5	21	52.5	18	45	14	35	12	30	12	30
2	Parterre	69	138	33	66	43	86	42	84	31	62	31	62	26	52
2	Deuxième galerie	27	54	5	10	5	10	20	40	9	18	2	4	12	24
2	Troisièmes loges	–		–		1	2	–		–		–		1	2
1½	Deuxième balcon	22	33	9	13.5	8	12	11	16.5	4	6	4	6	2	3
1¼	Premier amphithéâtre	9	11.25	3	3.75	1	1.25	18	22.5	5	6.25	10	12.5	5	6.25
¾	Deuxième amphithéâtre	33	24.75	14	10.5	7	5.25	37	27.75	11	8.25	8	6	13	9.75

Mai 1852	Jeudi 20	Vendredi 21	Samedi 22	Dimanche 23	Lundi 24	Mardi 25	Mercredi 26
Location suivant la feuille	259	338	246	203	225	202	228
Supplémens	13.50	9.75	14	5.25	5	24.5	6..50
Billets vendus la veille après la recette	29.25	28.75	26.25	17	34	17	13.50
Billets d'administration avec droit	2	1.50	4.25	-	-	5	-
Billets d'auteur en sus du droit	-	-	-	-	-	-	-

NIGHTLY BOX-OFFICE TAKINGS 1852

	Mai 1852	Jeudi 27		Vendredi 28		Samedi 29		Dimanche 30		Lundi 31	
6	Billets à toutes places	18	108	12	72	13	78	8	48	13	78
5	Loges de la galerie	11	55	8	40	15	75	20	100	20	100
5	Stalles d'orchestre	25	125	33	165	61	305	53	265	45	225
5	Stalles de balcon	4	20	8	40	13	65	15	75	6	30
4	Deuxièmes loges de face	6	24	4	16	6	24	9	36	14	56
4	Stalles de première galerie	1	4	4	16	24	96	38	152	39	156
4	Orchestre	6	24	17	68	18	72	21	84	16	64
3	Loges intermédiaires	12	36	5	15	14	42	22	66	17	51
2½	Deuxièmes loges de côté	5	12.5	5	12.5	3	7.5	45	112.5	17	42.5
2½	Pourtour	17	42.5	10	25	22	55	59	147.5	38	95

	Mai 1852	Jeudi 27		Vendredi 28		Samedi 29		Dimanche 30		Lundi 31	
2	Parterre	32	64	22	44	38	76	128	256	87	174
2	Deuxième galerie	12	24	4	8	17	34	42	84	20	40
2	Troisièmes loges	-				-		7	14	4	8
1½	Deuxième balcon	17	25.5	7	10.5	8	12	21	31.5	22	33
1¼	Premier amphiéâtre	6	7.5	2	2.5	12	15	52	65	12	15
¾	Deuxième amphiéâtre	16	12	11	8.25	17	12.75	129	96.5	42	31.50
	Location suivant la feuille		89		142		295		518.50		431
	Supplémens		16.75		9.50		12.50		73.50		26
	Billets vendus la veille après la recette		7		41		-		71.00		15
	Billets d'administration avec droit		4.50		2.25		5.25		-		4
	Billets d'auteur en sus du droit				0.5		-		-		0.25

NIGHTLY BOX-OFFICE TAKINGS 1852

	Juin 1852	Mardi 1ᵉʳ		Mercredi 2		Jeudi 3		Vendredi 4		Samedi 5		Dimanche 6		Lundi 7	
6	Billets à toutes places	24	144	20	120	–	–	–	–	13	78	10	60	–	–
5	Loges de la galerie	15	75	17	85	1	5	17	85	9	45	12	60	23	115
5	Stalles d'orchestre	37	185	24	120	9	45	17	85	35	175	30	150	62	310
5	Stalles de balcon	7	35	7	35	–	–	22	110	5	25	8	40	8	40
4	Deuxièmes loges de face	10	40	5	20	–	–	13	52	4	16	13	52	–	–
4	Stalles de première galerie	10	40	14	56	1	4	18	72	14	56	14	56	17	68
4	Orchestre	11	44	3	12	3	12	10	40	9	36	10	40	7	28
3	Loges intermédiaires	5	15	7	21	2	6	–	–	2	6	4	12	6	18
2½	Deuxièmes loges de côté	8	20	7	17.5	–	–	3	7.50	9	22.50	9	22.50	13	32.50
2½	Pourtour	12	30	8	20	–	–	14	35	12	30	18	45	22	55
2	Parterre	61	122	24	48	7	14	39	78	30	60	40	80	55	110
2	Deuxième galerie	6	12	19	38	1	2	3	6	14	28	14	28	8	16

	Juin 1852	Mardi 1er	Mercredi 2	Jeudi 3	Vendredi 4	Samedi 5	Dimanche 6	Lundi 7
2	Troisièmes loges	3 6	- -	- -	- -	1 2	- -	3 6
1½	Deuxième balcon	6 9	3 4.5	28 42	12 18	3 4.5	11 16.5	11 16.5
1¼	Premier amphithéâtre	8 10	6 7.5	26 32.5	14 17.5	15 18.75	18 22.5	18 22.5
¾	Deuxième amphithéâtre	12 9	20 15	36 27	21 15.75	14 10.5	31 23.25	33 24.75
	Location suivant la feuille	201	159	1135.50	911	365	107	710
	Supplémens	11.50	22	-	3.25	6.75	2.75	11.75
	Billets vendus la veille après la recette	45.75	54	21	2	20	16.50	42.75
	Billets d'administration avec droit	10.50	13	2	-	-	2	3.50
	Billets d'auteur en sus du droit	-	-	-	-	-	-	4

NIGHTLY BOX-OFFICE TAKINGS 1852

	Juin 1852	Mardi 8		Mercredi 9		Jeudi 10		Vendredi 11		Samedi 12		Dimanche 13		Lundi 14	
6	Billets à toutes places	7	42	4	24	11	66	10	60	19	114	13	78	9	54
5	Loges de la galerie	20	100	22	110	12	60	18	90	20	100	17	85	11	55
5	Stalles d'orchestre	89	445	63	315	95	475	45	225	56	280	72	360	75	375
5	Stalles de balcon	7	35	8	40	13	65	7	35	17	85	10	50	8	40
4	Deuxièmes loges de face	3	12	10	40	2	8	4	16	6	24	8	32	5	20
4	Stalles de première galerie	25	100	17	68	13	52	24	96	21	84	30	120	23	92
4	Orchestre	19	76	3	12	18	72	10	40	26	104	17	68	28	112
3	Loges intermédiaires	7	21	4	12	7	21	4	12	8	24	40	120	11	33
2½	Deuxièmes loges de côté	3	7.5	3	7.5	7	17.5	10	25	3	7.5	36	90	14	35
2½	Pourtour	23	57.5	18	45	18	45	17	42.5	21	52.5	45	112.5	29	72.5
2	Parterre	63	126	41	82	65	130	25	50	53	106	101	202	55	110
2	Deuxième galerie	25	50	6	12	14	28	12	24	1	2	44	88	9	18
2	Troisièmes loges	1	2	-	-	-	-	-	-	-	-	5	10	-	-

	Juin 1852	Mardi 8		Mercredi 9		Jeudi 10		Vendredi 11		Samedi 12		Dimanche 13		Lundi 14	
1½	Deuxième balcon	9	13.5	1	1.5	12	18	4	6	16	24	50	75	4	6
1¼	Premier amphithéâtre	5	6.25	13	16.25	9	11.25	5	6.25	–	–	42	52.5	11	13.75
¾	Deuxième amphithéâtre	31	23.25	20	15	24	18	20	15	33	24.75	99	74.25	41	30.75
	Location suivant la feuille	475		340		213		246		305		437		259	
	Supplémens	17.50		5.25		9		29		15.25		43.50		22	
	Billets vendus la veille après la recette	36.75		46.50		69.25		72		18.25		9		12.25	
	Billets d'administration avec droit	–		10.75		3		12.50		5.50		–		11.50	
	Billets d'auteur en sus du droit	–		0.25		–		0.25		–		–		–	

Juin 1852		Mardi 15		Mercredi 16		Jeudi 17		Vendredi 18		Samedi 19		Dimanche 20		Lundi 21	
6	Billets à toutes places	19	114	13	78	15	90	8	48	6	36	27	162	12	72
5	Loges de la galerie	31	155	13	65	4	20	10	50	11	55	18	90	-	-
5	Stalles d'orchestre	56	280	47	235	33	165	36	180	25	125	50	250	32	160
5	Stalles de balcon	18	90	7	35	12	60	8	40	3	15	4	20	2	10
4	Deuxièmes loges de face	5	20	-	-	10	40	1	4	-	-	11	44	-	-
4	Stalles de première galerie	14	56	6	24	5	20	13	52	8	32	21	84	10	40
4	Orchestre	22	88	23	92	21	84	9	36	8	32	20	80	6	24
3	Loges intermédiaires	11	33	6	18	18	54	13	39	4	12	12	36	4	12
2½	Deuxièmes loges de côté	4	10	7	17.5	5	12.5	9	22.5	8	20	30	75	7	17.5

	Juin 1852	Mardi 15		Mercredi 16		Jeudi 17		Vendredi 18		Samedi 19		Dimanche 20		Lundi 21	
2½	Pourtour	21	52.5	14	35	20	50	22	55	14	35	53	132.5	12	30
2	Parterre	43	86	63	126	21	42	27	54	36	72	86	172	29	58
2	Deuxième galerie	6	12	12	24	13	26	6	12	6	12	36	72	12	24
2	Troisièmes loges	–	–	–	–	–	–	1	2	–	–	6	12	–	–
1½	Deuxième balcon	9	13.5	5	7.5	3	4.5	6	9	9	13.5	28	42	9	13.5
1¼	Premier amphithéâtre	12	15	9	11.25	1	1.25	4	5	4	5	47	58.75	6	7.5

NIGHTLY BOX-OFFICE TAKINGS 1852

	Juin 1852	Mardi 15		Mercredi 16		Jeudi 17		Vendredi 18		Samedi 19		Dimanche 20		Lundi 21	
¾	Deuxième amphithéâtre	35	26.25	19	14.25	25	18.75	13	9.75	5	3.75	92	69	24	18
	Location suivant la feuille	270		268		141		178		202		165		320	
	Supplémens	7		9		13.75		3.50		8.50		35.50		2	
	Billets vendus la veille après la recette	66		54.75		36.25		22.50		11.25		32		23.50	
	Billets d'administration avec droit	9		–		9.50		11		8		–		16.75	
	Billets d'auteur en sus du droit	0.25		–		12.00		–		–		–		0.25	

Juin 1852	Mardi 22		Mercredi 23		Jeudi 24		Vendredi 25		Samedi 26		Dimanche 27		Lundi 28	
Billets à toutes places	11	66	13	78	4	24	7	42	1	6	10	60	8	48
Loges de la galerie	6	30	14	70	4	20	13	75	9	45	–	–	9	45
Stalles d'orchestre	41	205	33	165	16	80	15	65	14	70	17	85	19	95
Stalles de balcon	13	65	12	60	8	40	2	10	13	65	2	10	7	35
Deuxièmes loges de face	3	12	2	8	1	4	–	–	4	16	–	–	4	16
Stalles de première galerie	11	44	9	36	7	28	6	24	5	20	11	44	10	40
Orchestre	7	28	13	52.	5	20	7	28	19	76	7	28	7	28
	6		5		5		5		4		4		4	

NIGHTLY BOX-OFFICE TAKINGS 1852

	Juin 1852	Mardi 22		Mercredi 23		Jeudi 24		Vendredi 25		Samedi 26		Dimanche 27		Lundi 28	
3	Loges intermédiaires	9	27	8	24	6	18	4	12	5	15	13	39	3	9
2½	Deuxièmes loges de côté	13	32.5	7	17.5	6	15	7	17.5	7	17.5	4	10	4	10
2½	Pourtour	12	30	13	32.5	13	32.5	2	5	5	12.5	9	22.5	4	10
2	Parterre	40	80	35	70	34	68	23	46	39	78	25	50	19	38
2	Deuxième galerie	3	6	18	36	6	12	4	8	13	26	5	10	17	34
2	Troisièmes loges	–	–	2	4	2	4	1	2	–	–	–	–	–	–
1½	Deuxième balcon	10	15	3	4.5	6	9	2	3	2	3	12	18	1	1.5

Juin 1852		Mardi 22		Mercredi 23		Jeudi 24		Vendredi 25		Samedi 26		Dimanche 27		Lundi 28	
1¼	Premier amphithéâtre	6	7.5	9	11.25	4	5	8	10	5	6.25	6	7.5	12	15
¾	Deuxième amphithéâtre	10	7.5	31	23.25	20	15	14	10.5	20	15	31	23.25	10	7.5
	Location suivant la feuille	168		150		168		56		112		29		81	
	Supplémens	18.50		7		7		6.75		11.25		8.25		1	
	Billets vendus la veille après la recette	32.75		20		27.50		20.50		20		27		31	
	5illets d'administration avec droit	5		2.75		3		3		-		-		-	
	Billets d'auteur en sus du droit	-		-		0.25		-		-		-		0.25	

NIGHTLY BOX-OFFICE TAKINGS 1852

	Juin / Julliet 1852	Mardi 29		Mercredi 30		Jeudi 1er		Vendredi 2		Samedi 3		Dimanche 4	
6	Billets à toutes places	11	66	3	18	9	54	9	54	6	36	–	–
5	Loges de la galerie	5	25	9	45	2	10	6	30	3	15	2	10
5	Stalles d'orchestre	8	40	8	40	33	165	24	120	9	45	7	35
5	Stalles de balcon	2	10	2	10	5	25	8	40	6	30	2	10
4	Deuxièmes loges de face	2	8	–	–	–	–	–	–	2	8	–	–
4	Stalles de première galerie	–	–	6	24	5	20	3	12	6	24	–	–
4	Orchestre	6	24	1	4	3	12	13	52	3	12	2	8
3	Loges intermédiaires	6	18	2	6	4	12	4	12	1	3	–	–
2½	Deuxièmes loges de côté	5	12.5	–	–	1	2.5	2	5	1	2.5	3	7.5
2½	Pourtour	7	17.5	4	10	5	12.5	8	20	5	12.5	3	7.5
2	Parterre	24	48	23	46	26	52	22	44	18	36	18	36
2	Deuxième galerie	6	12	9	18	6	12	18	36	9	18	5	10

	Juin / Julliet 1852	Mardi 29	Mercredi 30	Jeudi 1er	Vendredi 2	Samedi 3	Dimanche 4
2	Troisièmes loges	– –	– –	– –	– –	2 4	1 2
1½	Deuxième balcon	4 6	3 4.5	5 7.5	6 9	8 12	10 15
1¼	Premier amphithéâtre	4 5	1 1.25	6 7.5	1 1.25	2 2.5	4 5
¾	Deuxième amphithéâtre	6 4.5	8 6	14 10.5	12 9	4 3	12 9
	Location suivant la feuille	103	85	273	155.50	158.50	6
	Supplémens	–	3.50	5	15.50	4.50	2
	Billets vendus la veille après la recette	30	15.75	10.75	16.50	7.75	26.75
	Billets d'administration avec droit	6,50	4.25	1.50	–	2	–
	Billets d'auteur en sus du droit	–	–	–	–	–	–

NIGHTLY BOX-OFFICE TAKINGS 1852

	Julliet 1852	Lundi 5		Mardi 6		Mercredi 7		Jeudi 8		Vendredi 9		Samedi 10 Bénéfice de Mlle Fitz-James		Dimanche 11 No performance
6	Billets à toutes places	-	-	4	24	1	6	2	12	3	18	2	12	
5	Loges de la galerie	3	15	-	-	4	20	-	-	-	-	11	55	
5	Stalles d'orchestre	11	55	3	15	14	70	13	65	11	55	12	60	
5	Stalles de balcon	-	-	1	5	5	25	-	-	1	5	11	55	
4	Deuxièmes loges de face	-	-	-	-	7	28	-	-	-	-	-	-	
4	Stalles de première galerie	1	4	1	4	2	8	1	4	5	20	11	44	
4	Orchestre	1	4	2	8	-	-	1	4	2	8	16	64	
3	Loges intermédiaires	3	9	-	-	-	-	-	-	-	-	6	18	
2½	Deuxièmes loges de côté	-	-	1	2.5	3	7.5	4	10	2	5	1	2.5	
2½	Pourtour	1	2.5	5	12.5	3	7.5	-	-	-	-	9	22.5	
2	Parterre	14	28	10	20	13	26	23	46	12	24	62	124	
2	Deuxième galerie	7	14	6	12	4	8	4	8	3	6	8	16	

Julliet 1852		Lundi 5		Mardi 6		Mercredi 7		Jeudi 8		Vendredi 9		Samedi 10 Bénéfice de Mlle Fitz-James		Dimanche 11 No performance
2	Troisièmes loges													
1½	Deuxième balcon	6	9	7	10.5	3	4.5	–	–	3	4.5	7	10.5	
1¼	Premier amphithéâtre	2	2.5	3	3.75	3	3.75	8	10	–	–	–	–	
¾	Deuxième amphithéâtre	10	7.5	3	2.25	4	3	7	5.25	4	3	8	6	
	Location suivant la feuille	57		11		28		15		–		169		

Julliet 1852	Lundi 5	Mardi 6	Mercredi 7	Jeudi 8	Vendredi 9	Samedi 10 Bénéfice de Mlle Fitz-James	Dimanche 11 No performance
Supplémens	0.75	–	4.50	0.75	1.50	14	
Billets vendus la veille après la recette	2	8	10.50	25.75	40.50	–	
Billets d'administration avec droit	–	–	–	2	–	–	
Billets d'auteur en sus du droit	–	0.25	2.00	–	10.50	–	

	Julliet 1852	Lundi 12		Mardi 13		Mercredi 14		Jeudi 15		Vendredi 16		Dimanche 18		Lundi 19	
6	Billets à toutes places	-	-	-	-	1	6	-	-	3	18	5	30	2	12
5	Loges de la galerie	1	5	-	-	1	5	-	-	-	-	4	20	4	20
5	Stalles d'orchestre	6	30	7	35	8	40	4	20	11	55	10	50	22	110
5	Stalles de balcon	-	-	1	5	1	5	1	5	-	-	2	10	2	10
4	Deuxièmes loges de face	-	-	1	4	3	12	-	-	-	-	-	-	-	-
4	Stalles de première galerie	4	16	3	12	2	8	1	4	3	12	12	48	5	20
4	Orchestre	1	4	2	8	3	12	1	4	-	-	7	28	9	36
3	Loges intermédiaires	5	15	-	-	-	-	5	15	4	12	5	15	8	24
2½	Deuxièmes loges de côté	-	-	-	-	2	5	6	15	2	5	4	10	8	20
2½	Pourtour	2	5	-	-	3	7.5	1	2.5	3	7.5	10	25	1	2.5
2	Parterre	4	8	9	18	15	30	7	14	9	18	29	58	25	50
2	Deuxième galerie	4	8	3	6	3	6	5	10	5	10	24	48	6	12
2	Troisièmes loges	-	-	-	-	3	6	-	-	2	4	1	2	-	-

NIGHTLY BOX-OFFICE TAKINGS 1852

	Julliet 1852	Lundi 12		Mardi 13		Mercredi 14		Jeudi 15		Vendredi 16		Dimanche 18		Lundi 19	
1½	Deuxième balcon	6	9	–	–	10	15	3	4.5	1	1.5	17	25.5	11	16.5
1¼	Premier amphithéâtre	5	6.25	2	2.5	5	6.25	2	2.5	5	6.25	13	16.25	6	7.5
¾	Deuxième amphithéâtre	2	1.5	1	0.75	6	4.5	4	3	5	3.75	32	24	22	16.5
	Location suivant la feuille	35		–		25		–		5		6		18	
	Supplémens	2.50		2		2		3		8.50		12.50		7.50	
	Billets vendus la veille après la recette	46		–		9		12.75		26		32.25		48.75	
	Billets d'administration avec droit	–		–		0.75		6.50		2		–		3	
	Billets d'auteur en sus du droit	–		–		–		–		–		–		–	

Julliet 1852		Mardi 20	Jeudi 22	Vendredi 23	Samedi 24	Dimanche 25	Lundi 26	Mardi 27
6	Billets à toutes places	– –	3 18	– –	4 24	13 78	9 54	11 66
5	Loges de la galerie	– –	– –	2 10	2 10	7 35	2 10	6 30
5	Stalles d'orchestre	14 70	16 80	11 55	9 45	28 140	14 70	21 105
5	Stalles de balcon	4 20	– –	4 20	6 30	7 35	1 5	6 30
4	Deuxièmes loges de face	– –	– –	– –	– –	8 32	– –	– –
4	Stalles de première galerie	– –	7 28	2 8	– –	31 124	2 8	3 12
4	Orchestre	2 8	2 8	3 12	5 20	20 80	4 16	13 52
3	Loges intermédiaires	2 6	– –	2 6	1 3	22 66	3 9	8 24
2½	Deuxièmes loges de côté	3 7.5	11 27.5	1 2.5	4 10	26 65	2 5	2 5
2½	Pourtour	4 10	7 17.5	3 7.5	3 7.5	30 75	2 5	24 60
2	Parterre	14 28	25 50	15 30	16 32	62 124	15 30	46 92

	Julliet 1852	Mardi 20	Jeudi 22	Vendredi 23	Samedi 24	Dimanche 25	Lundi 26	Mardi 27
2	Deuxième galerie	1	9	3	5	28	1	6
		2	18	6	10	56	2	12
2	Troisièmes loges	–	–	–	–	2	–	–
		–	–	–	–	4	–	–
1½	Deuxième balcon	1	7	5	–	46	3	8
		1.5	10.5	7.5	–	69	4.5	12
1¼	Premier amphithéâtre	–	3	1	11	29	11	4
		–	3.75	1.25	13.75	36.25	13.75	5
¾	Deuxième amphithéâtre	2	7	15	9	62	22	22
		1.5	5.25	11.25	6.75	46.5	16.5	16.5

Julliet 1852	Mardi 20	Jeudi 22	Vendredi 23	Samedi 24	Dimanche 25	Lundi 26	Mardi 27
Location suivant la feuille	2	21	82	18	100	6	73
Supplémens	–	7	1.50	2	28.25	1.50	16.75
Billets vendus la veille après la recette	48.75	5.75	6	5.75	10.25	62.25	28.50
Billets d'administration avec droit	3.50	1.00	–	–	–	1.50	2
Billets d'auteur en sus du droit	–	–	–	–	–	–	0.25

21st no performance

NIGHTLY BOX-OFFICE TAKINGS 1852

	Julliet / Août 1852	Mercredi 28		Vendredi 30		Dimanche 1er		Lundi 2		Mardi 3		Mercredi 4	
6	Billets à toutes places	3	18	3	18	4	24	6	36	-	-	-	-
5	Loges de la galerie	5	25	2	10	4	20	-	-	-	-	37	185
5	Stalles d'orchestre	7	35	5	25	6	30	14	70	-	-	16	80
5	Stalles de balcon	6	30	-	-	1	5	5	25	-	-	7	35
4	Deuxièmes loges de face	-	-	-	-	2	8	1	4	-	-	22	88
4	Stalles de première galerie	8	32	-	-	6	24	7	28	-	-	13	52
4	Orchestre	7	28	2	8	3	12	5	20	-	-	5	20
3	Loges intermédiaires	2	6	3	9	3	9	-	-	-	-	14	42
2½	Deuxièmes loges de côté	2	5	4	10	2	5	8	20	-	-	4	10
2½	Pourtour	18	45	9	22.5	14	35	5	12.5	2	5	19	47.5
2	Parterre	15	30	13	26	20	40	19	38	16	32	54	108
2	Deuxième galerie	5	10	1	2	19	38	-	-	9	18	21	42
2	Troisièmes loges	-	-	1	2	-	-	-	-	-	-	-	-

	Juillet / Août 1852	Mercredi 28		Vendredi 30		Dimanche 1er		Lundi 2		Mardi 3		Mercredi 4	
1½	Deuxième balcon	11	16.5	6	9	7	10.5	10	15	21	31.5	26	39
1¼	Premier amphithéâtre	2	2.5	5	6.25	5	6.25	1	1.25	83	103.75	14	17.50
¾	Deuxième amphithéâtre	18	13.5	6	4.5	37	27.75	16	12	176	132	59	44.25
	Location suivant la feuille		50		34.50		39		30		750.50		985.50
	Supplémens		4		6.25		5.25		3		9.50		15
	Billets vendus la veille après la recette		30.50		15		14		–		18		–
	Billets d'administration avec droit		–		3.75		–		–		–		–
	Billets d'auteur en sus du droit		–		–		–		–		–		–

29 Juillet no performance   31 Juillet no performance

NIGHTLY BOX-OFFICE TAKINGS 1852

	Août 1852	Jeudi 5		Vendredi 6		Samedi 7		Dimanche 8		Lundi 9		Mardi 10		Mercredi 11	
6	Billets à toutes places	13	78	9	54	16	96	2	12	7	42	9	54	12	72
5	Loges de la galerie	13	65	13	65	24	120	-	-	20	100	9	45	8	40
5	Stalles d'orchestre	66	330	78	390	53	265	17	85	39	195	44	220	57	285
5	Stalles de balcon	10	50	3	15	13	65	2	10	3	15	12	60	25	125
4	Deuxièmes loges de face	2	8	-	-	1	4	4	16	5	20	5	20	5	20
4	Stalles de première galerie	16	64	17	68	23	92	18	72	29	116	19	76	49	196
4	Orchestre	12	48	26	104	20	80	13	52	16	64	25	100	26	104
3	Loges intermédiaires	24	72	9	27	14	42	4	12	10	30	20	60	19	57
2½	Deuxièmes loges de côté	12	30	17	42.5	5	12.5	10	25	11	27.5	20	50	14	35
2½	Pourtour	25	62.5	30	75	42	105	20	50	24	60	16	40	48	120
2	Parterre	82	164	79	158	85	170	35	70	52	104	60	120	83	166
2	Deuxième galerie	9	18	22	44	20	40	19	38	15	30	17	34	22	44
2	Troisièmes loges	-	-	-	-	-	-	1	2	6	12	-	-	1	2

Août 1852		Jeudi 5		Vendredi 6		Samedi 7		Dimanche 8		Lundi 9		Mardi 10		Mercredi 11	
1½	Deuxième balcon	17	25.5	13	19.5	10	15	26	39	8	12	10	15	9	13.5
1¼	Premier amphithéâtre	18	22.5	15	18.75	6	7.5	31	38.75	17	21.25	18	22.5	10	12.5
¾	Deuxième amphithéâtre	35	26.25	44	33	42	31.50	59	44.25	59	44.25	40	30	9	6.75
	Location suivant la feuille		557		546		475.50		32.50		262		340		213
	Supplémens		24.50		33		11.25		14		15.25		28.25		16
	Billets vendus la veille après la recette		13.75		6		6.75		3.75		–		23.50		27.25
	Billets d'administration avec droit		3		3.50		2		–		–		–		2
	Billets d'auteur en sus du droit		–		–		0.50		–		1.75		0.25		0.25

NIGHTLY BOX-OFFICE TAKINGS 1852

	Août 1852	Jeudi 12		Vendredi 13		Samedi 14		Dimanche 15		Lundi 16		Mardi 17		Mercredi 18	
6	Billets à toutes places	23	138	4	24	6	36	-	-	4	24	19	114	18	108
5	Loges de la galerie	15	75	18	90	17	85	-	-	13	65	4	20	8	40
5	Stalles d'orchestre	47	235	36	180	23	115	3	15	27	135	41	205	28	140
5	Stalles de balcon	23	115	5	25	8	40	-	-	9	45	8	40	6	30
4	Deuxièmes loges de face	8	32	3	12	8	32	-	-	-	-	7	28	15	60
4	Stalles de première galerie	14	56	21	84	20	80	5	20	5	20	19	76	18	72
4	Orchestre	20	80	19	76	16	64	1	4	13	52	6	24	12	48
3	Loges intermédiaires	17	51	24	72	19	57	4	12	14	42	12	36	22	66
2½	Deuxièmes loges de côté	5	12.5	8	20	2	5	3	7.5	27	67.5	23	57.5	18	45
2½	Pourtour	11	27.5	46	115	16	40	-	-	30	75	24	60	35	87.5
2	Parterre	85	170	90	180	97	194	4	8	93	186	69	138	84	168
2	Deuxième galerie	29	58	36	72	18	36	-	-	39	78	42	84	47	94
2	Troisièmes loges	5	10	4	8	6	12	-	-	-	-	-	-	-	-

	Août 1852	Jeudi 12	Vendredi 13	Samedi 14	Dimanche 15	Lundi 16	Mardi 17	Mercredi 18
1½	Deuxième balcon	8 12	36 54	7 10.5	2 3	20 30	18 27	41 61.5
1¼	Premier amphithéâtre	20 25	8 10	9 11.25	5 6.25	21 26.25	10 12.50	32 40
¾	Deuxième amphithéâtre	33 24.75	24 18	14 10.5	10 7.5	59 44.25	30 22.5	16 12
	Location suivant la feuille	119	253	73	–	163	135	190
	Supplémens	17.50	58	15	3.75	56	28.50	35.75
	Billets vendus la veille après la recette	2	11.50	3.50	2.25	26	4.50	14
	Billets d'administration avec droit	3.75	–	3	–	5.25	–	5
	Billets d'auteur en sus du droit	–	1.25	0.25	–	–	0.25	–

NIGHTLY BOX-OFFICE TAKINGS 1852

	Août 1852	Jeudi 19		Vendredi 20		Samedi 21		Dimanche 22		Lundi 23		Mardi 24		Mercredi 25	
6	Billets à toutes places	6	36	19	24	7	42	16	96	9	54	3	18	–	–
5	Loges de la galerie	3	15	30	150	14	70	12	60	–	–	5	25	8	40
5	Stalles d'orchestre	31	155	50	250	41	205	19	95	15	75	19	95	16	80
5	Stalles de balcon	8	40	9	45	13	65	17	85	4	20	6	30	1	5
4	Deuxièmes loges de face	8	32	3	12	6	24	5	20	4	16	4	16	–	–
4	Stalles de première galerie	14	56	40	160	10	40	27	108	4	16	15	60	9	36
4	Orchestre	8	32	31	124	19	76	7	28	13	52	9	36	4	16
3	Loges intermédiaires	4	12	29	87	16	48	21	63	13	39	4	12	8	24
2½	Deuxièmes loges de côté	12	30	26	65	12	30	18	45	6	15	7	17.5	11	27.5
2½	Pourtour	18	45	63	157.5	16	40	52	130	12	30	21	52.5	13	32.5
2	Parterre	66	132	100	200	62	124	75	150	35	70	47	94	28	56
2	Deuxième galerie	34	68	43	86	22	44	45	90	17	34	13	26	22	44
2	Troisièmes loges	–	–	–	–	–	–	4	8	–	–	–	–	–	–

	Août 1852	Jeudi 19		Vendredi 20		Samedi 21		Dimanche 22		Lundi 23		Mardi 24		Mercredi 25	
1½	Deuxième balcon	22	33	41	61.5	16	24	47	70.5	6	9	8	12	5	7.5
1¼	Premier amphithéâtre	9	11.25	23	28.75	10	12.5	52	65	6	7.5	6	7.5	14	17.5
¾	Deuxième amphithéâtre	30	22.5	49	36.75	31	23.25	95	71.25	30	22.5	21	15.75	20	15
	Location suivant la feuille		84		318.50		238		227		176		50		119
	Supplémens		7.50		54.75		16.75		46.50		3		8.25		11.50
	Billets vendus la veille après la recette		0.75		17.75		23		8.50		19.25		–		–
	Billets d'administration avec droit		5.25		10.50		2		–		4		1.75		–
	Billets d'auteur en sus du droit		–		–		1		0.25		–		0.50		–

NIGHTLY BOX-OFFICE TAKINGS 1852

	Août/Septembre 1852	Vendredi 27	Samedi 28	Dimanche 29	Lundi 30	Jeudi 2	Vendredi 3
6	Billets à toutes places	7 42	4 24	9 54	9 54	- -	9 54
5	Loges de la galerie	- -	13 65	8 40	10 50	- -	25 125
5	Stalles d'orchestre	21 105	18 90	27 135	10 50	- -	52 160
5	Stalles de balcon	- -	4 20	13 65	6 30	- -	5 25
4	Deuxièmes loges de face	- -	- -	2 8	8 32	- -	2 8
4	Stalles de première galerie	7 28	7 28	14 56	15 60	- -	15 60
4	Orchestre	13 52	5 20	10 40	7 28	- -	11 44
3	Loges intermédiaires	11 33	2 6	8 24	17 51	- -	4 12
2½	Deuxièmes loges de côté	4 10	3 7.5	13 32.5	3 7.5	- -	5 12.5
2½	Pourtour	14 35	15 37.5	18 45	16 40	- -	4 10
2	Parterre	38 76	39 78	62 124	46 92	20 40	50 100
2	Deuxième galerie	20 40	10 20	35 70	22 44	5 10	15 30
2	Troisièmes loges	- -	3 6	- -	- -	- -	- -

	Août/Septembre 1852	Vendredi 27		Samedi 28		Dimanche 29		Lundi 30		Jeudi 2		Vendredi 3	
1½	Deuxième balcon	20	30	4	6	34	51	7	10.5	13	19.5	8	12
1¼	Premier amphithéâtre	8	10	3	3.75	38	47.5	17	21.25	25	31.25	8	10
¾	Deuxième amphithéâtre	26	19.5	16	12	71	53.25	48	36	25	18.75	22	16.5
	Location suivant la feuille		62		111		66.50		96		1159.50		462
	Supplémens		7.50		6		15.50		8.50		–		2
	Billets vendus la veille après la recette		–		10		4.75		31		–		3.25
	Billets d'administration avec droit		3.50		3		–		6		–		–
	Billets d'auteur en sus du droit		–		–		–		0.25		–		–

26 No performance 31 No performance 1 Sept No performance

NIGHTLY BOX-OFFICE TAKINGS 1852

Septembre 1852		Samedi 4		Dimanche 5		Lundi 6		Mardi 7		Mercredi 8		Jeudi 9		Vendredi 10	
Billets à toutes places	6	19	114	22	132	4	24	36	216	3	18	20	120	16	96
Loges de la galerie	5	7	35	14	70	21	105	15	75	23	115	24	120	20	100
Stalles d'orchestre	5	29	145	67	335	60	300	63	315	76	380	74	370	74	370
Stalles de balcon	5	5	25	20	100	15	75	17	85	11	55	23	115	19	95
Deuxièmes loges de face	4	5	20	10	40	-	-	4	16	7	28	10	40	9	36
Stalles de première galerie	4	17	68	54	216	5	20	16	64	12	48	33	132	16	64
Orchestre	4	6	24	32	128	9	36	14	56	17	68	35	140	20	80
Loges intermédiaires	3	5	15	30	90	2	6	2	6	5	15	16	48	12	36
Deuxièmes loges de côté	2½	6	15	48	120	9	22.5	15	37.5	7	17.5	21	52.5	7	17.5
Pourtour	2½	19	47.5	82	205	14	35	31	77.5	38	95	48	120	30	75
Parterre	2	27	54	110	220	32	64	64	128	53	106	92	184	64	128
Deuxième galerie	2	9	18	68	136	7	14	21	42	12	24	17	34	27	54
Troisièmes loges	2	-	-	3	6	-	-	2	4	-	-	7	14	-	-

	Septembre 1852	Samedi 4		Dimanche 5		Lundi 6		Mardi 7		Mercredi 8		Jeudi 9		Vendredi 10	
1½	Deuxième balcon	4	6	68	102	27	40.5	14	21	6	9	20	30	13	19.5
1¼	Premier amphithéâtre	9	11.25	71	88.75	15	18.75	8	10	4	5	11	13.75	4	5
¾	Deuxième amphithéâtre	15	11.25	151	113.25	26	19.50	24	18	41	30.75	34	25.50	35	26.25
	Location suivant la feuille		219		285.50		421		277		281		403		258.50
	Supplémens		12		81.75		4		14.25		7.75		28.50		14.50
	Billets vendus la veille après la recette		17.25		9.50		8.75		39.25		37.50		34		65.75
	Billets d'administration avec droit		–		–		–		–		1.50		12.75		5.25
	Billets d'auteur en sus du droit		–		–		0.75		0.50		0.50		–		1.25

NIGHTLY BOX-OFFICE TAKINGS 1852

	Septembre 1852	Samedi 11		Dimanche 12		Lundi 13		Mardi 14		Mercredi 15		Jeudi 16		Vendredi 17	
6	Billets à toutes places	17	102	14	84	13	78	11	66	19	114	16	96	20	120
5	Loges de la galerie	15	75	18	90	14	70	26	130	18	90	6	30	17	85
5	Stalles d'orchestre	51	255	82	410	53	265	51	255	48	240	51	255	69	345
5	Stalles de balcon	13	65	25	125	8	40	4	20	6	30	11	55	8	40
4	Deuxièmes loges de face	7	28	12	48	8	32	-	-	2	8	2	8	6	24
4	Stalles de première galerie	37	148	51	204	18	72	20	80	16	64	12	48	24	96
4	Orchestre	15	60	36	144	19	76	11	44	12	48	24	96	20	80
3	Loges intermédiaires	1	3	43	129	16	48	22	66	11	33	8	24	5	15
2½	Deuxièmes loges de côté	7	17.5	45	112.5	15	37.5	12	30	18	45	6	15	6	15
2½	Pourtour	39	97.5	77	192.5	28	70	20	50	16	40	18	45	20	50
2	Parterre	63	126	95	190	45	90	51	102	56	112	54	108	32	64
2	Deuxième galerie	27	54	62	124	9	18	20	40	19	38	28	56	24	48
2	Troisièmes loges	-	-	9	18	-	-	-	-	-	-	1	2	-	-

		Septembre 1852	Samedi 11		Dimanche 12		Lundi 13		Mardi 14		Mercredi 15		Jeudi 16		Vendredi 17	
1½		Deuxième balcon	16	24	62	93	11	16.5	15	22.5	20	30	2	3	10	15
1¼		Premier amphithéâtre	6	7.5	69	86.25	14	17.5	10	12.5	2	2.5	7	8.75	15	18
¾		Deuxième amphithéâtre	29	21.75	130	97.5	32	24	31	23.25	18	13.5	5	3.75	40	30
		Location suivant la feuille		385		614		364		197		190		173		198
		Supplémens		11.50		88		9.50		12.75		26.50		9.50		16
		Billets vendus la veille après la recette		30		31		12		10		23.75		24.75		32
		Billets d'administration avec droit		3.75		—		2		12.50		9		4		5
		Billets d'auteur en sus du droit		0.50		—		0.25		2		0.50		—		

NIGHTLY BOX-OFFICE TAKINGS 1852

	Septembre 1852	Samedi 18		Dimanche 19		Lundi 20		Mardi 21		Mercredi 22		Jeudi 23		Vendredi 24	
6	Billets à toutes places	13	78	19	96	13	78	25	150	6	36	19	114	35	210
5	Loges de la galerie	7	35	22	110	18	90	13	65	9	45	18	90	13	65
5	Stalles d'orchestre	25	125	48	240	38	190	36	180	55	275	41	205	55	245
5	Stalles de balcon	3	15	34	170	7	35	7	35	9	45	9	45	6	30
4	Deuxièmes loges de face	3	12	5	20	6	24	11	44	6	24	10	40	7	28
4	Stalles de première galerie	18	72	51	204	24	96	11	44	20	80	17	68	18	72
4	Orchestre	9	36	31	124	19	76	15	60	18	72	23	92	20	80
3	Loges intermédiaires	2	6	23	69	30	90	14	42	9	27	20	60	14	42
2½	Deuxièmes loges de côté	19	47.5	34	85	4	10	10	25	1	2.5	7	17.5	5	12.5
2½	Pourtour	29	72.5	52	130	21	52.5	18	45	22	55	25	62.5	20	50
2	Parterre	35	70	77	154	64	128	69	138	68	136	53	106	38	76
2	Deuxième galerie	16	32	90	180	13	26	17	34	15	30	4	8	25	50
2	Troisièmes loges	2	4	2	4	5	10	-	-	-	-	-	-	-	-

	Septembre 1852	Samedi 18		Dimanche 19		Lundi 20		Mardi 21		Mercredi 22		Jeudi 23		Vendredi 24	
1½	Deuxième balcon	3	4.5	66	99	16	24	6	9	19	28.5	12	18	3	4.5
1¼	Premier amphithéâtre	3	3.75	87	108.75	10	12.5	3	3.75	16	20	9	11.25	–	–
¾	Deuxième amphithéâtre	18	13.5	97	72.75	40	30	35	25.5	40	30	21	15.75	10	7.5
	Location suivant la feuille		215		389.50		249		174		630.50		271		142
	Supplémens		2		28.25		18.50		6.50		8.75		13.50		12
	Billets vendus la veille après la recette		2.75		34		3.75		36		22.25		24.50		34.75
	Billets d'administration avec droit		3.50		–		12.50		5.50		–		7		9
	Billets d'auteur en sus du droit		0.75		–		–		–		3.25		–		

NIGHTLY BOX-OFFICE TAKINGS 1852

	Septembre 1852	Samedi 25		Dimanche 26		Lundi 27		Mardi 28		Mercredi 29		Jeudi 30	
6	Billets à toutes places	23	138	21	126	12	72	11	66	15	90	20	120
5	Loges de la galerie	19	95	23	115	7	35	24	120	9	45	14	70
5	Stalles d'orchestre	42	210	42	210	36	180	37	185	49	245	25	125
5	Stalles de balcon	7	35	7	35	8	40	4	20	20	100	7	35
4	Deuxièmes loges de face	–	–	4	16	2	8	10	40	8	32	13	52
4	Stalles de première galerie	6	24	22	88	9	36	14	56	8	32	19	76
4	Orchestre	10	40	21	84	11	44	11	44	20	80	15	60
3	Loges intermédiaires	2	6	24	72	11	33	11	33	18	54	8	24
2½	Deuxièmes loges de côté	3	7.5	14	35	5	12.5	3	7.5	10	25	4	10
2½	Pourtour	24	60	47	117.5	17	42.5	16	40	17	42.5	24	60
2	Parterre	37	74	57	114	40	80	33	66	56	112	47	94
2	Deuxième galerie	11	22	46	92	9	18	9	18	27	54	9	18
2	Troisièmes loges	4	8	–	–	–	–	–	–	8	16	–	–

	Septembre 1852	Samedi 25		Dimanche 26		Lundi 27		Mardi 28		Mercredi 29		Jeudi 30	
1½	Deuxième balcon	2	3	46	69	5	7.5	3	4.5	2	3	17	25.5
1¼	Premier amphithéâtre	14	17.5	50	62.5	22	27.5	3	3.75	2	2.5	5	6.25
¾	Deuxième amphithéâtre	9	6.75	74	55.5	36	27.5	22	16.5	21	15.75	15	11.25
	Location suivant la feuille	220		254.50		187		155		283		256.50	
	Supplémens	4.75		14.50		13.50		8		16		12	
	Billets vendus la veille après la recette	66.75		20.50		18.50		4.25		40.50		23.50	
	Billets d'administration avec droit	–		–		10.50		–		1.50		5.50	
	Billets d'auteur en sus du droit	–		–		4		–		–		–	

NIGHTLY BOX-OFFICE TAKINGS 1852

	Octobre 1852	Vendredi 1er		Samedi 2		Dimanche 3		Lundi 4		Mardi 5		Mercredi 6		Jeudi 7	
6	Billets à toutes places	10	60	16	96	17	102	17	102	19	114	11	66	14	84
5	Loges de la galerie	22	110	13	65	24	120	13	65	15	75	9	45	22	110
5	Stalles d'orchestre	44	220	40	200	46	230	47	235	33	165	48	240	73	365
5	Stalles de balcon	8	40	15	75	12	60	4	20	13	65	6	30	12	60
4	Deuxièmes loges de face	2	8	4	16	11	44	6	24	-	-	3	12	8	32
4	Stalles de première galerie	24	96	20	80	46	184	9	36	15	60	25	100	41	164
4	Orchestre	16	64	15	60	24	96	14	56	16	64	8	32	30	120
3	Loges intermédiaires	13	39	6	18	33	99	10	30	-	-	4	12	17	51
2½	Deuxièmes loges de côté	5	12.5	17	42.5	30	75	11	27.5	5	12.5	4	10	6	15
2½	Pourtour	23	57.5	25	62.5	74	185	13	32.5	5	12.5	22	55	43	107.5
2	Parterre	57	114	60	120	75	150	51	102	52	104	40	80	70	140
2	Deuxième galerie	8	16	14	28	76	152	22	44	21	42	8	16	14	28
2	Troisièmes loges	1	2	1	2	9	18	3	6	2	4	-	-	-	-

	Octobre 1852	Vendredi 1er		Samedi 2		Dimanche 3		Lundi 4		Mardi 5		Mercredi 6		Jeudi 7	
1½	Deuxième balcon	17	25.5	9	13.5	76	114	2	3	1	1.5	13	19.5	26	39
1¼	Premier amphithéâtre	5	6.25	6	7.5	79	98.75	20	25	6	7.50	-	-	5	6.25
¾	Deuxième amphithéâtre	18	13.5	22	16.5	126	94.5	51	38.25	11	8.25	20	15	22	16.50
	Location suivant la feuille	367		220.50		313		90		233		224		604	
	Supplémens	6		10.25		63.25		20.75		19.50		4.50		6.50	
	Billets vendus la veille après la recette	11.75		45.75		28.75		4		15		59.25		0.50	
	Billets d'administration avec droit	1.50		7.00		-		7.25		-		1.50		-	
	Billets d'auteur en sus du droit	4.50		0.25		-		-		-		2.00		3.50	

NIGHTLY BOX-OFFICE TAKINGS 1852

	Octobre 1852	Vendredi 8	Samedi 9	Dimanche 10	Lundi 11	Mardi 12	Mercredi 13	Jeudi 14
6	Billets à toutes places	17 102	7 42	12 72	9 54	3 18	24 144	13 78
5	Loges de la galerie	36 180	14 70	20 100	18 90	19 95	12 60	21 105
5	Stalles d'orchestre	69 345	52 260	60 300	66 330	70 350	60 300	50 250
5	Stalles de balcon	24 120	6 30	7 35	8 40	24 120	13 65	17 85
4	Deuxièmes loges de face	- -	9 36	9 36	2 8	11 44	5 20	6 24
4	Stalles de première galerie	13 52	25 100	39 156	19 76	36 144	30 120	22 88
4	Orchestre	27 108	15 60	24 96	19 76	29 116	18 72	13 52
3	Loges intermédiaires	22 66	11 33	32 96	2 6	9 27	13 39	9 27
2½	Deuxièmes loges de côté	6 15	9 22.5	20 50	10 25	12 30	11 27.5	12 30
2½	Pourtour	22 55	29 72.5	61 152.5	28 70	37 92.5	21 52.5	44 110
2	Parterre	63 126	81 162	89 178	56 112	60 120	45 90	45 90
2	Deuxième galerie	12 24	35 70	68 136	34 68	21 42	22 44	13 26
2	Troisièmes loges	- -	3 6	8 16	- -	- -	- -	- -

	Octobre 1852	Vendredi 8		Samedi 9		Dimanche 10		Lundi 11		Mardi 12		Mercredi 13		Jeudi 14	
1½	Deuxième balcon	10	15	8	12	94	141	15	22.5	12	18	12	18	11	16.5
1¼	Premier amphithéâtre	17	21.25	14	17.5	48	60	11	13.75	11	13.75	10	12.5	6	7.5
¾	Deuxième amphithéâtre	29	21.75	16	12	117	87.75	57	42.75	31	23.25	22	16.5	13	9.75
	Location suivant la feuille		681.50		546		334		372		428		293		382
	Supplémens		8.75		12.50		44.25		12		34.50		9.25		9
	Billets vendus la veille après la recette		9.25		19		3.50		35.75		21.75		34.25		16
	Billets d'administration avec droit		2		4.50		–		6		1.50		5.50		1.50
	Billets d'auteur en sus du droit		–		0.25		0.25		6		–		–		–

NIGHTLY BOX-OFFICE TAKINGS 1852

	Octobre 1852	Vendredi 15		Samedi 16		Dimanche 17		Lundi 18		Mardi 19		Mercredi 20		Jeudi 21	
6	Billets à toutes places	11	66	12	72	28	168	14	84	-	-	20	120	10	60
5	Loges de la galerie	19	95	19	95	27	135	20	100	19	95	18	90	37	185
5	Stalles d'orchestre	76	380	38	190	70	350	48	240	73	365	82	410	80	400
5	Stalles de balcon	11	55	4	20	12	60	11	55	10	50	15	75	9	45
4	Deuxièmes loges de face	5	20	1	4	20	80	7	28	15	60	6	24	11	44
4	Stalles de première galerie	24	96	13	52	35	140	19	76	17	68	20	80	19	76
4	Orchestre	22	88	12	48	24	96	23	92	22	88	12	48	29	116
3	Loges intermédiaires	12	36	3	9	36	108	15	45	4	12	8	24	14	42
2½	Deuxièmes loges de côté	5	12.5	19	47.5	23	57.5	24	60	15	37.5	10	25	10	25
2½	Pourtour	23	57.5	23	57.5	72	180	26	65	46	115	34	85	37	92.5
2	Parterre	39	78	73	146	80	160	37	74	72	144	57	114	74	148
28	56uxième galerie	28	56	29	58	57	114	11	22	35	70	11	22	7	14
2	Troisièmes loges	-	-	-	-	14	28	-	-	5	10	-	-	-	-

Octobre 1852		Vendredi 15		Samedi 16		Dimanche 17		Lundi 18		Mardi 19		Mercredi 20		Jeudi 21	
1½	Deuxième balcon	19	28.5	21	31.5	45	67.5	10	15	8	12	20	30	15	22.5
1¼	Premier amphithéâtre	5	6.25	32	40	56	70	13	16.75	6	7.5	6	7.5	14	17.5
¾	Deuxième amphithéâtre	22	16.5	69	51.75	127	95.25	40	30	39	29.25	18	13.5	27	20.25
	Location suivant la feuille	394.50		241.50		518		195		869		481		474.50	
	Supplémens	13.50		19.75		32		19.25		5.50		18.25		29	
	Billets vendus la veille après la recette	37.50		2		12.50		10.25		–		7		–	
	Billets d'administration avec droit	3.50		2		12.50		6.75		–		3		–	
	Billets d'auteur en sus du droit	–		2		12.50		2.50		0.50		–		2.75	

NIGHTLY BOX-OFFICE TAKINGS 1852

	Octobre 1852	Vendredi 22	Samedi 23	Dimanche 24	Lundi 25	Mardi 26	Mercredi 27	Jeudi 28
6	Billets à toutes places	4	24	10	60	20	120	17	102	14	84	27	162	13	78
5	Loges de la galerie	23	115	24	120	37	185	32	160	31	155	17	85	21	105
5	Stalles d'orchestre	73	365	50	250	68	340	71	355	48	240	57	285	53	265
5	Stalles de balcon	10	50	16	80	23	115	13	65	5	25	20	100	13	65
4	Deuxièmes loges de face	11	44	5	20	17	68	2	8	14	56	6	24	9	36
4	Stalles de première galerie	45	180	28	112	52	208	16	64	24	96	27	108	15	60
4	Orchestre	19	76	21	84	30	120	11	44	18	72	18	72	13	52
3	Loges intermédiaires	7	21	14	42	23	69	4	12	13	39	17	51	13	39
2½	Deuxièmes loges de côté	16	40	10	25	43	107.5	13	32.5	10	25	–	–	2	5
2½	Pourtour	36	90	34	85	71	177.5	29	72.5	23	72.5	15	37.5	32	80
2	Parterre	52	104	65	130	107	214	76	152	55	110	66	132	68	136
2	Deuxième galerie	16	32	19	38	69	138	12	24	18	36	4	8	4	8
2	Troisièmes loges	–	–	–	–	9	18	2	4	–	–	–	–	4	8

	Octobre 1852	Vendredi 22		Samedi 23		Dimanche 24		Lundi 25		Mardi 26		Mercredi 27		Jeudi 28	
1½	Deuxième balcon	11	16.5	16	24	67	100.5	28	42	9	13.5	15	22.5	19	28.5
1¼	Premier amphithéâtre	14	17.5	6	7.5	73	91.25	19	23.75	5	6.25	-	-	2	2.5
¾	Deuxième amphithéâtre	14	10.5	19	14.25	169	126.75	76	57	17	12.75	18	13.5	32	24
	Location suivant la feuille	489		460		610		348.50		305		453		292	
	Supplémens	5		15.50		58		13.25		13		9.50		11.50	
	Billets vendus la veille après la recette	14.50		15.75		4.75		7.50		17		13.25		25.50	
	Billets d'administration avec droit	8		6.75		-		9.00		2		1.00		1.50	
	Billets d'auteur en sus du droit	-		0.25		-		0.50		2		1.00		0.75	

NIGHTLY BOX-OFFICE TAKINGS 1852

Octobre / Novembre 1852		Vendredi 29 Bénéfice de M. Ch. Perey *Not* two performances; some prices up for this performance; second column redone accounts		Samedi 30		Dimanche 31		Lundi 1er Novembre		Mardi 2	
6	Billets à toutes places	-	-	-	-	8	48	13	78	6	36	4	24
5	Loges de la galerie	-	-	-	-	36	180	44	220	31	155	18	90
5	Stalles d'orchestre	24	120	24	144	78	390	73	365	65	325	57	285
5	Stalles de balcon	7	35	7	42	12	60	21	105	29	145	1	5
4	Deuxièmes loges de face	22	88	22	88	12	48	17	68	12	48	2	8
4	Stalles de première galerie	20	80	20	100	19	76	34	136	34	136	16	64
4	Orchestre	11	44	11	55	19	76	30	120	34	136	23	92
3	Loges intermédiaires	20	60	20	60	13	39	50	150	37	111	8	24
2½	Deuxièmes loges de côté	9	22.5	9	22.5	4	10	38	95	34	85	13	32.5
2½	Pourtour	24	60	24	72	31	77.5	69	172.5	73	182.5	26	65

	Octobre / Novembre 1852	Vendredi 29 Bénéfice de M. Ch. Perey *Not* two performances; some prices up for this performance; second column redone accounts			Samedi 30		Dimanche 31		Lundi 1er Novembre		Mardi 2	
2	Parterre	58	116	58	145	65	130	99	198	106	212	59	118
2	Deuxième galerie	25	50	25	50	11	22	64	128	71	142	8	16
2	Troisièmes loges	-	-	-	-	6	12	13	26	8	16	-	-
1½	Deuxième balcon	33	49.5	33	49.5	13	19.5	64	96	61	91.5	17	25.5
1¼	Premier amphithéâtre	22	27.5	22	27.5	14	17.5	84	105	62	77.5	22	27.5
¾	Deuxième amphithéâtre	80	60	80	60	31	23.25	154	115.5	159	119.25	51	38.25

Octobre / Novembre 1852	Vendredi 29 Bénéfice de M. Ch. Perey *Not* two performances; some prices up for this performance; second column redone accounts		Samedi 30	Dimanche 31	Lundi 1er Novembre	Mardi 2
Location suivant la feuille	1718.50	2095.50	665	874.50	984	387
Supplémens	10.50	11.50	7	95.25	91.75	9.25
Billets vendus la veille après la recette	8.00	8.00	7	26.25	18	19.75
Billets d'administration avec droit	8.00	8.00	–	–	–	–
Billets d'auteur en sus du droit	8.00	8.00	–	0.50	–	0.50

	Novembre 1852	Mercredi 3		Jeudi 4		Vendredi 5		Samedi 6		Dimanche 7		Lundi 8		Mardi 9	
6	Billets à toutes places	17	102	15	90	13	78	12	72	15	90	21	126	17	102
5	Loges de la galerie	29	145	31	155	29	145	26	130	21	105	19	95	33	165
5	Stalles d'orchestre	45	225	47	235	58	290	76	380	33	165	50	250	20	100
5	Stalles de balcon	10	50	8	40	7	35	6	30	16	80	7	35	9	45
4	Deuxièmes loges de face	3	12	5	20	-	-	13	52	21	84	5	20	9	36
4	Stalles de première galerie	11	44	22	88	15	60	40	160	40	160	13	52	39	156
4	Orchestre	10	40	25	100	14	56	15	60	26	104	10	40	15	60
3	Loges intermédiaires	5	15	17	51	6	18	15	45	50	150	1	3	2	6
2½	Deuxièmes loges de côté	9	22.5	10	25	7	17.5	14	35	46	115	17	42.5	5	12.5
2½	Pourtour	23	57.5	46	115	17	42.5	31	77.5	71	177.5	26	65	12	30
2	Parterre	35	70	65	130	60	120	54	108	106	212	49	98	50	100
2	Deuxième galerie	13	26	8	16	19	38	20	40	51	102	33	66	19	38
2	Troisièmes loges	-	-	-	-	-	-	-	-	11	22	-	-	1	2

Novembre 1852	Mercredi 3		Jeudi 4		Vendredi 5		Samedi 6		Dimanche 7		Lundi 8		Mardi 9	
1½ Deuxième balcon	3	4.5	12	18	1	1.5	11	16.5	78	117	22	33	9	13.5
1¼ Premier amphithéâtre	7	8.75	12	15	8	10	13	16.25	87	108.75	18	22.5	12	15
¾ Deuxième amphithéâtre	24	18	20	15	19	14.25	22	16.5	124	93	61	45.75	15	11.25
Location suivant la feuille		314		272		147		495.50		460		226.50		233
Supplémens		9.25		39		3.75		27.75		78		13.50		1
Billets vendus la veille après la recette		12.75		31		23.50		15		10		15.75		9
Billets d'administration avec droit		6.50		–		2		7		–		5.50		–
Billets d'auteur en sus du droit		4.25		–		4.50		–		–		3.50		–

	Novembre 1852	Mercredi 10		Jeudi 11		Vendredi 12		Samedi 13		Dimanche 14		Lundi 15		Mardi 16	
6	Billets à toutes places	12	72	24	144	17	102	–	–	27	162	–	–	5	30
5	Loges de la galerie	10	50	14	70	27	135	–	–	7	35	18	90	28	140
5	Stalles d'orchestre	30	150	46	230	35	175	–	–	53	265	45	225	72	360
5	Stalles de balcon	4	20	8	40	10	50	–	–	19	95	15	75	9	45
4	Deuxièmes loges de face	5	20	1	4	–	–	–	–	10	40	14	56	23	92
4	Stalles de première galerie	24	96	25	100	25	100	–	–	35	140	20	80	29	116
4	Orchestre	23	92	16	64	14	56	–	–	26	104	14	56	18	72
3	Loges intermédiaires	4	12	17	51	2	6	–	–	24	72	10	30	14	42
2½	Deuxièmes loges de côté	20	50	2	5	4	10	–	–	53	132.5	4	10	20	50
2½	Pourtour	15	37.5	25	62.5	18	45	–	–	71	177.5	30	75	23	57.5
2	Parterre	52	104	36	72	39	78	41	82	89	178	75	150	84	168
2	Deuxième galerie	12	24	11	22	9	18	25	50	58	116	26	52	21	42
2	Troisièmes loges	–	–	4	8	–	–	–	–	7	14	2	4	–	–

NIGHTLY BOX-OFFICE TAKINGS 1852

	Novembre 1852	Mercredi 10		Jeudi 11		Vendredi 12		Samedi 13		Dimanche 14		Lundi 15		Mardi 16	
1½	Deuxième balcon	15	22.5	18	27	16	24	30	45	65	97.5	43	64.5	31	46.5
1¼	Premier amphithéâtre	11	13.75	1	1.25	13	16.25	35	43.75	61	76.25	35	43.75	28	35
¾	Deuxième amphithéâtre	24	18	24	18	20	15	63	47.25	100	75	122	91.5	45	33.75
	Location suivant la feuille	112		88		155		1344.50		407.50		1355		863	
	Supplémens	14		20.5		15.75		2.75		68		21.75		33.5	
	Billets vendus la veille après la recette	10		13.75		27.50		–		21.25		4.25		31	
	Billets d'administration avec droit	–		12.50		–		–		–		–		8	
	Billets d'auteur en sus du droit	–		–		–		–		–		–		0.75	

	Novembre 1852	Mercredi 17		Jeudi 18		Vendredi 19		Samedi 20		Dimanche 21		Lundi 22		Mardi 23	
6	Billets à toutes places	8	48	8	48	7	42	-	-	17	102	-	-	11	66
5	Loges de la galerie	23	115	18	90	21	105	22	110	31	155	10	50	17	85
5	Stalles d'orchestre	75	375	79	395	53	265	70	350	60	300	50	250	53	265
5	Stalles de balcon	6	30	16	80	19	95	8	40	10	50	10	50	11	55
4	Deuxièmes loges de face	3	12	2	8	6	24	2	8	14	56	5	20	3	12
4	Stalles de première galerie	21	84	27	108	20	80	27	108	42	168	14	56	32	128
4	Orchestre	19	76	17	68	14	56	23	92	18	72	27	108	23	92
3	Loges intermédiaires	13	39	6	18	4	12	8	24	21	63	12	36	4	12
2½	Deuxièmes loges de côté	8	20	7	17.5	21	52.5	9	22.5	26	65	13	32.5	5	12.5
2½	Pourtour	23	57.5	46	115	35	87.5	33	82.5	50	125	25	62.5	38	95
2	Parterre	81	162	87	174	71	142	94	188	85	170	67	134	82	164
2	Deuxième galerie	11	22	21	42	11	22	7	14	60	120	36	72	9	18
2	Troisièmes loges	-	-	-	-	-	-	-	-	13	26	4	8	-	-

NIGHTLY BOX-OFFICE TAKINGS 1852

	Novembre 1852	Mercredi 17		Jeudi 18		Vendredi 19		Samedi 20		Dimanche 21		Lundi 22		Mardi 23	
1½	Deuxième balcon	10	15	9	13.5	4	6	11	16.5	57	85.5	25	37.5	18	27
1¼	Premier amphithéâtre	10	12.5	8	10	14	17.5	13	16.25	51	63.75	25	31.25	31	38.75
¾	Deuxième amphithéâtre	62	46.5	38	28.5	47	35.25	41	30.75	111	83.25	113	84.75	71	53.25
	Location suivant la feuille	796		686		644		614		538.75		850		467	
	Suppléments	16.75		12		12.75		27		27.75		40.75		15	
	Billets vendus la veille après la recette	9		5		12		7		5		19		8.5	
	Billets d'administration avec droit	11.50		–		–		8		–		–		4	
	Billets d'auteur en sus du droit	15.75		–		0.50		–		16		–		–	

	Novembre 1852	Mercredi 24		Jeudi 25		Vendredi 26		Samedi 27		Dimanche 28		Lundi 29		Mardi 30	
6	Billets à toutes places	15	90	20	120	22	132	17	102	16	96	10	60	13	78
5	Loges de la galerie	25	125	19	95	15	75	24	120	21	105	15	75	18	90
5	Stalles d'orchestre	47	235	68	340	50	250	42	210	30	150	49	245	35	175
5	Stalles de balcon	9	45	16	80	11	55	13	65	11	55	9	45	8	40
4	Deuxièmes loges de face	2	8	11	44	2	8	11	44	10	40	4	16	11	44
4	Stalles de première galerie	17	68	32	128	20	80	29	116	30	120	10	40	24	96
4	Orchestre	18	72	19	76	18	72	17	68	18	72	9	36	9	36
3	Loges intermédiaires	15	45	24	72	6	18	17	51	20	60	5	15	10	30
2½	Deuxièmes loges de côté	13	32.5	10	25	8	20	7	17.5	30	75	4	10	10	25
2½	Pourtour	11	27.5	37	92.5	32	80	28	70	33	82.5	36	90	34	85
2	Parterre	77	154	71	142	61	122	56	112	81	162	64	128	55	110
2	Deuxième galerie	11	22	24	48	16	32	3	6	71	142	25	50	15	30
2	Troisièmes loges	–	–	3	6	–	–	–	–	2	4	–	–	7	14

NIGHTLY BOX-OFFICE TAKINGS 1852

	Novembre 1852	Mercredi 24		Jeudi 25		Vendredi 26		Samedi 27		Dimanche 28		Lundi 29		Mardi 30	
1½	Deuxième balcon	9	13.5	8	12	7	10.5	6	9	40	60	23	34.5	15	22.5
1¼	Premier amphithéâtre	8	10	18	22.5	19	23.75	12	15	46	57.5	28	35	10	12.5
¾	Deuxième amphithéâtre	41	30.75	33	24.75	53	39.75	39	29.25	123	92.25	50	37.5	24	18
	Location suivant la feuille		447		377		295		473		444		385		232
	Supplémens		15.25		19		11.75		24		18.25		7.50		20.50
	Billets vendus la veille après la recette		7.50		25.75		9.75		10.75		35		18.75		27.50
	Billets d'administration avec droit		–		5.50		8.25		3		–		11		5
	Billets d'auteur en sus du droit		2.00		0.50		–		–		4.50		–		0.50

	Décembre 1852	Mercredi 1er		Jeudi 2		Vendredi 3		Samedi 4		Dimanche 5		Lundi 6		Mardi 7	
6	Billets à toutes places	9	54	8	48	19	114	27	162	14	84	21	126	12	72
5	Loges de la galerie	20	100	17	85	15	75	32	160	27	135	8	40	9	45
5	Stalles d'orchestre	49	245	24	120	43	215	72	360	50	250	40	200	26	130
5	Stalles de balcon	12	60	2	10	5	25	18	90	10	50	12	60	9	45
4	Deuxièmes loges de face	12	48	3	12	6	24	5	20	14	56	7	28	–	–
4	Stalles de première galerie	6	24	18	72	17	68	18	72	39	156	30	120	20	80
4	Orchestre	14	56	18	72	15	60	19	76	16	64	20	80	16	64
3	Loges intermédiaires	29	87	25	75	4	12	14	42	24	72	3	9	3	9
2½	Deuxièmes loges de côté	15	37.5	24	60	10	25	11	27.5	43	107.5	13	32.5	3	7.5
2½	Pourtour	35	87.5	18	45	22	55	24	60	53	132.5	23	57.5	24	60
2	Parterre	57	114	88	176	57	114	70	140	77	154	91	182	41	82
2	Deuxième galerie	7	14	33	66	15	30	12	24	48	96	42	84	11	22
2	Troisièmes loges	2	4	2	4	–	–	1	2	2	4	6	12	2	4

NIGHTLY BOX-OFFICE TAKINGS 1852

	Décembre 1852	Mercredi 1ᵉʳ		Jeudi 2		Vendredi 3		Samedi 4		Dimanche 5		Lundi 6		Mardi 7	
1½	Deuxième balcon	9	13.5	27	40.5	5	7.5	16	24	57	85.5	31	46.5	21	31.5
1¼	Premier amphithéâtre	14	17.5	27	33.75	10	12.5	13	16.25	87	108.75	56	70	18	22.5
¾	Deuxième amphithéâtre	36	27	77	57.75	30	22.5	33	24.75	138	103.5	133	99.75	21	15.75
	Location suivant la feuille		322		443		103.50		214		460.50		194		264.50
	Supplémens		23.75		38.50		10.50		9.50		57.50		30.75		10.25
	Billets vendus la veille après la recette		23		5.75		17		17		40.50		19.25		30.50
	Billets d'administration avec droit		7		–		0.75		10		–		9.50		7.50
	Billets d'auteur en sus du droit		–		–		–		–		8.75		–		0.75

Décembre 1852		Mercredi 8		Jeudi 9		Vendredi 10		Samedi 11		Dimanche 12		Lundi 13		Mardi 14	
6	Billets à toutes places	7	42	9	54	19	114	-	-	21	126	23	138	19	114
5	Loges de la galerie	4	20	11	55	25	125	6	36	32	160	17	85	21	105
5	Stalles d'orchestre	39	195	34	170	29	145	25	200	59	295	54	270	42	210
5	Stalles de balcon	8	40	3	15	12	60	11	88	29	145	19	95	19	95
4	Deuxièmes loges de face	-	-	4	16	8	32	7	35	11	44	2	8	13	52
4	Stalles de première galerie	9	36	17	68	25	100	5	30	45	180	18	72	7	28
4	Orchestre	2	8	12	48	10	40	24	144	27	108	10	40	9	36
3	Loges intermédiaires	2	6	11	33	12	36	8	32	36	108	2	6	1	3
2½	Deuxièmes loges de côté	6	15	10	25	15	37.5	9	22.5	62	155	2	5	4	10
2½	Pourtour	17	42.5	40	100	16	40	18	54	61	152.5	14	35	24	60
2	Parterre	29	58	96	192	59	118	49	122.5	82	164	43	86	40	80
2	Deuxième galerie	14	28	44	88	18	36	16	32	91	182	13	26	18	36
2	Troisièmes loges	2	4	-	-	-	-	5	10	9	18	-	-	-	-

NIGHTLY BOX-OFFICE TAKINGS 1852

	Décembre 1852	Mercredi 8		Jeudi 9		Vendredi 10		Samedi 11		Dimanche 12		Lundi 13		Mardi 14	
1½	Deuxième balcon	2	3	28	42	14	21	10	15	69	97.5	23	34.5	13	19.5
1¼	Premier amphithéâtre	3	3.75	18	22.5	16	20	14	17.5	98	122.5	24	30	11	13.75
¾	Deuxième amphithéâtre	22	16.5	24	18	26	19.5	48	36	135	101.75	52	39	33	24.75
	Location suivant la feuille	217		289		201		2252.50		474.50		365		283.50	
	Supplémens	–		32.50		18		10.25		75.50		7.50		4.50	
	Billets vendus la veille après la recette	11.75		5		8.50		–		–		22.50		84.25	
	Billets d'administration avec droit	4.50		5		10.25		–		–		1.50		15	
	Billets d'auteur en sus du droit	–		3		–		–		–		–		1	

Samedi, 11 Décembre: some of the prices were increased for the *bénéfice* of Mlle Boisgontier.

	Décembre 1852	Mercredi 15		Jeudi 16		Vendredi 17		Samedi 18		Dimanche 19		Lundi 20		Mardi 21	
6	Billets à toutes places	3	18	10	60	15	90	17	102	25	150	–	–	–	–
5	Loges de la galerie	7	35	12	60	28	140	12	60	23	115	–	–	6	30
5	Stalles d'orchestre	46	230	45	225	53	265	46	230	42	210	–	–	21	105
5	Stalles de balcon	6	30	5	25	11	55	10	50	3	15	–	–	6	30
4	Deuxièmes loges de face	3	12	5	20	2	8	3	12	2	8	–	–	8	32
4	Stalles de première galerie	19	76	13	52	16	64	13	52	23	92	–	–	8	32
4	Orchestre	11	44	9	36	11	44	13	52	8	32	–	–	5	20
3	Loges intermédiaires	1	3	13	39	7	21	10	30	16	48	–	–	15	45
2½	Deuxièmes loges de côté	4	10	5	12.5	1	2.5	11	27.5	21	52.5	–	–	23	57.5
2½	Pourtour	27	67.5	9	22.5	27	67.5	13	32.5	24	60	–	–	49	122.5
2	Parterre	38	76	39	78	66	132	35	70	54	108	54	108	77	154
2	Deuxième galerie	11	22	10	20	11	22	10	20	33	66	20	40	21	42
2	Troisièmes loges	–	–	–	–	–	–	–	–	–	–	–	–	2	4

NIGHTLY BOX-OFFICE TAKINGS 1852

	Décembre 1852	Mercredi 15		Jeudi 16		Vendredi 17		Samedi 18		Dimanche 19		Lundi 20		Mardi 21	
1½	Deuxième balcon	1	1.5	20	30	7	10.5	10	15	57	85.5	40	60	10	15
1¼	Premier amphithéâtre	7	8.75	6	7.5	12	15	6	7.5	42	52.5	18	22.5	14	17.5
¾	Deuxième amphithéâtre	18	13.5	10	7.5	20	15	19	14.25	93	69.75	68	51	37	27.75
	Location suivant la feuille	182		177		279		231		189.50		1538.50		1884.50	
	Supplémens	1.75		9		6		7.50		26		-		25.50	
	Billets vendus la veille après la recette	36		39.50		14.75		38.50		20.50		-		15.50	
	Billets d'administration avec droit	3		4.50		2.25		11		-		-		-	
	Billets d'auteur en sus du droit	-		-		0.50		-		4.50		-		-	

	Décembre 1852	Mercredi 22		Jeudi 23		Vendredi 24		Samedi 25		Dimanche 26		Lundi 27		Mardi 28	
6	Billets à toutes places	–	–	–	–	–	–	22	132	–	–	2	12	–	–
5	Loges de la galerie	2	10	–	–	14	70	29	145	17	85	25	125	33	165
5	Stalles d'orchestre	12	60	63	315	67	335	63	315	61	305	88	440	98	490
5	Stalles de balcon	27	135	25	125	16	80	35	175	4	20	13	65	14	70
4	Deuxièmes loges de face	33	132	5	20	11	44	24	96	10	40	12	48	3	12
4	Stalles de première galerie	15	60	31	124	29	116	10	40	30	120	17	68	15	60
4	Orchestre	18	72	22	88	40	160	24	96	46	184	30	120	24	96
3	Loges intermédiaires	12	36	10	30	12	36	23	69	20	60	16	48	12	36
2½	Deuxièmes loges de côté	10	25	8	20	16	40	47	117.5	29	72.5	5	12.5	11	27.5
2½	Pourtour	39	97.5	49	122.5	45	112.5	55	137.5	34	85	20	50	25	62.5
2	Parterre	76	152	91	182	78	156	93	186	83	166	75	150	63	126
2	Deuxième galerie	14	28	7	14	24	48	54	108	48	96	10	20	15	30
2	Troisièmes loges	4	8	–	–	–	–	3	6	3	6	2	4	–	–

NIGHTLY BOX-OFFICE TAKINGS 1852

	Décembre 1852	Mercredi 22		Jeudi 23		Vendredi 24		Samedi 25		Dimanche 26		Lundi 27		Mardi 28	
1½	Deuxième balcon	12	18	16	24	5	7.5	29	43.5	40	60	3	4.5	10	15
1¼	Premier amphithéâtre	5	6.25	19	23.75	10	12.5	37	46.25	27	33.75	10	12.5	9	11.25
¾	Deuxième amphithéâtre	42	31.5	48	36	39	29.25	81	60.75	67	50.25	32	24	37	27.25
	Location suivant la feuille	1750.50		1552.00		1246.00		1335.00		1299.00		779		875	
	Supplémens	10.50		18.50		22.75		38.75		25.75		10.50		23.50	
	Billets vendus la veille après la recette	9.75		5.50		23		11.25		18.75		33		21.25	
	Billets d'administration avec droit	–		–		–		–		–		–		6	
	Billets d'auteur en sus du droit	–		–		–		–		–		3.25		–	

	Décembre 1852	Mercredi 29		Jeudi 30		Vendredi 31	
6	Billets à toutes places	10	60	15	90	16	96
5	Loges de la galerie	20	100	11	55	13	65
5	Stalles d'orchestre	79	395	78	390	40	200
5	Stalles de balcon	7	35	11	55	10	50
4	Deuxièmes loges de face	6	24	6	24	-	-
4	Stalles de première galerie	19	76	9	36	16	64
4	Orchestre	24	96	23	92	16	64
3	Loges intermédiaires	20	60	25	75	8	24
2½	Deuxièmes loges de côté	10	25	19	47.50	15	37.50
2½	Pourtour	18	45	12	30	21	52.5
2	Parterre	75	150	61	122	55	110
2	Deuxième galerie	10	20	6	12	11	22
2	Troisièmes loges	-	-	6	12	-	-

NIGHTLY BOX-OFFICE TAKINGS 1852

	Décembre 1852	Mercredi 29		Jeudi 30		Vendredi 31	
1½	Deuxième balcon	6	9	7	10.5	13	19.5
1¼	Premier amphithéâtre	7	8.75	11	13.75	8	10
¾	Deuxième amphithéâtre	20	15	14	10.5	16	12
	Location suivant la feuille		624.50		468		388
	Supplémens		32		15		11.50
	Billets vendus la veille après la recette		38		11.75		19.25
	Billets d'administration avec droit		2.75		8		1.50
	Billets d'auteur en sus du droit		–		–		–

IX
TABLES

I) Nightly Box-office Totals For 1852

MONDAY		TUESDAY		WEDNESDAY		THURSDAY		FRIDAY		SATURDAY		SUNDAY	
date	francs	date	francs	date	francs	date	francs	date	francs	date	francs	date	francs
						JANUARY							
						1	1509.00	2	1585.75	3	1454.25	4	1462.00
5	1025.50	*6	1166.50	7	1176.50	8	785.50	9	805.00	10	818.00	11	915.50
12	594.50	13	704.75	14	432.00	15	761.25	16	–	*17	1432.00	18	1431.00
19	1835.00	20	1601.50	21	1743.50	22	1653.75	23	1640.50	24	1570.25	**25	2097.00
26	2012.25	27	1875.50	28	1397.00	29	1637.25	30	1432.75	31	1691.50	FEBRUARY 1	2530.75

NIGHTLY BOX-OFFICE TOTALS FOR 1852

| MONDAY | | TUESDAY | | WEDNESDAY | | THURSDAY | | FRIDAY | | SATURDAY | | SUNDAY | |
date	francs	date	francs	date	francs	date	francs	date	francs	date	francs	date	francs
2	1774.25	3	1525.25	4	1026.75	5	1175.75	6	1070.75	7	1569.50	8	1866.50
9	1119.00	10	1738.75	11	1362.25	12	1315.00	13	1970.75	14	1357.25	*15	1808.00
16	1413.75	17	1163.25	18	902.25	19	1807.00	20	1485.25	21	801.75	*22	2428.00
*23	3048.75	24	4202.00	25	2025.00	26	2273.25	27	3517.00	28	2339.25	29	2309.50
MARCH													
1	2712.50	2	2087.25	3	2527.50	4	2400.25	5	2503.50	6	2657.50	7	1658.50
8	2248.00	9	2255.75	10	1683.75	11	2263.50	12	2031.75	13	2207.00	14	2022.00
15	1859.50	16	1582.00	17	1644.25	18	2514.75	19	1300.75	20	1627.25	21	2205.50
22	1406.00	23	1088.25	*24	1044.50	25	1132.75	26	1629.50	27	1480.25	28	2551.75
29	2354.00	30	1960.25	31	1749.25	APRIL 1	-	2	2228.75	3	1961.00	4	2081.00
5	1754.00	6	1639.50	7	1436.00	8	1482.25	9	1412.25	10	1514.75	11	1747.00
12	2276.00	13	2060.25	14	2396.25	15	1578.75	16	2153.75	*17	3222.75	18	2840.75

	MONDAY		TUESDAY		WEDNESDAY		THURSDAY		FRIDAY		SATURDAY		SUNDAY
date	francs	date	francs	date	francs	date	francs	date	francs	date	francs	date	francs
19	1931.75	20	1708.50	21	1651.25	22	1371.50	23	1148.75	24	1268.00	25	2133.25
26	1485.75	27	1573.50	28	1404.50	29	1802.50	30	1777.75	MAY 1	1730.00	2	2612.00
3	1828.25	4	1629.75	5	1792.00	6	1257.25	7	1563.00	8	1245.00	9	1504.50
10	1698.00	11	2060.75	**12	2191.50	13	452.25	14	1601.75	15	1106.50	16	985.00
*17	621.50	18	1389.50	19	2082.00	20	1286.25	21	983.75	22	938.50	23	811.00
24	807.00	25	933.50	26	829.00	27	701.25	28	738.00	29	1283.00	30	2296.25
*31	1675.25	JUNE 1	1064.75	2	867.50	*3	1348.00	4	1538.00	5	1005.00	6	836.00
7	1634.25	8	1646.25	9	1203.00	10	1381.00	11	1102.00	12	1375.75	13	2106.75
14	1371.75	15	1403.50	16	1114.25	17	900.50	18	833.25	19	698.00	20	1631.75
21	849.00	22	879.75	23	871.75	24	600.25	25	444.25	26	614.50	27	471.50

NIGHTLY BOX-OFFICE TOTALS FOR 1852

MONDAY date	francs	TUESDAY date	francs	WEDNESDAY date	francs	THURSDAY date	francs	FRIDAY date	francs	SATURDAY date	francs	SUNDAY date	francs
28	545.25	29	436.00	30	341.25	JULY 1	692.75	2	631.75	3	436.25	4	189.75
5	210.25	6	138.75	7	262.25	8	207.75	*9	201.00	10	672.50	11	–
12	191.25	13	93.25	14	205.00	15	121.75	16	194.50	17	–	18	460.50
19	434.25	20	208.75	21	–	22	301.25	23	266.50	24	237.75	25	1204.25
26	320.00	*27	642.00	28	381.00	29	––	30	211.75	31	–	AUGUST 1	352.75
2	314.75	*3	1100.25	4	1810.75	5	1662.00	6	1702.25	7	1641.50	8	616.25
9	1172.00	10	1338.50	11	1557.25	12	1264.00	13	1363.75	14	923.00	15	89.25
16	1140.25	17	1112.75	18	1316.75	19	817.25	20	1979.00	21	1148.50	22	1467.00
23	662.25	24	577.75	25	531.50	26	–	27	553.50	28	553.75	29	932.00

MONDAY		TUESDAY		WEDNESDAY		THURSDAY		FRIDAY		SATURDAY		SUNDAY	
date	francs	date	francs	date	francs	date	francs	date	francs	date	francs	date	francs
30	748.00	31	–	SEPTEMBER 1	–	*2	1279.00	3	1246.25	4	857.25	5	2478.75
6	1226.75	7	1502.00	8	1342.50	9	2037.00	10	1547.50	11	1515.00	12	2880.75
13	1342.25	14	1175.50	15	1157.75	16	1064.75	17	1296.75	18	850.75	19	2318.25
*20	1255.75	22	1122.25	*23	1570.75	24	1269.00	25	1200.25	26	1038.25	27	1581.00
28	896.50	29	887.50	*30	1289.75	31	1084.50	OCTOBER 1	1275.00	2	1186.25	3	2227.25
4	968.25	5	1002.75	6	1023.75	7	1952.75	8	1952.50	9	1587.75	10	2094.25
11	1465.75	12	1739.25	13	1423.00	14	1407.25	15	1540.25	16	1185.50	17	2471.75
18	1236.00	**19	2038.25	20	1677.25	21	1814.00	22	1702.00	23	1590.00	24	2871.25
25	1596.50	26	1365.00	27	1578.25	28	1323.25	29 **i) *ii)	2549.50 3030.50	30	1907.75	31	3174.50

NIGHTLY BOX-OFFICE TOTALS FOR 1852

MONDAY date	francs	TUESDAY date	francs	WEDNESDAY date	francs	THURSDAY date	francs	FRIDAY date	francs	SATURDAY date	francs	SUNDAY date	francs
NOVEMBER													
1	3111.50	2	1331.25	3	1187.00	4	1455.00	5	1106.50	6	1784.00	7	2433.25
8	1258.50	9	1135.25	10	917.75	11	1053.50	12	1028.50	*13	1615.25	14	2276.50
15	2483.75	16	2266.00	17	1963.50	18	1918.50	19	1711.00	20	1758.50	*21	2291.25
22	1942.25	23	1618.00	24	1450.00	25	1755.50	26	1342.75	27	1545.50	*28	1875.00
29	1339.25	30	1191.50	DECEMBER 1	1364.75	2	1464.25	3	991.25	4	1551.00	5	2226.00
6	1500.75	7	1003.75	8	751.00	9	1281.00	10	1181.75	*11	3137.25	12	2708.75
13	1366.00	14	1275.25	15	870.00	16	925.00	17	1254.00	18	1072.75	19	1400.75
*20	1819.50	21	2659.75	22	2642.00	23	2700.25	24	2538.50	25	3158.50	26	2727.00
27	2029.25	28	2154.75	29	1816.00	30	1578.00	31	1246.75				

* indicates a new production ** indicates two new productions

II) Monthly Totals and Daily Averages

Monthly totals (Daily average)			Average daily takings throughout the year	
January	40,246.75	(1,341)	Monday	1,421
February	52,926.50	(1,825)	Tuesday	1,412
March	60,389.00	(1,948)	Wednesday	1,339
April	53,042.00	(1,829)	Thursday	1,356
May	42,632.25	(1,375)	Friday	1,421
June	31,114.75	(1,037)	Saturday	1,438
July	9,116.25	(351)	Sunday	1,817
August	30,448.50	(1,049)		
September	40,314.25	(1,390)		
October	55,956.25	(1,748)		
November	50,146.00	(1,671)		
December	54,395.00	(1,755)		
	505,208.70			

X

A List of Authors used in 1852

The following list is sketchy. Only a few of the authors (Duvert, Clairville, Thiboust, Bayard, Lauzanne are the obvious ones) achieved anything more than an ephemeral reputation (even though the majority of them wrote a considerable number of comédie-vaudevilles). Most, however, do manage a mention in one or more of the nineteenth-century's dictionaries of biography.

What the list is intended to show is simply the number of writers involved in keeping only *one* theatre supplied with plays (and the list can take no account of those writers whose work was rejected by the director and the reading committee).

	Name	Dates	Comments
	Althoy, P.-M.	c.1802–56	
	Arago, J.-E.-V.	1790–1855	traveller, writer.
[?]	d'Artois, F.-V.-A.	1788–1867	
	Barrière, Th.	1823[25?]–77	
	Battu, L.	1829–57	
	Bayard, J.-F.-A.	1796–1853	wrote more than 200 plays.
	Beauvallet, L.	1828[29?]–85	
	Béraud, A.-N.	1792–1860	designer, director of the Théâtre de l'Ambigu, 1839–49.
[?]	Bercioux		
[?]	Bergeret		
	Berthoud, S.-H.		scientific journalist, novelist.
	Besselièvre, C.		journalist (*Le Corsaire*).

Name	Dates	Comments
[?] Boniface		
[?] Bourdois		
Bourgeois, A.-A.	1806–71	wrote everything in collaboration.
[?] Boyer, E. PARTOUT (dit)	?–1862	
Brisebarre, E.-L.-A.	1818–71	
Carmouche, P.-F.-A.	1797–1868	
Carré, M.	1819–72	
[?] Chapelle		
Clairville, L.-F. NICHOLAÏ (dit)	1811–79	actor at Bobino and L'Ambigu; prolific writer of vaudevilles.
[?] Colliot		
Commerson, J.-J.	1802–79	journalist.
Cormon, P.-E. PIESTRE (dit Eugène)	1810–?	
Decourvelle, P.-A.	1821[22?]–92	inspector of the Paris cemeteries.
Delacour, A.-C. LARTIGUE (dit)	1815[17?]–83	doctor, wrote medical encyclopaedias.
Delaporte, P.-M.	1806–72	
Dennery, A. PHILIPPE (dit)	1811–99	collector of objets d'art from the Orient; wrote opera libretti, including *Le Cid* (Massenet) and *Si j'étais roi* (Adam).
Desarbres, N.	1822–72	
Deslandes, R.	1825–90	

A LIST OF AUTHORS USED IN 1852

	Name	Dates	Comments
	Dupeuty, C.-D.	1798–1865	founder member of the Société des auteurs dramatiques.
[?]	Duprat		
[?]	Dutertre		
	Duvert, F.-A.	1795–1876	one of the best writers of vaudevilles.
[?]	Faulquemont		
	Galoppe d'Onquaire, H.-A.-C.	1805–67	
	Gautier, T.	1811–72	poet, novelist, critic.
	Grangé, P.-E.-B. (dit Eugène)	1810–87	
	Guénée, A.	1818–77	
	Jouslin de la Salle, A.-F.	1797–1863	
	Labiche, E.-M.	1815–88	prolific and popular.
[?]	Labie		
	Lafitte, J.-B.-P.	1796–1879	
[?]	Langlois		
	La Rounat, A.-N.-C. ROUVENAT de	1818–84	
	Laurençot, C.-H.-L.	1805–62	
	Lauzanne, A.-Th. Chevalier de	1805–77	prolific and popular.
[?]	Lefèbre, E.		
[?]	Lelarge, L.		

	Name	Dates	Comments
	Lemoine, G.	1802–83	
	Lemoine, A. dit LEMOINE-MONTIGNY	1805–80	
[?]	Leprévost		
[?]	Marchais		
	Martin, E.	c.1828–66	
	Michel, M.-A.-A.	1812–68	journalist (*La Revue des Théâtres*)
[?]	Monnier, A.		
[?]	Montheau, G. de		
	Muret, Th.-C.	1818–66	miliary historian, novelist, trained as lawyer.
	Murger, H.	1822–61	collaborated with the *Revue des Deux Mondes*
	Musset, A. de		
	Narrey, C.	1825–92	
	Nus, E.	1816–[?]	journalist.
	Myon, E.	1812–70	
	Pérey, Ch.		actor, writer (with the Variétés in 1852 as an actor).
[?]	Rougemont, B. de		
[?]	Royez		
	Siraudin, P.	1813–83	

A LIST OF AUTHORS USED IN 1852

Name	Dates	Comments
Thiboust, L.	1826–67	actor at the Odéon and the Beaumarchais. Popular writer of vaudevilles.
Vaëz, J.-N.-G. VAN NIEUWENHUYSEN (dit)	1812–62	
Varin, C.	1798–69	
Varney, P.-J.-A.	1811–79	composer

In all there are 71 names listed above. Those with [?] beside them have eluded my [rather perfunctory] searches. There will be information, but it hardly seems totally necessary for a work of this nature.

XI
Bibliography

Reference material (côtes) consulted at the Bibliothèque de l'Arsenal

Bache. Rt.5695(1) and 5695(2).
Bardou aîné. Rt.5730.
Boisgonthier. Rt.6057.
Boulenger, J. *Les Dandys.*
Buguet, Henry. Rt.3433.
Dantan, J.P. Rt.12.994.
Fitz-James, Cara. Rt.7574.
Fournier (ed.). *La Semaine théâtrale (1843-1875).* Rj.3860.
La France théâtrale. Rj.156, Rj.265.
Galerie des artistes dramatiques de Paris, 2 vols, Rt.5329.
Galerie illustrée des célébrités contemporains. 2 vols, Rt.5331.
Gazette des théâtres. Rj.115.
Histoire anecdotique des théâtres de Paris. Rj.310.
Inventaire sommaire des recueils, répertoires et collections de pièces a théâtre. Rec.1 à 315.
Kopp. Rt.8345.
Leclère. Rt.8614.
Lemaître, Frédérick. Recueil d'articles concernant Frédérick-Lemaître dar *Taconnet.* Rt.8881.
Lemaître, Frédérick. Recueil d'articles concernant Frédérick-Lemaître dar *Le Roi des Drôles.* Rt.8882.
Miroy, Clarisse. Rt.9500, Rt.9501.
Nos Théâtres. Rj.386.
Nouvelle galerie des artistes dramatiques vivants, 2 vols, Rt.5332.
Ozy, Alice. Rt.9834.
Page, Adèle. Rt.9845.
Pérey. Rt.9915.
Le Petit Chansonnier du vaudeville (Paris, Delarue, 1850). Rj.736.

Répertoire de pièces représentées sur le Théâtre des Variétés (1834-61).
188 brochures gravées in 8°. Rec.283.
Sigaux, G. *La Comédie et le Vaudeville de 1850 à 1900.*
Souvenirs de la vie de théâtre. Rt.5992.
Théâtre des Variétés: 1813-1866. 3 vols. in 4°. Rec.309.
Les Variétés. Rj.281.
Vaudeville. Recueil factice: documents, bibliographie, articles, presse. Rt.4417.

Books and Articles

Abraham, E. *Acteurs et actrices de Paris* (Paris, Michel Lévy, 1861).
Annuaire théâtral illustré dramatique et musical: 1852-53, 2 vols (rédigé par Duverger).
Anon. *Paris vivant — Le Théâtre — Mémoires d'un jeune homme* (Paris, Gonet, 1858).
Arago, J. *Foyers et coulisses* (Paris, Librairie Nouvelle, 1852).
Arnal. *Iconographie.* B.N. catalogue, Duplessis, N°·1659.
d'Aurevilly, Barbey. *Les Vieilles actrices* (Paris, Chacornac, 1889).
Beauvoir, Roger de. *Les Soupeurs de mon temps* (Paris, Achille Faure, 1868).
B.N. *Guide dans les théâtres* (Paris, Paulin et Le Chevalier, 1855).
Boucher, H. *Souvenirs d'un Parisien pendant la seconde république* (Paris, Perrin, 1908).
———. *Souvenirs d'un Parisien pendant la seconde république*, deuxième série (Paris, Perrin, 1909).
Buguet, Henry. *Foyers et coulisses* (Paris, Tresse, 1873).
Chansonnier nouveau pour 1852.
Chants et chansons de la Bohême (Paris, Bry aîné, 1853).
Les Courtisanes du Second Empire, 3 vols (Brussels, Office de publicité, 1871).
Dantan jeune: caricatures et portraits de la société romantique (Paris musées, Maison de Balzac, 1989).
Darthenay, V. *Les Acteurs et les actrices de Paris* (Paris, chez les éditeurs, rue Grange-Batelière, 13, 1853).

Dash, La Comptesse, *Mémoires des autres*. 6 vols (Paris, s.d., [1896-97]).
Duflot, Joachim. *Les Secrets des coulisses des théâtres de Paris* (Paris, Lévy, 1865).
Foucher, Paul Henri. *Entre cour et jardin* (Paris, Amyot, 1867).
———. *Les Coulisses du passé* (Paris, Dentu, 1873).
Fournel, Victor. *Curiosités théâtrales*, nouvelle édition (Paris, Garnier, 1878).
Galerie Historique et critique du dix-neuvième siècle (Paris, 1858).
Gautier, Th. *Celle-ci et celle-là* (Paris, Didier, 1853).
———. *Histoire de l'art dramatique en France* (Paris, Hetzel, 1859) [especially 6th series, October 1848-April 1852].
———. *Ecrivains et artistes dramatiques* (Paris, Tallandier, s.d.).
———. *Les Maîtres du théâtre français* (Paris, Payot, 1929).
Goncourt, E & J., Holff, Cornélius. *Mystères des théâtres* (Paris, Librairie Nouvelle, 1853).
Grivel, Lucien. *Du Boulevard du crime à la Comédie Française* (Chenove, editions Bayadère, 1986).
Heilly, Georges d'. *Le Scandale au théâtre* (Paris, Jules Taride, 1861).
Hemmings, F.W.J. *The Theatre Industry in Nineteenth-Century France* (Cambridge University Press, 1993).
Hercé, J. (trans.). *Un Anglais à Paris* (Paris, Plon, 1893).
Hervey. *Les Théâtres de Paris* (Pairs, Galignani et Cie, 1847).
Hostein, N. *Historiettes et souvenirs d'un homme de théâtre* (Paris, Dentu, 1878).
Houssaye, A. *Les Confessions. Souvenirs d'un demi-siècle*, 6 vols (Paris, Dentu, 1885-91).
———. *Les Comédiens sans le savoir* (Paris, Librairie illustrée, 1886).
Janin, J.G. *Histoire de la littérature dramatique*, 6 vols (Paris, Michel Lévy, 1855-58).
———. *Critique dramatique* (Vol. 1, *La Comédie*) (Paris, Librairie des Bibliophiles, 1877).
Lacombe, P. *Actrices d'autrefois — Les Etoiles du passé* (   ).
Laroque, A. *Acteurs et actrices de Paris* (Paris, Aux Bureaux de l'Entracte, 1888).
Lecomte, L.-H. *Frédérick-Lemaître: un comédien au XIXe siècle*, 2 vols (Paris, chez l'auteur, 1888).

Long, Joseph. *[Le] Théâtre des Variétés* (Cambridge, Chaldwyck-Healey; New Jersey, Teaneck, 1980).
McCormick, J. *Popular Theatres of Nineteenth-Century France* (London, Routledge, 1993).
Maurice, Charles. *Histoire anecdotique du théâtre*, 2 vols (Paris, Plon, 1856).
Mirecourt, Eugène de. *Arnal* (Series: Les Contemporains, N°·92) (Paris, chez l'auteur, 1857).
Mogador, Céleste. *Mémoires*. 4 vols. (Paris, Librairie Nouvelle, 1858).
Montagne, E. *Le Manteau d'Arlequin* (Paris, Librairie Internationale, 1866).
Monvel, Boutet de. *Les Variétés, 1850-1870* (Paris, Plon-Nourrit, 1905).
d'Onquaire, Galoppe C. *Le Musée musical de Dantan jeune* (Paris, Au ménéstral, 1862).
Palianti M. (ed.). *Almanach des spectacles pour 1853* (Paris, Librarie Nouvelle).
Planche, G. *Portraits littéraires*. 2 vols. (Paris, Charpentier, 1853). See vol. II.
Pougin, A. *Acteurs et actrices d'autrefois* (Paris, Juven et Cie, 1897).
Rambaud, Y. *Les Théâtres en robe de chambre: les comédiens* (Paris, A. Faure, 1866).
Rinaudo, Simone. *Le Vaudeville et la société bourgeoise du XIXe siècle* (Paris, Théâtre de la Ville, N°·42, 1978).
Rochefort, A de. *Mémoires d'un vaudevilliste* (Paris, Charlieu et Huillery, 1863).
Sarcey, F. *Comédiens et comédiennes: théâtres divers* (Paris, Librairie des Bibliophiles, 1884).
———. *Quarante ans de théâtre*, 6 vols, especially volume 4, *Les Modernes: le drame de le vaudeville* (Paris, Imprimerie des Annales, 1900-2).
———. *Journal de jeunesse* (Paris, Bibliothèque des 'Annales politiques et littéraires', s-d.).
Séchan, C. *Souvenirs d'un homme de théâtre 1831-1855* (Pais, Calmann-Lévy, 1883).
Seligman, J. *Figures of Fun: the Caricature-statuettes of J.P. Dantan* (Oxford, O.U.P., 1957).

Sorel, Philippe. 'Les Dantan du Musée carnavalet: Portraits — charges sculptés de l'époque romantique', *Gazette des Beaux-Arts*, Vol.107 (January 1986), pp.1-38; (February 1986), pp.87-102.
Vacquerie, A. *Profils et grimaces* (Paris, Michel Lévy, 1856).
Villemessant, J.A.H. de. *Les Cancans* (Paris, Dentu, 1852).
—————. *Mémoires d'un journaliste*, 6 vols. (Paris, Dentu, 1872-78).
Viro, P. *Charges et bustes de Dantan jeune* (Paris, ? , 1863).
Wild, Nicole. *Les Arts du spectacle en France, affiches illustrées* (Catalogue, B.N., 1976).
—————. *Dictionnaire des théâtres parisiens au XIXe siècle: les théâtres et la musique* (Paris, Aux Amateurs de livres, 1989).

Journals

Le Corsaire.
La Chronique de Paris.
L'Eclair.
Le Figaro.
L'Illustration.
Le Siècle.

DURHAM MODERN LANGUAGES SERIES

French

FM1   Richard D. Burton, *The Context of Baudelaire's 'Le Cygne'*. 1980, 102 pp. ISBN 0 907310 01 X. £4.95

FM2   R.J. Howells, *Pierre Jurieu: Antinomian Radical*. 1983, 90 pp. ISBN 0 907310 04 4. £4.95

FT1   Malherbe, Théophile de Viau, and Saint-Amant, *A Selection*. R.G. Maber (ed.), 1983, repr. 1985, 1987; second edition revised, 1991, 132 pp. ISBN 0 907310 08 7. £3.95

FM3   James S. Munro, *Mademoiselle de Scudéry and the 'Carte de Tendre'*. 1986, 97 pp. ISBN 0 907310 12 5. £4.95

FT2   Michel-Jean Sedaine, *Le Philosophe sans le savoir*. Graham E. Rodmell (ed.), 1987, 122 pp. ISBN 0 907310 15 X. £4.95

FM4   David Hillery, *Verlaine: Fixing an Image*. 1988, 105 pp. ISBN 0 907310 18 4. £4.95

FT3   Molière, *Dépit amoureux*. Noël Peacock (ed.), 1990, 150 pp. ISBN 0 907310 20 6. £4.95

FM5   H. Gaston Hall, *Molière's 'Le Bourgeois Gentilhomme': Context and Stagecraft*. 1990, 98 pp. ISBN 0 907310 21 4. £4.95

FM6   Anthony Cheal Pugh (ed.), *France 1940: Literary and Historical Reactions to Defeat*. 1992, 133 pp. ISBN 0 907310 23 0. £6.95

FM7   David Hillery, *Lamartine: The 'Méditations Poétiques'*. 1993, 132 pp. ISBN 1 870530 55 1. £6.95

FM8   Nichola Anne Haxell, *Reflections of the Revolution: Poetry and Prose for the Second French Republic*. 1993, 147 pp. ISBN 0 907310 24 9. £7.95

The illustration of the Théâtre des Variétés on the front cover is reproduced with the kind permission from Bowes Museum, Barnard Castle, Co. Durham.

FT4	La Mothe Le Vayer, *'Lettre sur la Comédie de L'Imposteur'*. Robert Mc Bride (ed.), 1994, 170 pp. ISBN 0 907310 25 7. £8.95
FM9	Christopher Lloyd and Robert Lethbridge (ed.), *Maupassant conteur et romancier*. 1994, 201 pp. ISBN 0 907310 26 5. £9.95
FM10	Richard Maber (ed.), *Nouveaux Mondes: from the Twelfth to the Twentieth Century*. 1994. 149 pp. ISBN 0 907310 27 3. £7.95
FM11	Richard Burton, *Le Flâneur*, 1994. 80pp. ISBN 0907310 28 1. £5.50
FM12	Henry Phillips, *Racine: Language and Theatre*, 1994. 157pp. ISBN 0907310 29 X. £8.95
FM13	Paul Andrew Tipper, *The Dream Machine: Avian Imagery in 'Madame Bovary'*. 1994. 35pp. ISBN 0907310 30 3. £2.95.
FM14	Christopher Lloyd (ed.), *Epidemics and Sickness in French Literature and Culture*. 1995. 199pp. ISBN 0907310 31 1. £8.95.
FM15	Christopher Lloyd, *Mirbeau's Fictions*. 1996. 118pp. ISBN 0 907310 35 4. £8.95.

German

GT1	Hans Sachs, *Selections*. Mary Beare (ed.), 1983, 242 pp. ISBN 0 907310 06 0. £3.50
GM1	Howard Gaskill, *Hölderlin's 'Hyperion'*. 1984, 68 pp. ISBN 0 907310 07 9. £4.95
GM2	Patrick Bridgwater, *The Poet as Hero and Clown: A Study of Heym and Lichtenstein*. 1986, 82 pp. ISBN 0 907310 13 3. £4.95
GM3	Patrick Bridgwater, *George Moore and German Pessimism*. 1988, 81 pp. ISBN 0 907310 17 6. £4.95

GM4   Mark G. Ward, *Laughter, Comedy and Aesthetics: Kleist's 'Der zerbrochne Krug'*. 1989, 87 pp. ISBN 0 907310 22 2. £4.95
GM5   Neil Thomas, *Reading the Nibelungenlied*. 1995, 119 pp. ISBN 0 907310 32 X. £7.95
GM6   Neil Thomas and Françoise Le Saux, *Myth and its Legacy in European Literature* . 1996, 169 pp. ISBN 0 907310 33 8. £8.95

Hispanic

HM1   R.P. Calcraft, *The Sonnets of Luis de Góngora*. 1980, 127 pp. ISBN 0 907310 00 1. £4.95
HM2   Keith Whinnom, *La Poesia amatoria de la época de los Reyes Católicos*. 1981, 112 pp. ISBN 0 907310 02 8. £4.95
HM3   H. Ramsden, *Pío Baroja: 'La busca' 1903 to 'La busca' 1904*. 1982, 90 pp. ISBN 0 907310 05 2. £4.95
HM4   Jack M. Flint, *The Prose Works of Roberto Arlt*. 1985, 96 pp. ISBN 0 907310 09 5. £4.95
HT1   Carlos Fuentes, *Aura*. Peter Standish (ed.), 1986, 53 pp. ISBN 0 907310 10 9. £3.95
HM5   John Crosbie, *A lo divino Lyric Poetry: An Alternative View*. 1989, 92 pp. ISBN 0 907310 19 2. £4.95

Slavonic

SM1   Terence Wade, *Prepositions in Modern Russian*. 1983, repr. 1984, 136 pp. ISBN 0 907310 03 6. £3.95
ST1   V.V. Mayakovsky, *Klop*. Robert Russell (ed.), 1985, 127 pp. ISBN 0 907310 11 7. £3.95
ST2   V.F. Odoyevsky, *Pyostryye skazki*. Neil Cornwell (ed.), 1988, 98 pp. ISBN 0 907310 14 1. £4.95
ST3   Aleksandr Blok, *The Twelve*. Avril Pyman (ed.), 1989, viii + 136 pp. ISBN 0 907310 16 8. £4.95

Further titles in preparation.

All titles may be ordered direct from:

The General Editor, Tel: 0191 374 2744
Durham Modern Languages Series, Fax: 0191 374 2716
Elvet Riverside, New Elvet,
Durham DH1 3JT

Lightning Source UK Ltd.
Milton Keynes UK
UKOW050621150213

206326UK00001B/40/P